Signposts to
French Literature

Signposts to French Literature

Colin Radford, Christopher Shorley
and Mary Hossain

Hutchinson

London Melbourne Auckland Johannesburg

Hutchinson Education

An imprint of Century Hutchinson Ltd

62–65 Chandos Place, London WC2N 4NW

Century Hutchinson Australia Pty Ltd
P O Box 496, 16–22 Church Street, Hawthorn,
Victoria 3122, Australia

Century Hutchinson New Zealand Ltd
P O Box 40–086, Glenfield, Auckland 10,
New Zealand

Century Hutchinson South Africa (Pty) Ltd
P O Box 337, Bergvlei 2012, South Africa

First published 1988

© Colin Radford, Christopher Shorley and Mary Hossain 1988

Set in Garamond Stemple

Printed and bound in Great Britain by
Anchor Brendon Ltd, Tiptree, Essex

British Library Cataloguing in Publication Data
Radford, Colin
  Signposts to French literature.
  1. French literature, 1600–1970. Critical studies
  I. Title   II. Shorley, Christopher
  III. Hossain, Mary
  840.9
  ISBN 0-09-173075-9

Contents

Preface

The study of French literature remains a firm fixture on the map, both in schools and in higher education. Despite all the debates about the 'relevance' of literary texts, all the pressures to alter the established syllabus, and all the changes taking place in standards of literacy and reading habits, a literary element still offers something of crucial importance in any advanced modern language course.

It has been argued – with more feeling than sense – that the work of, say, Molière or Saint-Exupéry is of no use because it has precious little to do with life today. The argument falls apart on any close inspection. For one thing, a good education – in any discipline – is precisely one which extends and enriches students by liberating them from their immediate circumstances and helping them to see with fresh eyes; and literature – especially foreign literature – is a unique and economical way of showing how people have lived and thought, all over the world and throughout history. It is no doubt true that travel broadens the mind, and literature, whether exposing the foibles and obsessions of seventeenth-century Paris or conveying the insights of a pioneer pilot flying over remote oceans, deserts and mountain ranges, can yield a voyage of discovery which is every bit as enlightening. The other counter to the charge of irrelevance is that, on mature reflection, literature is, in fact, inevitably bound up with the central and permanent issues of real life. It may not always be factual, but it is none the worse for that: as Aristotle says, 'History treats of particular facts', while 'poetry [by which he means literature in general] is more concerned with universal truths'. It is certainly as authentic as, for example, laboratory experiments, psychological theories or political doctrines. No-one will read Proust intelligently without learning more than they thought possible about love; or Pascal without gaining new understanding of what religious belief is; or Rousseau without a sharpened vision of the nature of human society.

It has also been claimed that the study of literature in a modern

languages programme is an unnecessary distraction from the main
objective of fostering a high level of linguistic proficiency and
practical communication. This claim, too, becomes harder to
justify the more it is considered. One obvious factor is that French
men and women in all walks of life attach great importance to
literary culture, and that therefore a sound acquaintance with it
should be part of any linguist's basic equipment. Moreover,
literature is made up of language used in particularly intensified
and aesthetically pleasing ways, when the expressive powers of
sound and lexical variety, imagery and grammatical structure, are
marshalled to maximum effect. And anyone who aspires to even a
reasonable level of linguistic competence (as opposed to just
'getting by') simply cannot afford to ignore this dimension of the
subject. It would, in theory, be possible for a student of music to
approach the piano merely in terms of its construction, its physical
characteristics and its acoustic properties; but no-one can grasp
much about the piano without knowing what Beethoven or
Bartok composed for it, or how Brendel or Ashkenazy play it.
And so with the study of French: no-one can seriously expect to
understand the language in any depth unless they go beyond vocabulary lists and conjugations to some awareness of what French can
become in the hands of virtuosi such as Racine, Baudelaire or
Camus. Language and literature are interdependent: they cannot
be separated without both being seriously impoverished.

                    *   *   *

About this book

Signposts to French Literature is for newcomers, who may use it in
various ways in the early stages of what, it is hoped, will be a
lengthy, rewarding and enjoyable journey. It can, if read consecu-
tively, give an overall view of the topography, showing where the
major features fit into the literary landscape. Alternatively, it can
serve in a more piecemeal way, giving close-ups of the work of
individual authors. And those wishing to move on to fuller
investigations are directed from the sketch-maps offered here
towards more detailed material of the Ordnance Survey variety.

A number of English-language guides have, at different times,
suggested paths across the terrain, each with its own individual
purposes and orientations. Lytton Strachey's *Landmarks in
French Literature* (1912), for instance, gives the general reader of
an earlier age an enthusiastic guided tour of the prize exhibits.
Laurence Bisson, with his wartime paperback *A Short History of*

French Literature (1943) and Geoffrey Brereton, using the same
title (first edn 1954), adopt a more detached and comprehensive
manner. In their *Advice to the Student of French* (first edn 1955),
R. C. Knight and F. L. George present the Honours student with
a set of bearings in literature, along with much other information
on *explication de textes*, residence abroad and examination
technique. *French Literature and its Background*, edited by John
Cruickshank (1968–70) consists of six volumes of essays by
academic specialists, complete with chronologies and bibliographical information. *France: A Companion to French Studies*,
edited by D. G. Charlton (first edn 1972), like its predecessor,
edited by R. L. G. Ritchie (1937), is a comprehensive volume
covering history, ideas, literature, the visual arts and music. *The
Right Angle: Your Degree in French* by Malcolm Smith, Jean
Barron, Harry Cockerham and Mike Routledge (1987) draws on
the authors' experiences as teachers and examiners at London
University to explain the disciplines of modern language studies,
including the reading of literature and the writing of essays. The
present authors are well aware of all these predecessors and of the
many debts they owe to them.

Signposts to French Literature is a compact and accessible
general account, perhaps the first new one-volume survey in
English in the decades since Bisson and Brereton, and differing
markedly from them as it is designed specifically to meet the
present needs of sixth-formers, students in further education, and
undergraduates embarking on degree courses. To this end the
subject-matter is geared to a close analysis of recent GCE
Advanced Level syllabuses and those operating in the first year in
colleges and universities. The main text begins with a short
description of the sources of the language and literature of France
in the Middle Ages and the Renaissance. This sets the scene for the
seventeenth, eighteenth, nineteenth and twentieth centuries, each
of which is the subject of a separate chapter. These major chapters
open with an overview of the historical, political and cultural
developments, followed by a general summary of the literary
situation and a supplementary reading list. The second part of each
of these chapters consists of separate sections on the most
prominent writers, with a discussion of the writer's career and
major work, a short list of critical studies in English likely to be
available, and a series of 'Workpoints' – questions, quotations and
suggestions which lead the reader on to further exploration. The
final, brief chapter balances the first one on origins by looking
forward to possible future developments. There follows a glossary
of some of the more specialized terms occurring in the book, and
then a general bibliography. This latter includes bibliographical
guides, dictionaries, general works and series not necessarily

mentioned in relation to particular centuries or authors, and should therefore be consulted in conjunction with the more specific bibliographies. Here and throughout, the intention is to present the information simply, with a minimum of scholarly detail, and with an emphasis on the most approachable and, where possible, the most recent works.

1

Beginnings

No serious traveller starts a journey without a careful survey of the territory to be covered along the road; and anyone who merely wants to go from A to B will find the journey all the better for knowing something of the surroundings. Likewise, any student of French literature, even one mainly concerned with its later periods, will understand the whole area far more with a little awareness of the climate, the hills and the valleys, the ancient tracks which predated the classical palaces and the industrial cities, and some of which still exist today. It is important to have some idea of how the literary landscape gradually came about, rather than to take its recent shapes as permanent features. And it is as well to remember that the literary, like the natural landscape has its earthquakes and subsidence, floods and droughts, which cause fresh upheaval and change. Further, most contours remain visible even when covered with brick, concrete or tarmac: so that a grasp of underlying trends can help solve many apparently unique problems. Beyond which, as writers are endlessly conscious of their cultural environment, readers can scarcely afford to turn their backs on it: to identify the epic qualities of a modern novelist, or the rhetorical devices of a Symbolist poem, is to locate them in more senses than one.

The notion of France comes into focus only slowly over the centuries, when 'Francia' is used to indicate, roughly, the territory called 'Gallia', or Gaul (c. AD 400), and the tenth and eleventh centuries, when 'Francia' is used to indicate, roughly the territory in its modern form. In between, there had been various invaders including Norsemen, Huns, and a Germanic tribe called the Franks, who gave the country its name, and whose greatest ruler was the Emperor Charlemagne (reigned 771–814). This transitional period also sees the infancy of the French language. After the Romans left their various European provinces, Latin developed in two distinct directions: among the tiny, educated, clerical élite it persisted, little changed, for perhaps a thousand years; but with time the language of the ordinary inhabitants of many Roman provinces, Vulgar Latin, was transformed into the vernacular forms known collectively as the Romance languages. And with the growth of this popular idiom – the vehicle, of course, of a still essentially oral culture – literature (which might be loosely defined as a creative or artistic use of language) could come into being. The oldest surviving document written in Old French is the text of the Strasbourg Oaths (842), which seal a military alliance against the Holy Roman Emperor Lothair. Various religious texts are evidence of linguistic evolution over the following centuries, and by about 1100 this phase had reached a peak, allowing the spread of a great secular literature.

The emergence of a civilization

In the eleventh and twelfth centuries France, for all its intellectual and artistic pre-eminence, was still – like all other European countries – far from being a centralized state in any modern sense. The great warriors who had dominated barbarian societies now became hereditary landowners, often holding their fief (or *feuda* – hence the term 'feudal system') in exchange for loyalty and service to their king, but retaining a high degree of independence. The other major power in the land was the Church, which controlled not only people's beliefs, but also education and much of society's wealth. The medieval universities, cathedrals and monasteries still in existence today are impressive proof of this influence. An uncompromising and rigorous set of military, aristocratic and religious values is thus central to medieval civilization, and finds vivid practical expression in the Crusades in which, from the end of the eleventh century, Christian armies fought to recover the Holy Land. This same spirit also informs the long epic narratives of the period, known as *chansons de geste* (*chansons* because they were chanted or sung by minstrels; *geste* from the Latin *gesta*, or 'heroic exploits'). Typically, they recount, in ten-syllable assonanced verse, chivalric adventures supposed to have happened centuries earlier. Of the eighty or so extant *chansons de geste*, many relate to the age of Charlemagne, including the most famous of them, the *Chanson de Roland* (composed *c.* 1100). This transforms a minor military skirmish into a glorious triumph for the exceptionally valiant and divinely-inspired French army against the heathen Saracens. The crisp, economical narrative of the unknown author allows the emphasis to fall on the grandeur of the events and the spiritual ideal of the Christian heroes.

The courtly ideal

The relatively peaceful atmosphere of the courts of the Languedoc (the southern part of France where, in the Middle Ages, the word for 'yes' was *oc* rather than the northern *oïl*) was particularly favourable to another vital strand in this outstanding literary period. Parallel with the epics, which stressed the public issues of military and religious conflict, a more private and personal literature was also growing. The *troubadours* wrote delicate poems, short in length but again intended to be sung, celebrating the power of love, often as felt by a knight for an unattainable noble lady. In northern France this *fin'amor* is captured more in *romans*, or romances – poems with a setting remote from current reality, and in which love motivates the narrative action. The earliest of them used stories from classical literature, and included the *Roman d'Alexandre* which, because it has lines of twelve syllables (which would, much later, supersede the eight currently favoured in romance), yields the term alexandrine. Much of the subject-matter of this literature of courtly love is drawn from legends of King Arthur and his knights; the outstanding texts are those of Chrétien de Troyes, the most influential writer of Arthurian romance and author of the first story of the Grail, and the romances of Thomas and Béroul, both devoted to the doomed lovers Tristan and Iseut. In the thirteenth century, Guillaume de Lorris, in his *Roman de la Rose*, creates an allegory of love, while Jean de Meung uses his subsequent, encyclopaedic, continuation of the poem to question and debunk courtly values. A more earthy tone occurs in the *fabliaux*, humorous tales of trickery, cunning and marital infidelity. And gradually, fundamental changes became apparent: lyric poetry depends less and less on music; and more works are written in prose, including romances (a significant move towards the modern *roman*) and historical works such as Villehardouin's memoirs of the Crusades. The most striking indication of all, perhaps, is the disappearance, by about 1300, of the *chanson de geste*, which barely outlived the last Crusade.

Crisis and decline

The damaging events which overtook France during the fourteenth and fifteenth centuries inevitably had their effect on literature. There was the prolonged, if sporadic, conflict with England, known as the Hundred Years' War, from which emerged a national heroine in Joan of Arc; other upheavals included a peasants' revolt, famine and the Black Death. Epic and romance seemed out of tune with the prevailing atmosphere of fearful gloom. Other genres, such as didactic poetry and drama, flourished in their places, reflecting an increased need for reassurance, propaganda and instruction. From modest origins in the liturgical plays of the twelfth century – the earliest of them composed in Latin – drama became highly popular during the following 300 years, acted by members of guilds and religious confraternities, and staged in public squares and church porches. The *mystères* generally had sacred subjects – biblical stories or lives of saints – while the *moralités*, *farces* and *soties* were all secular genres, respectively moral instruction in allegorical form, comic scenes of contemporary life, and anarchic ridicule of figures in authority. The other great advance is in poetry, when fixed forms such as the *rondeau* and *ballade* set new standards of refinement. Interest shifts increasingly to the personalities of individual writers, and although many now appear secondary figures, Christine de Pisan stands out as a lyricist of the feminine point of view, and Charles d'Orléans as a skilled interpreter of the courtly tradition. Unquestionably, the great poet of the age is François Villon, who brilliantly distils irony, low-life experiences, pathos, fear of death, and hope of salvation. His major works are the *Lais* (1456) and the *Testament* (1461).

Renewal

A return to relative peace and, from 1515, the political stability of the monarchy of François I, himself a patron of the arts, offer a new beginning. And the influence of Renaissance humanism, by now long under way in Italy, gains ground rapidly from the end of the fifteenth century. Initially this was a movement of scholars, which renewed the understanding of classical Latin texts and revived the knowledge of Greek. With the growth of printing there was a swift spread of new ideas, discoveries and types of literature among a rapidly expanding audience. The new spirit of enquiry and the challenging of traditional authority also make for a crucial split in the Christian Church, when first Luther and then Calvin assert the individual's right to interpret the Bible and to communicate directly with God. At the same time as the emergence of what comes to be called Protestantism, revolutions are also taking place in geography (after Columbus) and cosmology (when Copernicus and Galileo argue that the earth is not the immovable centre of the universe).

This intellectual ferment is perfectly captured in the work of François Rabelais (*c.* 1494–*c.* 1553), philosopher, theologian, doctor, lawyer and much else besides. His stories of the adventures of the giant Pantagruel and his father Gargantua combine fantasy with realism, outlandish humour with subtle satire. Rabelais's language is a rich mixture of popular and learned styles, regionalisms and borrowings from Latin and Greek. Similarly wide-ranging, his narrative technique takes in monologue and dialogue, letters, set-piece speeches and poems. Rabelais marks another crucial step forward in fiction; and poetry, too, sees vital advances.

Following Rabelais's contemporary, Marot, who was among the first writers in French to adopt the Italian form called the sonnet, the *Pléiade* – a group of seven leading poets – sought to create a new poetry based on classical models, but using a renewed French language which they saw as the equal of Greek and Latin. Their manifesto was Du Bellay's *Deffense et Illustration de la langue françoyse* (1549), and their foremost poet Ronsard (1524–85), creator of some of France's finest lyrics, such as the tender 'Quand vous serez bien vieille' from the *Sonnets pour Hélène*. The classical influence makes itself felt in drama too: as the mystery and miracle plays fade out by the middle of the sixteenth century, so there appear the first tragedies in French, some based on Greek myth and others on Roman history – though subjects are also drawn from the Bible. However, for all their poetic virtues, even the best of these, say the plays of Robert Garnier, lacked the tension and conflict which would mark the great tragedies of the next century.

Dissension and controversy

The religious controversy had grave consequences in the latter half of the sixteenth century: between the death of Henri II in 1559 and the Edict of Nantes in 1598, which granted Huguenots freedom of worship, France was torn apart by the Wars of Religion and shattered by such horrors as the St Bartholomew's Eve massacre of Huguenots, ordered by Charles IX in 1572. Inevitably, the conflict is reflected in the literature of the period: Ronsard, among others, writes in favour of the Catholic position, while d'Aubigné and his co-religionists defend the Protestant cause. Meanwhile, the humanist enquiring spirit was turning to broad political and moral issues; the prose of La Boétie and Pasquier is an instrument for tackling the problems of tyranny and sovereignty, while Du Vair promotes stoicism, a philosophy of rationalism and resignation, through his translation of Epictetus. Stoicism is in fact a major element in the thought of the most important writer of the period, Michel de Montaigne (1533–92). His collections of *Essais*, which begin as little more than maxims and anecdotes drawn from classical authors, develop into a set of profound, if unsystematic, studies of the human mind. In the essay *Apologie de Raimond Sebond* he shows the limitations of reason, claims that nothing can be known for certain, and adopts the sceptical motto 'Que sçais-je?'. Elsewhere he argues for friendship, tolerance, broad-mindedness

and, above all, self-knowledge, such as he reveals in the increasingly
personal later essays. Not least because of their attractive, readable
style, the *Essais* have lived on when other writings expressing
similar ideas have not. In the seventeenth century, to go no further
than that, they had immense impact, both inspiring the free-
thinking *libertins* and moving writers as different as Descartes
and Pascal to try to counter his scepticism with their own beliefs.

But if, say, Descartes borrows bricks from the same place as
Montaigne to construct his own house, this is only one of the
countless examples of the past's decisive role in forming the more
recent landscape. Even the briefest of glimpses back into the
origins of French literature confirms the irresistible influence of
historical events and social change on language, and the way that
the state of the language determines and conditions literature. It
also highlights such basic watersheds as those dividing oral and
written codes, or verse and prose, and uncovers ancient battle-
grounds, ideological and technical. It becomes clear, moreover,
that all the main genres are built on deep foundations: that the
principal verse forms and metres were established long before
Malherbe; that drama, including tragedy, did not have to wait for
Corneille; that prose, as a vital medium for both ideas and fiction,
was not invented by Descartes or Madame de Lafayette. The
literary terrain of the post-1600 period may be scrutinized in fuller
detail and at greater length, but given some grasp of what
underlies or bears down on it, given some degree of orientation,
the approach must be both easier and more rewarding.

Further reading

J. Fox, *A Literary History of France*, vol. 1: *The Middle Ages*
(1974); L. Muir, *Literature and Society in Medieval France* (1985).

T. Cave, *The Cornucopian Text* (1979); A. Krailsheimer (ed.), *The
Continental Renaissance* (1971).

2

The seventeenth century

There exists a popular image of seventeenth-century France which conceals as much as it reveals. Generations of Hollywood scriptwriters have familiarized the public with a number of salient features, such as the iron rule of Cardinal Richelieu, aided surreptitiously by his 'éminence grise' Father Joseph, but thwarted by d'Artagnan and the three musketeers; or in the latter half of the century, the stylish ceremonial of court life under Louis XIV at Versailles. By their excessive concentration upon the spectacular and exceptional, these simplifications distort the historical reality as surely as cartoonists throughout the world have distorted the shape of Cyrano de Bergerac's nose. There were in the seventeenth century many triumphs – military, political, social, architectural, theatrical and literary – so many, in fact, that it is easy to neglect the difficulty with which they were achieved and to overlook the persistent problems which they disguised. By the time the graceful fountains at Versailles began to play, the cost of their construction in human lives was appalling. Like the formal beauty of classical architecture, the literature of this period can only be properly understood and fully appreciated in the context of political developments and political stagnation, of commercial endeavours and economic bankruptcy, of social refinement for one narrow social stratum and brutish misery for the bulk of the nation.

The closing years of Louis XIV's reign belong with the seventeenth century; so, too, at the end of the sixteenth century, do the opening years of Henri IV's reign, partly because this transitional period provides a yardstick against which change can be measured, and partly because the attempts of his successors to achieve order and stability were already sketched out in Henri IV's policies. The fundamental problems were more clearly visible before the magnificence and absolutism of Louis XIV managed to conceal or deflect attention from what was still unresolved. The fact, for example, that Henri's reign came about through the assassination of his predecessor and ended with his own murder is a mark of political instability; and the fact that, in order to take the throne, Henri was obliged to convert from Protestantism to Catholicism is a sign of the religious turmoil which overshadows the reigns of all three seventeenth-century monarchs.

The entire history of the period from 1589, the year of Henry IV's accession, to 1715, when Louis XIV died, can be seen as France's attempt to come to terms with two powerful influences: the Renaissance and the Reformation. The rebirth of learning and culture encouraged a reverence for the achievements of Greece and Rome together with an openness to new ideas, which acted as a stimulus to more scientific modes of thought, often at the expense of traditional religious beliefs. The growth of the Protestant faith led to struggles not only between Protestant and Catholic, but also within Catholicism itself. That is why much of French art and literature finds its subjects in Greek, Roman and biblical antiquity. Nor is it surprising that the confusions created by the variety of ideas and beliefs should at times militate against the efforts to achieve greater order in government, society and the national economy. The formal splendours of the gardens at Versailles, like the ordered beauty of classical literature, convey a compelling impression of stability. This veneer may conceal the variety and even confusion which lay beneath the surface where the new and the traditional were often bewilderingly entangled. The inter-twining of strands as the struggle for order affects every facet of life is visible even in the personal careers of many of the century's leading figures; Pascal, undoubtedly one of the most eminent scientists, is best remembered for his religious writings and the support he gave to the Jansenists of Port-Royal in their conflicts with the Jesuits; Racine, who had received a strict Jansenist upbringing at Port-Royal, disappointed his tutors by devoting his talents and the major part of his life to secular drama based on the myths and legends of pagan antiquity before turning to the Bible for the subjects of his last two works; and Descartes and La Rochefoucauld started on military careers before becoming writers.

A brief examination of the three reigns will throw into relief the efforts of successive monarchs and ministers to achieve order and greatness, and indicate many successful political moves to control or unite the various elements and factions. Such developments did not necessarily constitute progress, and certainly not a uniform progress, for the spirit of religious toleration and political judgement which prompted Henri IV to grant Protestants an immunity from religious persecution by the Edict of Nantes in 1598 was soon forgotten; and by the formal Revocation of the Edict of Nantes (Edict of Fontainebleau, 1685) Louis XIV effectively banished the Huguenots and so destroyed much of the commercial and industrial wealth that his ministers had painstakingly stimulated. It is important to remember such underlying tensions and contradictions when attempting to situate the work of important literary figures in a true social, political and religious climate, particularly as works of criticism tend quite correctly to stress the qualities of order and clarity in the principal artistic endeavours of the Classical age.

These were precisely the qualities advocated for French language and literature by Malherbe and Boileau; and if, in the examination of some literary giants, emphasis is placed above all upon three dramatists, Corneille, Racine and Molière, because theatre was the pre-eminent genre, these same qualities, the same desire for refinement of thought and clarity of expression, are apparent in other genres and other forms of art: in the philosophical writings of Descartes and Pascal, in the sermons of Bossuet, in the descriptions of society found in the works of Madame de Sévigné and La Bruyère.

In an attempt to understand the literature of French Classicism, these characteristics must not be minimized or neglected, provided also that due weight is given to the fact that any grand design will generate its own nonconformists. Those of an independent mind – the free-thinkers or *libertins* – were treated intolerantly, with the result that, if La Fontaine is the best known of seventeenth-century poets, others like Saint-Amant and Théophile de Viau were obliged to take refuge outside France. Even Descartes, in many ways the father of modern French philosophy, considered it prudent to live and publish his work abroad. Such international contacts were, of course, to bring their own immediate influences on French culture. Contact with the art and architecture of Roman antiquity is unmistakable in many French paintings and buildings which date from the sixteenth and seventeenth centuries, but there were at the same time more contemporary links with Italy: the influence of Italian drama on Molière's comedy is clear; and two of the greatest French painters, Poussin and Lorrain, settled in Rome. However, the example of architecture provides a further opportunity to warn against judgements which neglect the full complexity of the period; among the buildings which have survived 300 years are many which are attributable less to any particularly Italian influence than to Louis XIV's military ambitions: Vauban's fortress at Besançon, for example, is a reminder of political realities.

Three particularly important influences on the development of Classical language and literature need to be singled out for special comment: the first is the work of Malherbe to purify and regulate French poetry and the French language; the second is the Académie Française, established in 1635 by Cardinal Richelieu, to control and stimulate literary activity; and the third is the contribution both to language and to literature made by the *salons*, the regular gatherings organized by such leading social figures as Madame de Rambouillet and Mademoiselle de Scudéry at which particular attention was paid to refinement of language and the cultivation of literary style.

Malherbe (1555–1628) came to Paris in 1605 at the king's request after many years in Provence where he had established his reputation as a poet. He quickly became the authority on poetry and language. Not by a formal treatise but by the example of his own work, by his personal authority and by the reactions of his contemporaries, Malherbe was to carry out lasting reforms of French versification in two ways: he exercised a control over the poetic liberty introduced in the sixteenth century by Ronsard and the other poets in the Pléiade; and by his meticulous attention to the form of the alexandrine he established firm rules for the standard line of French verse and drama. More important even than his concern for poetry was Malherbe's attempt to regulate the French language. In place of the complicated sentence structures, the latinisms and the frequently slack use of language which were characteristic of literature in the previous century, Malherbe substituted a less ornamental, more precise French. His contribution is doubly important: for language, because he forged the basic tool on which the quality of Classical literature was to depend and, in so doing, paved the way for the further regulation and purification to be undertaken collectively by the Académie Française and individually by such influential grammarians as Vaugelas and Bouhours; and for literature, because he advocated many of the qualities, such as clarity, simplicity and control, which were to become the hallmarks of truly Classical literature.

Malherbe's work was to be continued in a more official way by the Académie Française, of which Vaugelas was one of the founder members. When Cardinal Richelieu heard of the regular meetings held at the home of Valentin Conrart to exchange ideas on linguistic and literary topics, he decided to formalize the proceedings: he was himself genuinely interested in literature; moreover, in the interests of national prestige, he wished to extend state control beyond the political and economic even as far as the intellectual and cultural activities of the country.

The Academy was formally established by royal command in 1635, Louis XIII nominating the founder members and outlining their original programme of activities and functions. The principal task, stated in Article 24 of the Statutes, was to provide 'des règles certaines à notre langue, et à la rendre pure, éloquente et capable de traiter des arts et des sciences'. In addition, the Academy was charged with the preparation of four works which would form and regulate the standards of language and literature. The publication of various editions of the dictionary, the first in 1694, shows that the Academicians have regularly addressed themselves to one of their tasks, even though the other three were neglected: the grammar was not finished until 1932, and no work on a Rhetoric or Poetic has ever appeared. Even so, the influence of the French Academy on literature, taste and culture has been considerable for over 350 years, and most major writers (with a few exceptions such as Molière, Diderot and Flaubert) have been members.

The third important, though less formal, influence on the language and literature of French Classicism was the private salon where men and women of taste and intellect would meet – partly for the social pleasures of good company and partly for the more serious purpose of stimulating their interest in literary activity and encouraging the development of more refined language and behaviour. The best known of these gatherings took place in the Hôtel de Rambouillet. In the celebrated *chambre bleue* of Arthénice – an anagram for Catherine, marquise de Rambouillet – the hostess would receive her intimate friends, usually aristocrats, together with influential literary and political figures, often – but not exclusively – from the middle class. Among her guests during fifty years in which her salon contributed to the artistic and cultural vitality of the nation were, for example, Richelieu and Corneille, Vaugelas and Conrart, Voiture and the Prince de Condé.

The fashion spread, and it is possible to suggest direct links between some of the other salons and a number of notable literary achievements: one of the entertainments at the salon of Madame de Sablé was the composition of maxims, and La Rochefoucauld was to develop this form into his major work; and to the short stories which were a popular diversion at the home of Mademoiselle de Montpensier can be traced the inspiration required for one of the first great writers of French fiction, Madame de Lafayette, to begin her work.

The fashion spread still further during the seventeenth and eighteenth centuries. At some gatherings the tone was essentially social, and into that category would go the salon of Ninon de Lenclos. At others the emphasis was supposedly intellectual; but it would be wrong to condemn the major salons for the sort of excesses that Molière portrays in *Les Femmes savantes* or *Les Précieuses ridicules*. The struggle for linguistic and social refinement had encouraged affectations and excesses of the sort most apparent in *préciosité* of language which, forbidding the use of base, vulgar and even commonplace terms, led to the use of such expressions as 'l'ameublement de la bouche' for teeth, and 'l'instrument de la propreté' for a broom. At these major Parisian salons, as at the *samedis de Sapho* where Mademoiselle de Scudéry presided, good sense, taste and judgement provided a control over tendencies to excess and exaggeration. The salons were, in fact, to stimulate the development in the seventeenth century of one of the most important influences not merely on literature but on culture and society in general: the role of woman.

It was largely the feminine touch that transformed the boorishness of court life under Henri IV, where the nobles, when not actually feuding, retained the manners and language of the barrack room, to the polish of Versailles under Louis XIV where the descendants of those nobles had become courtiers aspiring to the qualities of the *honnête homme*. The notion of behaviour controlled by standards known as *les bienséances* was to extend from society to the stage.

Henri IV (1553–1610)

When, in 1589, Henri of Navarre adopted the Catholic faith in order to become King of France and so begin the dynasty of Bourbon monarchs, the country was suffering from a long series of violent religious wars which had devastated the countryside, impeded economic development and led to such atrocities as the St Bartholomew's Eve massacre in 1572. The new king's description of his conversion ('Paris is worth a Mass') and his decision to govern through a chief minister, Sully, who remained a Protestant, are a clue to his political shrewdness and to the major endeavours of his reign: the removal of religious unrest and the restoration of order. Probably the most notable achievement of his reign was the promulgation in 1598 of the Edict of Nantes by which the Huguenots were granted freedom of worship and various safeguards and privileges, including control of the port of La Rochelle.

The accession of Henri IV can be taken as a decisive step towards the establishment of a political system which was to last until the French Revolution of 1789: the development of a unified and centralized nation ruled by an absolute monarch. Even if the policy of religious toleration was to prove only partially and temporarily successful, the reign of Henri IV was in many ways a preparation for the policies of Louis XIV. The province of Navarre which he brought with him to the throne consolidated French territories on the Spanish border and formed a stage in the establishment of natural frontiers, a strategy which Louis XIV was to pursue so successfully that, by 1700, the territorial boundaries of France as we now know it were almost complete. Other lasting and important, if less spectacular, achievements of Henri's reign were the strengthening of central government and the stimulus given to commerce and industry.

Progress was far from easy. Sully's efforts to restore some order and discipline, for example by modifying the collection of taxes or by simplifying the varied system of weights and measures, provoked hostility. Every attempt to increase uniformity or centralize power was interpreted as an attack on local privilege; and if some of Sully's work was to provide a basis for economic development, other policies, however well-intentioned, stimulated resentments which were to fester and, by the time Louis XIV came to the throne, erupt into the lengthy civil disturbances and hostilities known as the *Frondes*.

Although Henri's endeavours and the many successes of his reign earned him the title of 'Henri le grand', the civil and political dissensions persisted. As he prepared to join his armies battling to establish French supremacy in Europe, he nominated his wife, Marie de' Medici as Regent; the following day, having already survived seven earlier attempts on his life, Henri was assassinated. It was an irony that the knife snatched by Ravaillac from an inn called the Three Spoons as Henri passed along the rue Saint-Honoré should end a reign in the very town for which Henri had abjured the Protestant faith, the town which he had improved architecturally and established as the centre of a national government.

Louis XIII (1601–43)

As Louis was only 9 when he succeeded his father to the throne, there was a lengthy regency, a period of disorganization in which the country was so badly governed by the queen-mother and her Italian favourites that the political institution known as the States-General assembled in 1614 to protest at the defective government and the disorder created by the feuding of unruly aristocrats. This assembly, representing three social orders (nobility, church and *le tiers état*) was an impotent political force: it could neither find nor impose any solution and so it dispersed, never to meet again until the eve of the French Revolution, 175 years later. Such control as there was began to pass from Marie de' Medici to the young king himself when, in 1617, he ordered the assassination of Concini, the Regent's latest favourite; and then, in 1624, a period of sure and effective government began with the nomination as his principal minister of a young bishop, the Cardinal de Richelieu. For almost forty years France was to be governed by two churchmen: by Richelieu until the death of Louis XIII; and then, for eighteen years during the minority of Louis XIV, by Cardinal Mazarin. Both worked to strengthen royal authority, to increase national prestige and to extend French power throughout Europe.

As head of the King's Council Richelieu was able to influence, even control, most facets of life in France: he gave administrative power to an increasingly efficient middle-class civil service and so reduced the strength of obstreperous and hostile aristocrats as effectively as he reduced their feudal fortresses; he filled important posts with his own supporters, even his own relatives, giving a cousin command of the artillery and a nephew command of the navy; he brought the influential to a state of obedience and the poor to a state of tax-paying servitude; he judged political offenders at courts appointed by himself; he forbade duelling on pain of death and even the king's favourite, Cinq-Mars, was executed for that offence; he continued Sully's efforts to stimulate commerce; and – in some ways the most surprising feature of his work – he, a Catholic, involved France in a foreign policy based upon support for the Protestant princes of Germany against the Catholic countries of Spain and Austria. Richelieu's support of Protestantism in the Thirty Years War seems all the more surprising as a central feature of his domestic policy was based on the suppression of Huguenot influence and the destruction of their protected port of La Rochelle (1629). The paradox is, however, removed when it is realized that, in these policies as in everything he did, Richelieu was motivated only by his aim to establish the greatness of France: the Huguenots constituted an internal threat, an 'empire within an empire'; and support for German principalities was a method of reducing the military threat of the Hapsburg dynasty, France's traditional rival for European supremacy. When, by the Treaty of Westphalia in 1648, the Thirty Years War was ended, France had gained control of Alsace and Roussillon and so moved one step nearer to the establishment of 'natural frontiers'. Richelieu was by then dead, but this outcome of the war can be seen as posthumous confirmation of his military judgement and political shrewdness. His role had been successful: he had left France a stronger, more centralized and more unified country; at the heart of it was a capital that had grown in size and wealth and splendour. His own residence, the Palais-Cardinal (now the Palais-Royal), was the visible proof of his authority and achievement.

Inevitably there were continuing problems: as well as the massive deprivation of the vast peasant population, the religious unrest and turmoil persisted. In some ways, the intense religious activity brought numerous spiritual, educational and even architectural benefits: the foundation of convents in Paris at a rate of more than one per year; the establishment of important religious organizations such as the Oratoire to train young men for the priesthood (and to this sort of educational development can be attributed the remarkably powerful pulpit oratory of preachers like Bossuet and Bourdaloue); charitable organizations such as the Sisters of Charity, founded by Saint Vincent de Paul. The spread of missionaries led to valuable commercial settlements in Canada and the Near East.

However, the religious activity had less desirable consequences: in addition to the persistent persecution of the Protestant community, there were unproductive rivalries within the Catholic faith between, for example, the Jesuits and the Jansenists; and the power of 'faux dévots', who played on religious credulity and fanaticism while wearing a mask of piety to conceal self-interest, was so widespread that Molière could make it a subject of satirical attack in *Tartuffe*. Richelieu, the dominant force in Louis XIII's reign, was less a churchman and more a statesman and soldier. His outstanding administrative abilities were to open a way for the absolutism of Louis XIV; his failure to eliminate religious discord was to echo and re-echo later in the century.

Louis XIV (1638–1715)

The long reign of Louis XIV, which began in the year following Richelieu's death, can be considered in three stages: the first, from 1643 to 1661, was the Regency when Anne of Austria, the queen-mother, and Richelieu's successor, Cardinal Mazarin, governed the country; the second, a twenty-year period of grandeur which reached its climax with the transfer of the court from Paris to Versailles in 1682; and the last, a period of decline marred by the Sun King's extravagance and increasing intransigence, some thirty years characterized by such costly errors as the Revocation of the Edict of Nantes. The second stage coincides almost exactly with the quarter-century when Classical literature reached its peak.

The Regency gave an inauspicious start to Louis's reign: Mazarin was less able than Richelieu; the military successes could not compensate for the growing neglect of commerce; the dissatisfactions of the nobility and the frustration of Parisian and provincial *parlements* became increasingly intense, with the result that the young king was forced by two periods of civil disturbances known as the *Frondes* to take refuge a few miles from Paris at Saint-Germain-en-Laye. Louis did not forget the indignity; and the majority of the population who were not involved in either the *fronde parlementaire* (1649) or the *fronde des princes* (1650–2) were ready, almost relieved, to accept the autocratic control of domestic affairs which was contained in Louis's declaration: 'L'état, c'est moi.' With the death of Mazarin in 1661, Louis took personal charge of the affairs of France.

The twenty-year period of greatness is attributable in part to the foundations laid by the Cardinals, in part to the commanding personality of Louis himself. His marriage to the Infanta of Spain, Maria Theresa, ensured a time of relative calm in foreign affairs:

the king was free to govern at home. He chose to rule at court through men selected from the *noblesse de robe* of middle-class origin, such as Fouquet, the financier, and Colbert, a brilliant administrator who was able to undertake work equivalent to that of six or seven ministers in today's France; and in the provinces through governors, usually reliable aristocratic allies, and through *intendants*, again members of the bourgeoisie nominated by himself. This system of imposing a centralized authority had two important advantages: the king's nominees could be removed at will; their use was in itself a further way of reducing the power of the nobility. Among the notable achievements in this period are the improvement of commerce and communications, the establishment of a trained, regular army, the encouragement of Classical art in all its forms: painting, music, theatre, dance, literature and – most obviously by the magnificent palace of Versailles – architecture. From 1680 the king was officially known as 'Louis le Grand'. Soon afterwards began the period of decline.

The magnificence of Versailles where the court moved in 1682 was not matched by the greatness of the reign. The theatricality of the setting and the display of court life have become legendary. Unfortunately, by the time the stage was finally ready for royal and aristocratic parade, the age of Classical drama was virtually over: Molière had already been able to use the gardens for elaborate productions before he died in 1673; Racine had written all but two of his plays by 1677; Corneille was to die in 1684. The gallery opened when Poussin and Lorrain were dead. The extravagance continued but there was no longer a Colbert to create the necessary wealth. The formality, solemnity and punctilious etiquette for which court life at Versailles is famous tended to be an increasingly empty charade for the benefit of an increasingly autocratic monarch, an ageing widower who had married a devout widow, Madame de Maintenon; a failing ruler too imbued with the notion of his own divine rightness to see that he was unwise when he involved France in costly wars abroad and expelled the Huguenots who had always been a source of commercial wealth at home. By the end of the century they were dispersed throughout Europe, so that, for example, one in every five of the inhabitants of Berlin was French. The Huguenots who remained in France were outlawed. The revolt of those in the Cévennes (the 'Camisards'), was a measure of the social distress in the early years of the eighteenth century and a foretaste of the political discontent which was to result in the French Revolution.

*   *   *

The literature has outlived the monarchy. The impetus given to all forms of art by Richelieu and Louis XIV in their desire to establish greatness in every aspect of national life has proved more enduring than most of their political, social and economic achievements: art, architecture, music and literature provide a record of the genius, the grandeur, the splendour of French Classical culture. In a way, given Louis's personal taste for the spectacular, it is understandable that theatre, of which spectacle is an essential part, should be the major genre, even though Corneille, Racine and Molière, by their greater emphasis upon the psychological, were more visually restrained than dramatists in other periods.

These three playwrights together represent such a pinnacle of dramatic attainment that they, more than any other writers, are considered representative of French literary greatness in the seventeenth century. It is important to recognize that many of the qualities characteristic of their work, the concision and clarity of style, the remarkable psychological penetration, the elegance and subtlety of thought and expression, are characteristic also of other writers in what has been called the Golden Age of French literature. The greatness and importance of Classical theatre is undeniable, but it must be seen as complementing rather than eclipsing the attainments in other genres: the philosophical works of Descartes and Pascal; the evolution of the novel, from *L'Astrée* (1607–10), the vast pastoral romance by Honoré d'Urfé, to *Télémaque* (1699) in which Fénelon presented selected episodes from Virgil to Homer primarily for the benefit of his royal pupil, the grandson of Louis XIV; the penetrating portrait of social life and human psychology provided in the *Caractères* of La Bruyère, in the letters written by Madame de Sévigné to her daughter; in the *Mémoires* of the Duc de Saint-Simon; and, at a time when lyric poetry had declined in popularity, in the short yet telling *Fables* of La Fontaine.

The contemporary philosophical climate is, in many ways, quite as important for an understanding of seventeenth-century literature as the social and historical context. Two major figures, René Descartes and Blaise Pascal, demonstrate the most significant developments of thought in the century following the Renaissance. In very different ways, their work can be seen as attempts to come to terms with the problems posed by the Renaissance.

In broad terms, Montaigne's celebrated device or motto 'Que sçais-je?' was an indication of several features of his century: a confusion or uncertainty caused by the wealth of newly revealed material particularly from Greek and Roman antiquity, a sceptical rejection of traditional beliefs, and an openness to new ideas. The works of Descartes and Pascal, both brilliant scientists, are important elements within the pattern of seventeenth-century efforts to transform doubt into authority, and to search for answers to the intellectual and metaphysical uncertainties that are created when old beliefs are challenged but not fully replaced, when confidence in old certainties falters and is not fully restored.

The essential principle of Descartes's thought, as demonstrated in two major works, his *Discours de la méthode* (1637) and his *Méditations métaphysiques* (1641), was a repudiation of all accepted thought, a refusal of all authority except for what could be proven by the exercise of reason. His application of rational and scientific methods was not fully understood by many of his contemporaries; but in a Europe where Galileo had recently been condemned for challenging accepted astronomical theory, he was mistrusted. The proof of God's existence by human reason was seen by some to be heretical; he was attacked by the Sorbonne; his works were put on the Index in 1663. In spite of the hostility, however, his theories survived; and he is known as the father of French philosophy not simply because he was the first to write a philosophical text in the French language, nor because of the highly personal style which he created to convey his ideas, but principally because of his powerful influence upon French and European thought. Some literary critics have been tempted to relate Descartes's emphasis upon reason to the rational approach adopted by the heroes of Corneille's tragedies, but it is doubtful whether there was a more direct link than the mood of optimism and confidence in human potential which both writers shared with many of their contemporaries. The real influence of Descartes cannot be confined to the superficial effects of the sort portrayed in Molière's *Les Femmes savantes* where 'blue stockings' who dabble in fashionable philosophical chatter refer to Cartesian *vortices* with all the confidence of ignorance. Descartes's major contribution was to the fundamental transformation of mental attitudes and the development of a scientific outlook which was to reach a peak of importance some two centuries later.

One person who certainly understood Descartes as scientist and as philosopher, who criticized the implications of Cartesian reliance upon human reason and who, a little later in the century, failed to share the mood of optimism, was the second philosophical writer with whose works every student of French literature needs some familiarity. Blaise Pascal is best remembered for two works: the *Lettres provinciales* and the *Pensées*. By the former work he exerted a more direct and immediate influence than Descartes on his contemporaries, for these letters were his contribution to the defence of Jansenism and Port-Royal against attack from other forms of Catholicism. By the latter, he was to establish himself for all time as the defender of true Christianity against the mechanistic theories and rationalism of Descartes and others. Although a brilliant scientist whose mathematical genius alone would have earned him a distinguished reputation, Pascal is remembered particularly for his attempt, following an ecstatic experience in 1654, to write an Apologia for Christianity of which the *Pensées* are his original notes. For all its incompleteness, the enduring qualities of this work are its thought and the lucidity and force with which Pascal's views are expressed. His style is simple but vigorous, subtle but unaffected, lucid yet profound; and above all it has a particular combination of rigour and passion which has earned for his work the description of 'la géométrie enflammée'. By his penetrating insights into the workings of the human mind and soul and by his stylistic control, Pascal is closely related to those writers in the latter half of the seventeenth century whose work forms the high-water mark of French Classicism.

*   *   *

The evolution of the novel is also characterized by increasingly acute observation of human nature. Fictional writings at the start of the seventeenth century were, for all their variety of subject matter, far removed from the novel as it was to develop during the next two centuries in content, form and – most obviously – in length. There was considerable variety of subject matter, ranging from pastoral romances like d'Urfé's *L'Astrée*, which looked backward in the direction of the medieval romance (*roman*), to the fantastical journeys to the moon and the sun described by Cyrano de Bergerac, which look forward to our own science fiction. Only with the work of Madame de Lafayette does fiction begin to resemble the modern world.

The five parts of *L'Astrée* have as their central thread the love of a shepherdess for her beloved Céladon. In an idyllic rural setting, the scores of characters become involved in a bewildering set of adventures, write poetry, encounter nymphs and druids, and above all they discuss love and affairs of the heart. One distinctive feature of this pastoral novel which attaches it more to the literature of the seventeenth century than to its predecessor, the *roman courtois* of medieval times, is the increasingly perceptible concern for an analysis of human emotions.

This fiction was an aristocratic genre for a leisured reading public: fiction for a social élite. Another of the notable novels written at the same period for a similar audience was Mademoiselle de Scudéry's *Le Grand Cyrus* (1649–53). This can be described as a *roman à clef* since it was written about its own aristocratic audience. The ten volumes of this work, although supposedly dealing with events in Asian antiquity, depict the life of Parisian salons. Thinly disguised as Persians, the characters belong to the very social élite of which the author was herself a member, and the tone and mood of the novel capture the *galanterie* and *préciosité* that were fashionable in the 1650s.

The artificial and pretentious are always an inviting target for attack, and mockery of the sentimental novel is the basis for Scarron's *Le Roman comique* (1651–7), which describes in a somewhat more realistic manner the activities of an itinerant theatrical company. As the actors travel from town to town or wait in a variety of inns, there is opportunity for lengthy digressions and improbable adventures; above all there is, allowing for exaggeration, a fascinating account of the life to which a company of travelling players were subject: the taverns, the brawls, the 'attentions' inflicted upon the actresses, the physical hardship, the working conditions, all of which Scarron portrays with verve, humour and a refreshingly honest crudity.

Fiction, which started with the heroic romance, moves closer to the nineteenth-century novel with the work of Madame de Lafayette. *La Princesse de Clèves* (1678) concentrates upon the relationships between the heroine, her husband and the duc de Nemours. The plot is complicated, but there is a control of presentation which marks an important development. There are traces of the *préciosité* visible in earlier novels, and its subject is a historical one; but by its concern for the accurate analysis of human behaviour and by its more restrained style, this story of life at court in the sixteenth century belongs in spirit and style to the literature and court of Louis XIV. A study of human passion and suffering to the exclusion of external descriptions, it recalls the form and flavour of Classical French tragedy.

*   *   *

The same concern to provide a concise and elegant analysis of human psychology and social behaviour is characteristic of other writers of prose. The letters written by Madame de Sévigné to her daughter living away from Parisian society give an entertaining and accurate picture of court life, an incisive description of major events and minor incidents, of literary tastes and fashion and social scandal, rendered all the more human by the genuinely maternal concern and the personal nature of the basic relationship.

This precise and succinct portrayal of individual human beings was elevated to the status of an art by La Bruyère in his *Caractères* (1688). As tutor to the duc de Bourgogne, he was well placed to observe a wide range of behaviour at court: the social vanity, pretentiousness, eccentricities, self-seeking. Often under fictional names, the parasite and the parvenu, the fop and the glutton, are drawn with deft strokes and devastating accuracy. This social criticism is the pointed and perceptive work of a benevolent caricaturist, but the lines can be more vigorous and the strokes more trenchant when he comments on the oppression and poverty which surround and support the splendours of the capital.

A less localized and less sympathetic portrayal of mankind is given in the writings of La Rochefoucauld. Where La Bruyère wrote a paragraph, La Rochefoucauld wrote a sentence; where the former's *portraits* are tinged with a kindly, even sympathetic irony, the latter's observations are mordant. La Bruyère's subject could, in his embarrassment and confusion, still stumble from the room; La Rochefoucauld's subject is securely fastened to the operating table where there is no escape from the knife. With a surgeon's skill, La Rochefoucauld dissects; with a psychologist's insight, he penetrates and analyses human motivation. Human indolence, self-love, passion: one by one, our failings are stripped of pretence, our virtues are questioned. The picture of humankind is austere, sometimes bitter, always compelling.

A similarly skilful analysis of human and social behaviour, although presented in a more imaginative and entertaining way, is to be found, perhaps surprisingly, in some of the most memorable and enduring of French poetry, much of it taking as its subject not, in fact, human beings but creatures from the domain of the natural historian. In an age when tragedy was known as 'la poésie tragique' and many comedies were also written in alexandrine verse, it would be incorrect to view the seventeenth century as a period when poetry was neglected. Certain forms were less favoured; in particular, and partly as a reaction against the exuberance and variety of Renaissance poetry, there was little of a lyrical or personal nature. There were exceptions, but the poetry of Saint-Amant and Théophile de Viau met with little official favour.

Among the more favoured forms were poems with a religious basis, such as translations of the Psalms, and poems of a formal and official nature, such as the consolation written by Malherbe to M. du Périer on the death of his daughter or the prayers for the king's safety and success in battle. There were also many poems with a critical purpose, for example, the long satirical works of Régnier and Boileau. The value of these lengthy works lies nowadays more in their historical interest than in their intrinsic merits as poetry. The most memorable and most appealing of seventeenth-century poems are among the shortest: the *Fables* of La Fontaine.

These tales about foxes and storks, lions and frogs, insects and rabbits, may seem far removed not only from the poetry but also from every form of Classical art. By its apparent choice of subject matter, La Fontaine's work is certainly unique. In fact, the animal world he describes is, like all Classical art, a study of mankind, a study of contemporary society and of humankind in general, not confined to the occasional woodcutter or miller who features alongside the characters in a largely animal kingdom. This collection of anecdotes is not the bestiary of the scientist but the moral commentary of a consummate artist. What La Fontaine enjoyed in Molière's work was not just the humour but the accurate portrayal of human nature; and it was to that facet of nature that he drew attention in an evaluation of Molière's skill:

> Et maintenant il ne faut pas
> Quitter la nature d'un pas.

By his own inspired selection of character and incident, by the rapidity of the events and the telling concision of dialogue, La Fontaine employed many of the skills which characterize French Classical theatre.

Theatre is the major form of art for which the Classical age is remembered. However, although Corneille, Racine and Molière are now universally accepted as masters of their craft, their reputations were not established as smoothly or quickly as today's respect might suggest. Modern acclaim, modern attitudes towards the theatre, and the regular study of a few texts by these dramatists in schools and universities can easily disguise the difficulties faced by these playwrights during their working lives and so conceal the true extent of their remarkable achievements. The theatre is invariably a precarious endeavour and the giants of the seventeenth century were, like the great dramatists of every age, aware of the importance of the audience. Corneille's view that: 'notre premier but doit être de plaire à la cour et au peuple' is echoed by Racine's 'plaire et instruire' and by Molière's 'plaire, peindre et instruire'. There was an equally important, if negative, pole contained in the notion of 'plaire': it was important for the dramatist not to offend, a particularly difficult task in an age when the acting profession was widely viewed with suspicion or outright hostility. (Molière was initially refused a Christian burial and as late as 1730 the body of Adrienne Lecouvreur, a famous tragic actress, was thrown into the common ditch.)

Today, the fame of Corneille and Racine as masters of tragedy is assured, and Molière is respected above all as a writer of serious comedies, but their success came only after a struggle. In addition to the difficulties common to all theatrical work, there were various sets of constraints peculiar to the seventeenth century, which need to be considered if the twentieth-century reader is fully to appreciate the extent of their achievements. Of these it will be helpful to try and disentangle three: the physical conditions of performances, the cultural climate of the age, and the moral and religious attitudes. To understand how the dramatists came to terms with, and even benefited from, these constraints, it will be useful to consider briefly the broad development of French theatre and its state (not merely in theory but also in practice, for a play is always more than just a text) when Corneille embarked upon his dramatic career in the 1620s. Modern views are conditioned by three centuries of critical comment, but all three writers could well have been remembered differently by their contemporaries: Louis XIV and his court, for example, might particularly have savoured recollections of Molière as the producer of spectacular *divertissements* in the gardens of Versailles, whereas provincial audiences in Toulouse or Narbonne or Nantes, where Molière served his apprenticeship in a travelling repertory company, would recall the clowning, the buffoonery and slapstick more in tune with medieval farce or the *commedia dell'arte*. Even modern conceptions of theatre architecture and modern attitudes to theatre-going can cause confusion: in 1600 there was only one public theatre in Paris; as late as 1661 there were still only three. Consequently, some of Corneille's tragedies were first produced on an improvised stage in a *jeu de paume*, a sort of enclosed tennis court where the total space for audience and performers was approximately 35 metres by 12 metres. The first performance of one of Racine's later tragedies – a royal command performance with Louis XIV in attendance – was staged in a dormitory at Saint-Cyr, the fashionable college for young ladies directed by Madame de Maintenon, Louis's second wife.

The restricted physical conditions of seventeenth-century French theatre were to some extent caused by a monopoly upon all theatrical performances in Paris from 1402 to 1629. When, at the end of the dark ages, drama began to re-emerge, the Church was sympathetic to those performances based on religious subjects. As the treatment became broader and bawdier, some control was considered necessary, and the sole right to perform mystery plays in the Paris region was granted to the Confrérie de la Passion. Drama was not extinguished, as the performances of farces and soties by special licence at fairs and on feast-days indicate, and this comic tradition is particularly visible in the earliest of Molière's plays. When the performance even of mystery plays was forbidden in the sixteenth century (because anxieties about the spread of the Reformation made the authorities see the stage as a possible pulpit for Protestant ideas), this ban had two effects: the first was that the Confrérie was no longer able to use its theatre, leaving the Hôtel de Bourgogne available for lease to other companies; the second was that there was encouragement for the Renaissance writers to ignore the medieval tradition and to experiment, in drama as in poetry, with the forms inherited from Greek and Roman antiquity.

Alexandre Hardy was probably the dramatist who benefited most from the conjunction of these two factors: he stepped into the Hôtel de Bourgogne and wrote literally hundreds of plays which by the variety of plots, the spectacular events, and by its openness to Spanish and Italian drama, created a theatre which conveyed all the verve and energy of the Renaissance. The favourite play was the tragi-comedy: a tale packed with incidents – duels, and disguises, deaths and elopements – and ending happily. Although his prolific contribution was soon eclipsed by the major writers of Classical tragedy, Hardy had helped to prepare a popular audience and his style certainly had its influence upon the work of Corneille and other dramatists in the first half of the century.

Another important legacy of the Renaissance mood, in drama as in other forms of literature, was the influence of Greek and Roman antiquity. This is apparent in far more than the subjects chosen by Corneille and Racine, and its importance must not be minimized. It is understandable that, in a century striving for greatness and artistic perfection, the tragedies, the comedies and the dramatic theories of antiquity should provide an attractive model. The three great playwrights of the century, Corneille, Racine and Molière, are all, in different ways, indebted to the examples from Greece and Rome which the Renaissance had brought to light; Corneille concentrated largely upon the history of Rome for most of his tragedies; Racine's work drew upon myths and legends of Greece; clear links can be traced between Molière's comedies and those of Terence and Plautus, dramatists of pre-Christian Rome.

At the same time, the legacy of antiquity, filtered by the Renaissance, can sometimes be seen as impinging on some seventeenth-century dramatists in ways that were less welcome. To that extent the cultural climate can be taken as the second of the constraints experienced by Classical French dramatists. Respect for the past developed into reverence, with the result that the principles on which the earlier drama was based reappeared in the seventeenth century as prescriptions. Aristotle's *Poetics* had presented the author's observations on what made for good tragedy in pre-Christian Greece; but, with the approval of Richelieu's Academy, these observations were elevated to the status of rules which, in keeping with the disciplinary spirit of the times, were then imposed upon writers. For Corneille, these 'règles' were particularly irksome. His audience was not composed of learned critics; his reaction, ultimately one of prudence, was to 'ajouter les règles afin de ne déplaire aux savants'; his aim ('gagnons la voix publique') remained unchanged. Another illustration of this sort of artificial regulation is the *séparation des genres*: comedy and tragedy were, for two centuries, to be kept as

entirely distinct forms, with the result that tragi-comedy fell from
favour. Similarly, Corneille and Racine were faced with the
problem of reconciling the pagan divinities worshipped by Greek
and Roman characters with the Christian outlook of their
audiences. It is therefore important to bear in mind the conflicting
legacies of Classical antiquity: undeniably a source of inspiration
and yet, simultaneously, a source of constraint.

The differing attitudes of Corneille and Racine towards the 'rules'
of tragedy are illuminating: where Corneille chafed, Racine adapted to them and his work gains in power and intensity from the very
concentration which results when action is condensed and compressed to satisfy the unities. There are other important differences:
Corneille, who belonged to the more optimistic days of Descartes
at the start of the century, was closer in time and mood and spirit
to the exuberant drama of Hardy; Racine belongs to the more
pessimistic age of Pascal and La Rochefoucauld, when there was
less confidence in man's potential. This major distinction is
reflected not so much in their choice of subjects as in the choice
and treatment of character.

Corneille may have shown an interest, at the start of his career,
in comedy and tragi-comedy, but he is remembered above all for
tragedies to which he first turned in 1635 with *Médée*. The pattern
of his work, which really became apparent in *Le Cid* two years
later, depends upon central characters who are heroic and often
successful in their struggles to achieve 'la générosité' and 'la
gloire', and upon an 'action illustre, extraordinaire, sérieuse', even
'invraisemblable'. To demonstrate the power and grandeur of
these characters and their political ambitions, Corneille preferred a
plot based upon 'quelque grand intérêt de l'Etat ou quelque
passion plus noble et plus mâle que l'amour'. Racine frequently
chose love, and as they struggle with that destructive force his
characters reveal not strength but weakness, not an abnormal
ability to conquer but a fundamentally human fallibility. La
Bruyère drew a clear distinction between the two great writers of
tragedy when he said: 'Corneille nous assujettit à ses caractères et à
ses idées, Racine se conforme aux nôtres; celui-là peint les hommes
comme ils devraient être, celui-ci les peint tels qu'ils sont.'

However, the two dramatists were constantly vying with one
another and trespassing on each other's territory. Racine's
Britannicus was specifically written to show that he too could
write a political tragedy, and in 1670 two plays on the same subject
were produced within eight days of one another: Racine's *Bérénice*
and Corneille's *Tite et Bérénice*. The subject is typically Cornelian:
the heroic action of the Emperor Titus who, by sending away the
love of his life, the queen Bérénice, in obedience to the wishes of
Rome, follows the path of duty rather than love. But a closer

look shows that Corneille's characters have taken on some of the human weakness of Racine's, whereas Racine's show an almost Cornelian grandeur. At one point Corneille's emperor proclaims himself 'maître de l'univers sans l'être de moi-même' in a phrase more reminiscent of Phèdre's 'Moi régner! Moi ranger un état sous ma loi!/Quand ma faible raison ne règne plus sur moi', than of the self-control of Corneille's Cinna: 'Je suis maître de moi comme de l'univers'. And yet, in general, the tragic patterns remain distinct: Corneille's characters are eventually exhilarated by their choice of honour and duty, whereas Racine's are emotionally destroyed by their renunciation, and his play ends, not in triumph, but in sadness, evoking 'cette tristesse majestueuse qui fait tout le plaisir de la tragédie'.

Concentration upon human weakness forms the basis for the work of the third major dramatist, Molière, who delighted courtiers and country folk, Paris and the provinces with his plays and his performances. To the traditional craft of comedy which was based on farce and the Italian *commedia*, he brought a new ingredient: humour which depended on the accurate portrayal of psychologically authentic eccentricity located in a gallery of nobles and servants, doctors and lawyers, pedants and peasants. Molière's comedy achieves a blend of the contemporary and the permanent, and if we are today unable to appreciate much of the topicality, the laughter provoked by his universal targets is accessible to all centuries where humankind includes hypochondriacs and misers, snobs and social misfits.

This amazing universality is one of the major attributes of French culture in the seventeenth century, whose literature and theatre are also outstanding for their precise analysis of human thought, emotion and passion, for a power which depends more upon clarity and control than upon lyricism and exuberance, and for their penetrating and percipient examination of psychological and moral behaviour.

Further reading

J. Lough, *An Introduction to Seventeenth-Century France* (1954); H. Méthivier, *Le Siècle de Louis XIII* (1964); H. Méthivier, *Le Siècle de Louis XIV* (1960); R. Mettam, *Government and Society in Louis XIV's France* (1977).

A. Adam, *Grandeur and Illusion. French Literature and Society 1600–1715* (1972); R. Bray, *La Préciosité et les précieux* (1948); W. Moore, *French Classical Literature* (1962); P. Nurse, *Classical Voices. Studies of Corneille, Racine, Molière, Madame de Lafayette* (1971).

E. Kearns, *Ideas in Seventeenth-Century France* (1979); A. Krails-heimer, *Studies in Self-Interest. From Descartes to La Bruyère* (1962).

O. de Mourgues (ed.), *An Anthology of Seventeenth-Century Lyric Poetry* (1966).

C. Gossip, *An Introduction to French Classical Tragedy* (1981); T. Lawrenson, *The French Stage and Playhouse in the Seventeenth Century* (1966); W. Moore, *The Classical Drama of France* (1971).

Pierre CORNEILLE (1606–84)

By the age of 18, Pierre Corneille had graduated in law and started on a legal career in his home town as *avocat* at the *parlement de Rouen*. His father, a well-established lawyer holding a Crown appointment in the department responsible for *eaux et forêts*, purchased two appointments for his eldest son in 1628 and, for over twenty years, Corneille worked as a professional lawyer. However, law was certainly not an overwhelming attraction for, within a year of taking up these appointments, Pierre Corneille was to make a start in his parallel career as a dramatist. His first play was noticed by Montdory, an actor-manager who performed in Rouen; this comedy was produced with some success on an improvised stage (*jeu de paume*) in Paris; and within a few years Corneille's work had attracted the favourable attention of the Cardinal de Richelieu. Corneille was not prepared to work for long as a ghost-writer for the Cardinal's own plays: he preferred to develop his own style and his own dramatic theories; but these were soon to attract the Cardinal's less favourable attention when *Le Cid* (1637) offended Richelieu's views on drama and those adopted by the Académie Française which the Cardinal had established two years earlier.

Corneille's earliest plays were particularly influenced, like those of many a young writer, by contemporary taste: like his brother Thomas, who was also to become a celebrated dramatist, he was attracted to tragi-comedy rather in the manner of Hardy and other Renaissance playwrights, and to comedy. There are already in these early works signs of the genius which was to find its true expression in tragedy, on which Corneille began to concentrate in the mid 1630s.

His first major triumph was *Le Cid*, a play which can be seen as marking the start of French Classical tragedy, even though the action is set in Spain rather than, as was more usual, in Greek or Roman antiquity. The hero, Don Rodrigue, loves Chimène; but her father, the Count, insults his father, Don Diègue. So Rodrigue is immediately faced with a conflict between his duty and his inclination, the very dilemma with which Corneille confronts the majority of his heroes and heroines. Don Diègue being too old to fight a duel, family honour requires Rodrigue to avenge his father; but if he were to kill his future father-in-law he would lose Chimène's love. It might be argued that *Le Cid* would be a more conventional tragedy if the play were to end with the suffering of the young lovers when the hero sacrifices his personal feelings to his other responsibilities. In fact, the Count's death occurs at the end of the first act and therefore very early in a play which, by its five acts and use of alexandrine verse, is identical in form and structure to conventional tragedy. Corneille's personal and very distinctive interpretation of tragedy is developed in the four remaining acts: Rodrigue attempts to convince Chimène of his continuing love; he assumes command of the Spanish army (of which the Count had, until his death, been commander-in-chief); he saves his country overnight by his courage and leadership in a pitched battle against invading Moorish armies; he returns the next morning to fight a second duel, this time against a rival suitor for Chimène's affections; and he presents himself at court for judgement by the king.

Through these exceptional actions, all within some twenty-four hours, Rodrigue not only distinguishes himself from his fellow-countrymen, thereby earning the title of *El Cid*; he also establishes a model for the Cornelian hero which is quite distinct from the more standard tragic hero in classical antiquity or in seventeenth-century France. From the king's decision to pardon Rodrigue and from the final hint at a happy reunion of hero and heroine in the fullnes of time, it might seem that Corneille was influenced by traditional tragi-comedy (the tragedy with a happy ending). That is only a partial explanation. Like the heroes in Corneille's later tragedies, Rodrigue is faced with a heart-rending dilemma; by the exercise of his reason he decides which is the most honourable course of action; by the exercise of immense energy and will-power he follows that course, regardless of personal suffering. A similar pattern is discernible in, for example *Horace* (1640), where the hero's duty is not to his family alone but to the Roman state of which he has been selected as champion; and in *Polyeucte* (1641), where the hero's glory lies on an even higher plane and he sacrifices not only his personal love but also his family duties to the supreme vocation of Christian martyrdom.

Unfortunately for Corneille, *Le Cid* provoked bitter resentment and criticism. He had offended the Cardinal by his portrayal of duelling (which Richelieu had recently proscribed) and by his references to Spanish greatness at a time when France and Spain were at war. He had also ignored the precepts of Classical tragedy which an excessive reverence for Aristotle's theories had, by 1637, established as rules: *Le Cid* did not satisfy the unity of time, since its action exceeded one day; it did not satisfy the unity of place, since the scene changed from a square in Seville to Chimène's apartments and then to the royal palace; and by the inclusion of a minor love affair, it offended the unity of action. There followed the 'Querelle du *Cid*', and Corneille withdrew temporarily from the theatre to do battle with his critics and to meditate about the techniques of his art.

It is clear from his subsequent plays, from the *examen* or commentary which he wrote for every one of his tragedies, and from the three *Discours* which accompanied his complete works in 1660, that Corneille was never fully reconciled to the academic, largely theoretical and often pedantic views of those who attacked *Le Cid*. Rather than acquiesce in the imposition of sterile rules, Corneille preferred to write plays which satisfied a theatre audience. Never is the Aristotelian catharsis of pity and fear the culmination of his tragedy. Instead he presents a hero who transcends all difficulties, a hero notable more for his extraordinary power than for his downfall and failure, a hero in whose quest for glory the emphasis is placed more on energy, will and achievement than on frailty and suffering. This concentration upon human greatness rather than weakness gives to his theatre a mood of robust optimism. Furthermore, the refusal of his central characters to become the victims of passion has several effects: rarely, if ever, does love form the basis of the tragedy; invariably they present their views with a force, an eloquence and an order which mirror the hero's strength and self-control. As one of them explains: 'Je suis maître de moi comme de l'univers.'

Such exceptional prowess has encouraged some critics to see Corneille's characters as more than human, even superhuman. It is argued that his portraits are distorted by excessive stress upon the illustrious and the extraordinary. Corneille, however, considered himself to be a good craftsman, and, to such criticism, which was often based upon acquired theory rather than inborn talent and practical experience, his reply is that his plays fulfil their essential task of attracting and pleasing an audience.

Further reading

P. Yarrow, *Corneille* (1963); H. Barnwell, *Pierre Corneille: Writings on the Theatre* (1965); R. Knight, *Corneille: 'Horace'* (1981); H. Barnwell (ed.), *Pompée* (1971).

Workpoints

1   Key issues to be considered in Corneille's theatre are: *Gloire, Générosité, Devoir, Honneur, Raison, Volonté*. 'Corneille

made the tragedy a drama of conflicting loyalties in strong and resolute souls, on the theme of self-fulfilment through self-renunciation. The choice – love or duty, martyrdom or happiness – might be agonizing, but it was still free, guided by reason, sustained by will-power' (*F. Roe*).

2   Consider Corneille's use of history: *le vrai* or *le vraisemblable*?

3   The place of love in Corneille's tragedy: a tragedy should, according to Corneille, be based on 'une passion plus noble et plus mâle que l'amour'.

4   Characterization. Is the hero in Cornelian tragedy more heroic than tragic? Corneille 'asks us, not to recognize the ordinary, but to be awestruck by the superior' (*E. Bentley*).

5   Comparisons with Racine: 'Corneille's women characters are all but virile; Racine's are drawn with unsurpassed variety, tenderness and delicacy' (*F. Roe*). 'Corneille is a very great dramatist but not so richly tragic as Racine because of his lack of compassion. True, he avoids also the sentimentality of mere pity' (*E. Bentley*).

René DESCARTES (1596–1650)

Descartes is an extremely important figure in the history of philosophy and his ideas have influenced the whole development of Western thought. Educated by the Jesuits at one of the most famous colleges of the day, he became disillusioned with his studies, especially with their lack of certainty, and, as he tells us in Part 1 of the *Discours de la méthode* (1637), decided to read instead in the *grand livre du monde*. In 1618 he enrolled in the Dutch army, where he met and was encouraged by the Dutch scholar Isaac Beeckman. In 1619, now in the Bavarian army, he spent the cold winter days meditating in a *poêle* (a room heated by a large stove) and after a night of dreams on 10 November 1619 formed the project, as he tells us in Part 2 of the *Discours*, of constructing the edifice of knowledge single-handed. These thoughts matured over the next few years and, encouraged by the support of the Cardinal de Bérulle, who saw in Descartes a future defender of Catholicism through reason, Descartes started writing his ideas down. In order to escape from the pointless social round of Paris and think in peace, he moved in 1628 to Holland, where he spent the next twenty years writing the works for which he is now known. This tranquil and productive life was unfortunately brought to an end by pneumonia when Queen Christina of Sweden, in her thirst for knowledge, called Descartes to the court and required him to teach her philosophy at five in the morning in the depths of winter.

Mathematician, physicist, biologist and philosopher, he aimed to attack the outdated scholastic philosophy which he had been taught, replacing it with a scientific approach inspired by his enthusiasm for the clarity of mathematics. How he came to attempt this is recounted in the *Discours de la méthode*, a work of much wider popular appeal than its title would suggest or than philosophical works usually have for the ordinary reader. Intended for a mixed readership of specialists and educated people generally, including the fashionable ladies of the salons, it was written in French rather than Latin, a *discours* rather than a *traité*, appealing to the ability to reason shared by everyone rather than to the specialized knowledge of the professional philosopher, and written in an attractive style, personal, varied, full of images to explain his thought. Far from being a unified work, it is part intellectual autobiography, part philosophical argument and part practical illustration; an attempt to put forward some of his ideas in a tentative manner, carefully testing the water, as it were, in view of current attitudes. Galileo had recently (1633) been condemned by the Inquisition for supporting the Copernican theory that the earth moved round the sun, and Descartes foresaw that his projected book *Le Monde* might put him in the same kind of danger. The *Discours* was intended to give some indication of his recent work, while avoiding controversial subjects which might get him into trouble with the Church.

Descartes begins by recounting his unsuccessful search for truth in the various disciplines taught at college. Then in Part 2 he tells how he came to the conclusion that, just as an architect can design a better building if he does not have to accommodate existing structures or consult others, so one man, thinking on his own and starting from scratch, would be more likely to arrive at the truth. To conduct his thought correctly he outlines four rules, the first and most important being never to accept anything as true which he does not know clearly and distinctly to be so. Since he will have to lead a normal life while building up his new system of truth, he explains in Part 3 what codes of behaviour he will provisionally adopt. Part 4, the most important section of the *Discours*, contains the process now known as Cartesian doubt in which Descartes systematically doubts everything that can be doubted until he arrives at one certainty, the existence of the doubting, thinking mind. This he expresses in the famous sentence known as the *cogito* (Latin for 'I think'): 'je pense, donc je suis' or 'cogito ergo sum'. Since he perceives this clearly and distinctly, it gives him his criterion for other truths: whatever he perceives clearly and distinctly, like this, is true. This brings him to the proofs of the existence of God, which he finds as certain and as convincing as his own existence and more certain than mathematics. The existence of God then becomes a guarantee for all his certain truths in that a perfect God would not mislead him. Having established this firm foundation Descartes can now build up the edifice of knowledge again. In Part 5 he applies his method to a practical study of the circulation of the blood. He also develops the theory, so important for the materialism of the eighteenth century, that animals are merely machines and that the human body also is just a machine with the addition of an immortal soul. In Part 6 he reflects upon the general application of his method to science and his reasons for publishing at that particular time.

In 1641 (French translation 1647), in the *Méditations métaphysiques*, the arguments in the fourth part of the *Discours* concerning the existence of God and the human mind were elaborated and clarified.

Descartes stands as a crucial figure in the history of Western thought, between the scholasticism of the Middle Ages and the modern, scientific approach. By doubting everything in order to build up again from a certainty reached on his own, he encouraged a healthy scepticism about received opinions, but went beyond the negative scepticism popular since Montaigne, giving an optimistic view of the future in which science, built on firm metaphysical foundations would, by following his method, gradually provide a clear and thorough understanding of the world and – especially through medicine – improve it for mankind. At the same time he stressed the division between mind and matter which was subsequently to dominate philosophical thought and lead later philosophers to emphasize the theory of knowledge.

In religious thought he was seen as the originator of the materialism of the eighteenth century, but was also welcomed as contributing to the revival of natural theology through his emphasis on the proof of the existence of God and the importance of this as a cornerstone of his philosophy. Here he should be contrasted with that other great thinker of the seventeenth century, Pascal, who, seeing the dangers inherent in Descartes's abstract proofs of the existence of God, used instead a predominantly psychological approach to persuade the unbeliever of the necessity, not just of God, but of all the doctrines of Christianity. Descartes's influence, however, goes beyond specific disciplines of science, philosophy or religion and can be discerned behind any methodical and reasoned approach to a problem, even that of the traditional *explication de texte*, where analysis proceeds through a series of logical steps and divisions rather than through a loose association of thoughts and impressions. His influence was varied and far-reaching, and the interest of his work, especially of the *Discours*, endures as a readable and vivid account of one man's personal search for truth.

Further reading

P. France, *Rhetoric and Truth in France: Descartes to Diderot* (1972), ch. 2; B. Williams, *Descartes: the Project of Pure Enquiry* (1978); E. Kearns, *Ideas in Seventeenth-Century France* (1979), ch. 2; D. Curtis, *Descartes: 'Discours de la méthode'* (1984); T. Sorrell, *Descartes* (1987).

Workpoints

1 'It is very important that the Method of Doubt is not the whole of Descartes' Method. . . . Doubt introduces and forms the enquiry, but eventually makes way for a systematic vindication of knowledge and an orderly reconstruction of it' (*B. Williams*). Show how Descartes first demolishes the edifice of knowledge and then builds it up again.

2 'Descartes writes, not as a teacher, but as a discoverer and explorer, anxious to communicate what he has found' (*B. Russell*). Do you agree with this statement? What aspects of his style convey this enthusiasm?

3 'Although the structure of the *Discours* seems polished and well-knit together to the casual reader, . . . the homogeneity and coherence of the most famous of Cartesian writings is far from evident and its apparent simplicity and clearness constitute a formidable snare and delusion for the unwary' (*L. Beck*). Do you find the *Discours* clear, logical and simple? Can you find any inconsistencies or lack of structure?

Madame de LAFAYETTE (1634–93)

Madame de Lafayette came from a minor aristocratic background, and her marriage gave her higher rank. After the early years of married life, however, her husband lived mostly on his country estates, while she remained in Paris. She moved in court society, frequented the *précieux* circles of the salons, and surrounded herself with a group of intellectuals, notably La Rochefoucauld, who certainly contributed to the thinking behind her books and may well have helped to write them.

Apart from the derivative *Zaïde* (1669–71), Lafayette's works mark significant changes from the conventional fiction of the period. Where earlier writers dealt with themes of heroism and chivalry in a remote and unreal past, she generally opts for a recent, historically-based situation. And where many current novels were rambling and shapeless, her texts tend to be concise and carefully constructed. The short pieces, *La Princesse de Montpensier* (1662) and *La Comtesse de Tende* (1724), and the longer *La Princesse de Clèves* (1678) all present the same problem of the eternal triangle. But it is certainly in *La Princesse de Clèves* that this issue received its most mature treatment. The tight time-scheme concentrates the action within about a year (1558–9) and the whole book is of no more than 150 pages. There are vestiges of traditional story-telling devices: eavesdropping, a mislaid letter and a series of digressions; but they are intended to work in relation to the central story rather than as ends in themselves. One of the most effective technical features is the interplay of public and private scenes. The text begins by describing the atmosphere of Henri II's court with its passions, intrigues and jealousies, and this retains its importance even when the focus shifts to the personal concerns of the young and beautiful Princesse, a fictional character grafted onto the well-documented historical setting. But as her mother, Mme de Chartres, points out, at court 'ce qui paraît n'est presque jamais la vérité', and the essence of the book is to probe beneath outward appearances in search of psychological truth. By withdrawing her main characters to the intimacy of apartment or country house, and making subtle use of different narrative levels (dialogue, monologue, interior monologue), Lafayette seeks to analyse the motivating forces at work in their minds. The mother is shown to create the central situation through her ambition for a match her daughter does not really want, and through her insistence on the sanctity of marriage; the loving husband, an initially reasonable and balanced man, becomes a terrifying example of the power of jealousy when he realizes his wife loves another; the would-be lover, Nemours, is moved by a passion for the Princesse which blinds him to his other interests (as well as to hers), even if this passion eventually cools. At the centre of these conflicting pressures (and learning from all she sees and hears at court), the Princesse strives to find a correct course of conduct. She consistently resists Nemours's advances, despite her very real attraction to him, and, in a famous scene, partially admits her predicament to her husband. Even after the Prince's death, when ostensibly free to marry Nemours, she still refuses, as her complex emotions are dominated by guilt about her husband and doubts about Nemours's constancy: 'Les raisons qu'elle avait de ne point épouser M. de Nemours lui paraissaient fortes du côté de son devoir et insurmontables du côté de son repos.'

It is a measure of Lafayette's achievement that *La Princesse de Clèves* is the only contemporary novel to rank with the great seventeenth-century works of Corneille, Molière and Racine. And, even if it lacks realistic detail and local colour, this one text, by its basic credibility, depth of character analysis and capacity to embrace serious moral issues, marks the start of the novel's evolution towards the major genre into which, in later centuries, it will develop.

Further reading

J. Scott, *Madame de la Fayette: a selective critical bibliography* (1974); J. Scott, *Madame de Lafayette: 'La Princesse de Clèves'* (1983); J. Raitt, *Madame de la Fayette and 'La Princesse de Clèves'* (1971); P. Nurse, *Classical Voices* (1971) ch. 4.

Workpoints

1 How is the story put together? How far does it have a sense of unity? 'Even the interpolated stories . . . have their role to play in the preparation of the dénouement' (*J. Raitt*).

2 How does the Princesse develop in the course of the novel? What factors lead her to her final decision? 'J'avoue . . . que les passions peuvent me conduire; mais elles ne sauraient m'aveugler': how does she acquire the maturity implicit in this statement?

3 What picture of human nature emerges from the text? 'Dans ce roman, tout est calculé pour mettre en lumière la force destructrice et dégradante de l'amour' (*P. Clarac*). 'The view of the passions presented by the author . . . is not a glibly moralistic one, but *tragic*' (*J. Scott*).

Jean de LA FONTAINE (1621–95)

La Fontaine is one of the few seventeenth-century poets read with pleasure now and, although he wrote other works (*Contes*, 1665; *Les Amours de Psyché et de Cupidon*, 1669), it is for his *Fables* (1668–93) that he is read and loved. These were written quite late in his life, after he had left his provincial home in Château-Thierry and his post of *maître des eaux et forêts* and was living in Paris with the help and support of a series of influential patrons.

Like many of his contemporaries, he was writing for a select group of extremely sophisticated people at the highest level of society, in the salons and at court. Indeed, although he was a great individualist working in a minority genre, we can see many points of comparison with the other great writers of the second half of the seventeenth century, with the dramatic works of Molière and Racine, the analyses of human nature found in the *Maximes* of La Rochefoucauld and the *Pensées* of Pascal, and the psychological realism of *La Princesse de Clèves*. La Fontaine shares with them and his age an overriding interest in how human beings behave as individuals and in society. Resembling Philinte in Molière's *Le Misanthrope*, he has a tolerant, though cynical attitude to the world, a kind of resigned pessimism when faced with examples of foolishness or cruelty. La Fontaine's remark in Fable 1 of Book 9, 'Le dépositaire infidèle':

> Quand l'absurde est outré, l'on lui fait trop d'honneur
> De vouloir par raison combattre son erreur

corresponds to Philinte's criticism of Alceste:

> Et c'est une folie à nulle autre seconde
> De vouloir se mêler de corriger le monde.

A more positive philosophy and a more lyrical style emerge, however, from 'Le songe d'un habitant du Mogol' (Book 2, 4) with its praise of solitude similar to that found in another tradition of nature poetry represented in the early seventeenth century by Saint-Amant, Théophile de Viau and Tristan l'Hermite. This however is not the dominant tone of the *Fables*, which on the whole are ironic and humorous.

In common with Mme de Lafayette's, his observation of society is particularly applicable to the court of Louis XIV, but extends beyond that to a general study of human behaviour. Like Molière and Racine, he gives a dynamic presentation of human activity rather than a static analysis. His fables are little stories given a dramatic form, with characters talking and acting against a briefly sketched background:

> Une ample comédie à cent actes divers,
>   Et dont la scène est l'Univers.
>   *(Book 5, 1)*

The characters in these fables are usually taken from nature – birds, fish, trees – although human beings and human artefacts also figure: 'Je me sers d'animaux pour instruire les hommes' he says in a dedicatory poem to the king's son, Monseigneur le Dauphin. His actors are both animal-like and human, lightly outlined with an evocatory power that shows a sensitivity to nature:

> Un jour, sur ses longs pieds, allait, je ne sais où,
> Le Héron au long bec emmanché d'un long cou.
>   Il côtoyait une rivière.
> L'onde était transparente ainsi qu'aux plus beaux jours.
>   *('Le Héron', Book 7, 4)*

They are also given the human attributes usually bestowed on them by tradition: the sly fox, the foolish crow, the proud oak tree.

Just as other Classical writers claimed for their work a moral value in the sense that it teaches us about human nature, so these fables are meant not just to entertain but also to be instructive:

> Je chante les héros dont Esope est le père,
> Troupe de qui l'histoire, encor que mensongère,
> Contient des vérités qui servent de leçons.
> ('A Monseigneur le Dauphin')

In 'La Grenouille qui se veut faire aussi grosse que le bœuf' (Book 2, 3), for example, the frog tries to expand to match the size of the ox and explodes. At the end of the poem comes the moral:

> Le monde est plein de gens qui ne sont pas plus sages:
> Tout bourgeois veut bâtir comme les grands seigneurs,
>> Tout petit prince a des ambassadeurs,
>> Tout marquis veut avoir des pages.

In language also La Fontaine is typical of his century. The French language had gradually been purified by Malherbe and the newly-founded Académie Française, and a standard of perfection had been set. By the time La Fontaine was writing, the aim was naturalness and artistic perfection: nothing self-indulgent, exaggerated or pedantic. La Fontaine takes the prose fables of Aesop and the verse fables of the Latin writer Phædrus, among others, and turns them into masterpieces of precision, lightness and wit. Much of their success is attributable to his superb use of *vers libres*, which admirably suit the little dramatic scenes, with their quick changes of tone, that make up the *Fables*, as does the use of stylized colloquial French, slight archaisms and proverb-like aphorisms ('On a souvent besoin d'un plus petit que soi'), chiselled down to bare perfection.

Here is a language as perfect as Racine's, but varied as befits the fable genre:

> La cigale ayant chanté
>> Tout l'été,
> Se trouva fort dépourvue
> Quand la bise fut venue.
>> (Book 1, 1)

This creates a feeling of joyful lightness followed by a more sombre tone for the foolish cicada's deprived state in winter. The story starts in an extremely simple, unfussy way. Similarly, 'Le

Corbeau et le renard' (Book 1, 2) rejuvenates and gives perfect shape to the Aesop fable, with its jaunty parallel presentation of the two characters:

> Maître Corbeau, sur un arbre perché,
>   Tenait en son bec un fromage.
> Maître Renard, par l'odeur alléché,
>   Lui tint à peu près ce langage.

This is followed by variations in tone as the fox flatters the crow in an increasingly grandiloquent manner, reaching a climax with 'Vous êtes le phénix des hôtes de ce bois' before adopting a patronizing 'my dear fellow' once the cheese has been dropped:

> Le Renard s'en saisit, et dit: 'Mon bon Monsieur,
>   Apprenez que tout flatteur
> Vit aux dépens de celui qui l'écoute.'

Dramatic, ironic, amused and amusing, these poems elevate the old popular form of the fable to something perfect and unforgettable by La Fontaine's choice of character, incident and detail and by his mastery of rhythm and rhyme, of timing and tone.

Further reading

R. and D. Ledésert, *Fables by La Fontaine* (1951); O. de Mourgues, *La Fontaine: 'Fables'* (1960); M. Guiton, *La Fontaine, Poet and Counterpoet* (1961).

Workpoints

1   Odette de Mourgues has described the *Fables* as containing 'a rich blend of sympathy, tenderness and irony'. See if you can find these elements in some of the *Fables*.

2   Do you find the animals convincing as animals or as symbols of human beings? What is the point of using animals as characters? 'One of the privileges of the animal fable is simply that it provides the possibility of satirizing human nature with candour but without rancour, indeed with gaiety and good humour' (*A. Boase*).

3   Does La Fontaine depict seventeenth-century French society in particular or human society in general? Are there features in his poems which seem to relate more particularly to life at court under Louis XIV?

4   Analyse the dramatic qualities of some of these poems – the way the characters are introduced, their dialogue with its

different tones, the way the scene builds up to a climax. Show how the reader's interest is engaged.

5 Do you think these *Fables* are suitable for young children? Could children appreciate them fully? 'This book which is supposed to be intended for children denies at every page the existence of the most elementary forms of justice and loyalty' (*O. de Mourgues*).

Jean-Baptiste Poquelin MOLIÈRE (1622–73)

Molière (to use the stage name he adopted in the 1640s) came from a comfortable middle-class background in Paris and could easily have continued in his father's business as an upholsterer with a minor court appointment; or he could have consolidated his family's social status by entering the legal profession for which his schooling at the Collège de Clermont and a law degree from Orléans had prepared him by the age of 20. Fortunately for the French theatre in the seventeenth and later centuries, he chose the stage, a far harder profession judging by the description of life in struggling, provincial companies given in Scarron's *Le Roman comique* (1651–7). After a lengthy apprenticeship as dramatist and actor, Molière returned to Paris in 1658; there he quickly gained royal patronage and was able, despite various professional set-backs and ill-health, to write and perform plays which have earned him enduring fame as the father of modern French comedy.

Little can be said with absolute certainty about some of the earlier sketches and plays attributed to him, and his first major successes are generally taken as *Les Précieuses ridicules* (1659) and *L'Ecole des femmes* (1662). From these and later plays it is apparent that Molière's comic genius was to 'élever la comédie à un rang égal à celui de la tragédie' (R. Fernandez) and to give status to comedy which, in comparison with tragedy, was then considered a less worthy *genre*. Broadly speaking, his success is derived from the happy blending or fusion of two major elements: one old, one new. Molière's work continues the lusty traditions of popular French farce and the Italian *commedia dell'arte*; he was familiar with these and Spanish comedy through his long provincial apprenticeship, and so thoroughly had he learned the crafts of comedy, so well did they match his own talents for mime and slapstick that there are farcical elements even in his most 'serious' comedies. The second and novel strand was his introduction into French comedy of a more thoughtful, even intellectual mode which depended upon the careful study and accurate portrayal of human nature and human psychology. Whereas the Italian *commedia* had depended upon improvised dialogue, Molière's plays were written in a prose or verse style so literary that they earned the approval of Boileau, probably the severest critic of the late seventeenth century. The farcical elements appealed to conventional taste, and the replacement of stock characterization by the accurate depiction of human behaviour appealed to the more refined interests of many contemporaries. La Fontaine's comment on this innovation was: 'Et maintenant il ne faut pas/Quitter la nature d'un pas.'

With the acclaim of such influential critics and the very active support of Louis XIV, it would seem that, by 1662, Molière's position was secure: he had recently married Armande Béjart, a young and attractive member of his company; he was, by royal command, involved in the production of spectacular entertainments at Versailles; and in the next ten years he was to write a series of comedies which have endured for over three centuries as masterpieces of comic theatre rather than as monuments of literary history. Those for which he is best remembered are *Le Misanthrope* (1666), *L'Avare* (1668), *Tartuffe* (1669) and *Les Femmes savantes* (1672).

In fact, his life and professional career were far from easy. Quite apart from the personal problems created by his unhappy marriage, his work was frequently attacked by rival dramatists. Molière's answer was to write two short works, *La Critique de l'Ecole des femmes* and *L'Impromptu de Versailles* (1663), from both of which we can obtain a clear statement of his dramatic theory and artistic intentions. Other criticism came from those who were threatened or wounded by his mockery: as well as Molière's depiction of universal human failings and weaknesses such as pedantry, avarice and religious hypocrisy, his plays contain scathing comments on more immediate targets (recognizable to a seventeenth-century audience if not always to the twentieth century), such as medical incompetence, pretentious poetry and social fashions.

His most productive years were therefore marred by struggles and tensions. In 1665, the year when his company was designated by royal decree the *Troupe du roi*, the start of a serious illness is recorded; this was to cause a temporary interruption in his work two years later, and in 1673, overworked as actor, author and manager, he died virtually on stage during a performance of his latest play, *Le Malade imaginaire*. The irony of that title is matched by the fact that current religious attitudes towards the theatre would have prevented him from receiving a Christian burial, had it not been for the personal intervention of Louis XIV. There is a further irony which would not have escaped Molière's sense of humour: if the Church allowed him to be buried only by night, the literary world also seemed content to leave him in the dark, for he did not receive the official recognition of the Académie Française until 1778.

His plays have survived. For centuries he has continued to succeed in his principal aim which, as stated in the *Critique*, was to entertain: 'Je dis bien que le grand art est de plaire.' Molière's concern for the general public rather than for the specialist or for some narrow social or intellectual coterie meant that he must try to please a varied audience ranging from the educated courtier to the very common man. His solution was a blend of styles ranging from farce, which provokes the belly-laugh, to a more subtle form of humour, which produces the smile or inner laugh – what Donneau de Visé described as 'le rire dans l'âme'. So, in his plays, there is certainly scope for the sort of visual humour that depends upon the comic gestures and movements and facial expressions at which Molière the actor excelled; scope, too, for the verbal humour that depends upon such standard comic devices as repetition, contrast, anti-climax, parody and satire in which Molière the author also excelled. However, the major achievement was the fusion of traditional comedy with the accurate depiction of human behaviour in all its complexity for which Molière the psychologist will always be remembered. Humour is adjusted to the character: 'L'auteur n'a pas mis cela pour être de soi un bon mot, mais seulement pour une chose qui caractérise l'homme' (*La Critique*, scene 7). Comedy, according to Molière, needs to be anchored in human reality, and if some of his plays can be criticized for their perfunctory endings and for their slightness of plot, that is because his major structural concern was to arrange encounters between conflicting characters and so derive maximum humour from the portrayal of man's permanent weaknesses and, simultaneously, from the more immediate targets available in contemporary society. In Molière's opinion, true comedy is based on the permanent and the topical; and so firmly did he adhere to this precept that, as another speech from *La Critique* indicates, he even considered tragedy as the less demanding genre:

Lorsque vous peignez des héros, vous faites ce que vous voulez. Ce sont des portraits à plaisir. . . . Mais lorsque vous peignez les hommes, il faut peindre d'après nature . . . et vous n'avez rien fait, si vous n'y faites reconnaître les gens de votre siècle.

Further reading

W. Moore, *Molière, a New Criticism* (1949); B. Masters, *A Student's Guide to Molière* (1970); W. Howarth, *Molière: a Playwright and his Audience* (1982); J. Broome, *Molière: 'L'Ecole des femmes' and 'Le Misanthrope'* (1982); H. Barnwell, *Molière: 'Le Malade imaginaire'* (1982).

Workpoints

1 Examine the variety of Molière's devices for obtaining comic effects on stage. Comedy of character or comedy of manners?

2 Whereas Racine saw the twin aims of tragedy as 'plaire et instruire', Molière wrote of the need in comedy to 'plaire, peindre et instruire'. Consider the implications of the last two verbs:

peindre   How far are Molière's comedies a portrait of his own times, how far an expression of general truth?

instruire What are the practical lessons to be derived from Molière's plays? According to the preface he wrote for *Tartuffe*, Molière's aim was to 'travailler à rectifier et adoucir les passions'.

3 Molière's depiction of character: 'His plots are slight, his dénouements often clumsy or conventional, for he was less interested in these than in the exposition of character.'
'Interested as he was in the portrayal of human foibles for comic effect, Molière was unable to avoid the pitfall of all earnest dramatists: he has left us types.'

4 'Molière is much more than a writer of comedy: he is, in addition, a philosopher, a moralist, a keen observer of human foibles, a merciless critic of men' (*R. Wilson*).

5 According to Goethe, Molière's comedies 'touchent à la tragédie'. How does Molière handle the tragic potentialities of his subjects?

Blaise PASCAL (1623–62)

Pascal was a great scientist and religious writer whose *Pensées*, fragmentary and vivid, provide a most stimulating analysis of human nature and the human predicament as well as one of the best-known and most convincing arguments in favour of Christianity.

Educated at home by his scientist father, with a clear, practical approach to knowledge, Pascal, through Jansenist influence, was converted to a more intensely felt religious belief, first in 1646 and then more dramatically in an ecstatic spiritual experience on 23 November 1654, recorded on a scrap of paper known as the *Mémorial*. He took up the fight for Jansenism and Port-Royal, then under pressure from the Jesuits, in a series of witty, polemical letters, the *Lettres provinciales* (1656–7), and, while continuing his scientific work, started, in 1657, an Apology (praise and defence) upholding the Christian religion, intended to shake the indifferent out of their lethargy and draw to Christianity those inclined to the secular philosophies inherited from the Renaissance. The *Pensées*, unfinished and only partly classified at his death in 1662, constitute the preliminary work for this Apology. The fragmentary form, with its scope for individual response, has led to many different versions, but the basic ideas and method are clear.

Pascal, unlike Descartes, rejects as ineffective the method of first proving the existence of God. Instead he paints a dramatic picture of the human condition, the 'Misère de l'homme sans Dieu', stressing the duality, the 'étonnantes contrariétés', inherent in man's aspirations towards truth and happiness, combined with his inability to achieve them on his own. Man is hampered by the weakness of his reason and misled by imagination, the passions, habit, vanity and self-love. Faced with the paradoxical nature of man, Pascal demonstrates the inadequacy of the secular philosophies of scepticism and dogmatism, of Epicureanism and Stoicism, leading the reader to accept that only Christianity can provide the explanation and solution to the dilemma of the human condition.

Though emphasizing the weakness of reason, Pascal is not a sceptic. He points out the value of thought through which man dominates the material world: 'Pensée fait la grandeur de l'homme.' However this thought should lead not to pride but to a recognition of weakness and wretchedness: 'La grandeur de l'homme est grande en ce qu'il se connaît misérable: un arbre ne se connaît pas misérable.' If Pascal can make man aware of his inadequacy in this way he can also lead him to the doctrine of the Fall, by showing him, in the image of the 'roi dépossédé', that, just as only a deposed king will be wretched because he is no longer king, so man is wretched because he knows that he once enjoyed perfect truth and happiness, a state from which he has now fallen.

Pascal finds another way to certainty through *le cœur*: 'C'est le cœur qui sent Dieu et non la raison. Voilà ce que c'est que la foi. Dieu sensible au cœur et non à la raison.' This is however not an invitation to a blind leap of faith. 'Le cœur' is not a sentimental emotion but a valid intuitive faculty capable of giving certainty in science about first principles and in religion about the existence of God. Moreover, in the famous wager fragment Pascal attempts to show mathematically that, even if the reason cannot prove the existence of God, it is still more reasonable to wager for His existence. The mind is required to be active and reason to play its part (one heading reads: *Soumission et usage de la raison*), but in a hierarchy of separate 'orders' (body, mind and heart) the third is infinitely superior.

Pascal does not follow the order of someone like Descartes, who starts from first principles, and reasons logically, step by step.

Instead he organizes the *Pensées* according to what he calls the 'ordre du cœur', where each subject mentioned is related to the central point that he wishes to prove – a method sometimes called 'convergent proof'. It would therefore be a mistake to try and re-organize the *Pensées* into an order inappropriate to Pascal's aim. His approach is a dramatic one, his intention being to shake people out of their indifference or complacency. His style therefore is also dramatic, often based on the clash of opposites, on paradox, on undermining confidence by archetypal images of uncertainty and instability: 'Nous voguons sur un milieu vaste, toujours incertains et flottants, poussés d'un bout vers l'autre; quelque terme où nous pensions nous attacher et nous affermir, il branle, et nous quitte, et si nous le suivons il échappe à nos prises, nous glisse et fuit d'une fuite éternelle; rien ne s'arrête pour nous.' This kind of evocation of man lost in an infinite universe, combined with Pascal's acute and often witty psychological analysis, makes the *Pensées* compulsive reading even for those who do not share his Christian convictions.

Further reading
Editions
The two main ways of ordering the fragments are found in Pascal, *Pensées*, ed. Lafuma (1962), and Pascal, *Pensées*, ed. Brunschvicg (1897, 1972).

Critical works
J. Broome, *Pascal* (1965); P. Topliss, *The Rhetoric of Pascal* (1966); A. Krailsheimer, *Pascal* (1980); J.Cruickshank, *Pascal: 'Pensées'* (1983).

Workpoints
1   'No reader who wishes to realise once and for all the great qualities of French prose could do better than turn straight to the *Lettres provinciales*. Here he will find the lightness and the strength, the exquisite polish and the delicious wit, the lambent irony and the ordered movement, which no other language spoken by man has ever quite been able to produce' (*L. Strachey*).
    Find examples of these various qualities in the *Provinciales*.

2   Voltaire called Pascal a 'misanthrope sublime' and objected that people were neither as bad nor as unhappy as Pascal claimed. Is this your impression of Pascal and do you think it is a valid objection?

3   The *Pensées* can appear disorganized and rather daunting. See

if Pascal's reference to a kind of order different from the logical one of mathematics – 'Cet ordre consiste principalement à la digression sur chaque point qui a rapport à la fin, pour la montrer toujours' – can give shape to these apparently disconnected fragments.

4 Another indication of Pascal's intentions appears in this fragment:

> S'il se vante, je l'abaisse.
> S'il s'abaisse, je le vante.
> Et le contredis toujours.
> Jusqu'à ce qu'il comprenne
> Qu'il est un monstre incompréhensible.

Show how Pascal puts this plan into effect.

5 'Pascal's powers of persuasion are . . . almost wholly directed towards inducing in his reader consciousness of appalling inadequacy and intense disquietude in the face of the essential perplexities of man's condition' (*P. Topliss*).

Jean RACINE (1639–99)

Racine is the supreme writer of French Classical tragedy, frequently compared and contrasted with his older contemporary Corneille and with the vastly different genius of Shakespeare.

Brought up in the sombre atmosphere of Port-Royal, Racine then lived in high society and at court, learning to read and love Greek literature, and gaining the favour of the young Louis XIV. After two plays of minor interest, *La Thébaïde* (1664) and *Alexandre le Grand* (1665), Racine's genius crystallized in a series of tragic masterpieces from *Andromaque* (1667) to *Phèdre* (1677), with the addition of one comedy, *Les Plaideurs* (1668), and then, after a silence of twelve years, the two biblical dramas, *Esther* (1689) and *Athalie* (1691).

Racine's tragedies vary considerably in subject-matter and emphasis, but they all show vulnerable human beings crushed by fate. Some, as in *Bérénice* (1671), are destroyed through their very virtues and accept their destruction in a noble gesture of renunciation. Others, more characteristically, are driven to destruction by their own uncontrollable desires, notably ambition or love. Exceptionally, in *Phèdre*, we see an acute sense of guilt, as the main character struggles violently between uncontrollable passion and a sense of dignity and honour.

The plays usually begin at a moment of crisis when, triggered by an outward event, a step is taken by one of the characters which will lead inevitably to disaster. In the inexorable slide towards the tragic end, dramatic moments of profound psychological truth reveal the depths of their hearts. The logical structure and sense of inevitability create scenes of great irony as fate and the characters' own passions work against them.

In *Andromaque*, for example, based on events following the capture of Troy, we see a chain of unrequited love, where noble feelings almost vanish in a sea of passion, as Pyrrhus, in love with his Trojan captive Andromaque, threatens to hand over her son to the Greeks unless she marries him. Around the tragic figure of Andromaque, torn between betraying her dead husband and seeing her son killed, other, more violent characters are advancing towards their own self-destruction. The Greek princess Hermione sees Pyrrhus, her intended husband, in love with Andromaque, but loves him too much to leave, as self-respect demands. Oreste, in love with Hermione, follows her every whim, prepared even to kill Pyrrhus at her jealous request, only to be confounded by the staggering 'Qui te l'a dit?' as she refuses to take responsibility for the deed she had herself commanded. The characters, unlike those of Corneille, are not in control of their passions:

> Il peut, Seigneur, il peut, dans ce désordre extrême,
> Epouser ce qu'il hait, et punir ce qu'il aime,

says Pylade about Pyrrhus. Hatred is close to love, as Hermione warns Oreste when asking him to murder Pyrrhus: 'S'il ne meurt aujourd'hui, je puis l'aimer demain.'

In *Britannicus* (1669), taken from Roman history, the Emperor Néron, until now subservient to his mother Agrippine and his mentor Burrhus, and held in check by his 'trois ans de vertu', takes the first step towards tyranny. He arrests Britannicus's beloved Junie and we see his sadistic fascination with the spectacle of her brought in tears to the palace: 'J'aimais jusqu'à ses pleurs que je faisais couler.' He eventually watches impassively as Britannicus is poisoned. We follow the dramatic development of the 'monstre naissant'. We also witness the downfall of Agrippine, whose cunning treachery turns against her as her son perceives that she has only been working for her own ends.

Phèdre, the most profound and moving of all Racine's tragedies, shows the moment of crisis when Phèdre, on the point of death ('une femme mourante et qui cherche à mourir'), is, against her will and hating herself ('Je m'abhorre encore plus que tu ne me détestes'), propelled into a confession of love for her stepson Hippolyte. We see her frenzied search for help, yet all her lucidity and feeling of guilt cannot prevail against the strength of her passion and the weight of destiny bearing down on her entire race:

Puisque Vénus le veut, de ce sang déplorable,
Je péris la dernière et la plus misérable.

In *Athalie* this wider dimension is provided by biblical history, as Athalie is defeated by God ('Dieu des Juifs, tu l'emportes'), and the race of David is placed again on the throne. Yet within this biblical context, Athalie belongs, just as much as Phèdre, to the race of Racinian heroines torn apart by violent emotions. The characters move apparently inexorably towards disaster, whether through the logic of destructive love in *Andromaque*, the mythologically expressed passion of *Phèdre*, or the force of religious history in *Athalie*.

Racine worked brilliantly within certain conventions, most importantly the unities of action, time and place. He took unity of action to extremes of simplicity in *Bérénice*, writing in the preface that 'Toute l'invention consiste à faire quelque chose de rien' and deriving almost the whole action from one sentence of Suetonius: 'Titus reginam Berenicem . . . dimisit invitus invitam' (Titus sent away Queen Bérénice against his will and against hers). Unity of time, concentrating and intensifying the action, is ideal for the psychological drama of Racine where all attention is focused on the reactions of the characters. Yet although the action on stage takes place at one point of crisis, the past and the future loom large. The characters in *Andromaque* are haunted by the Trojan war: how can Andromaque forget the burning of Troy and the blood-stained eruption of Pyrrhus into the palace?

Songe, songe Céphise, à cette nuit cruelle
Qui fut pour tout un peuple une nuit éternelle.

Yet how can she accept in the future the death of her son?

Quoi? Céphise, j'irai voir expirer encor
Ce fils, ma seule joie, et l'image d'Hector?

Racine also turns to his advantage the unity of place, creating in *Britannicus* and *Bajazet* a court ambiance similar to that of *La Princesse de Clèves*, a claustrophobic atmosphere of spying where even the walls have ears. In *Phèdre*, the very nearness of the characters brings disaster: Phèdre has succeeded in banishing Hippolyte and, for a while, could control her passion for him, but fate throws them together again. The first words of the play express Hippolyte's intention to leave and so avoid the presence of Aricie, his illicit love, yet he is forced to stay. The potentially artificial rule of unity of place becomes an essential ingredient in the hot-house tragedy of Racine. However he can equally well evoke vast stretches of time and space, as Bérénice, for example, visualizes a world where she and Titus will be apart:

> Dans un mois, dans un an, comment souffrirons-nous
> Seigneur, que tant de mers me séparent de vous?

Indeed in *Phèdre* the whole cosmos opens up before her, from the sun to the darkness of Hades, as she can find no place to hide.

In Racine's tragedies movement is minimal, spectacle almost non-existent. The whole action is borne by the language, and the poetry in which these dramatic emotions are conveyed is untranslatable in its simplicity and power. Take, for example, the first words spoken by Phèdre:

> N'allons point plus avant. Demeurons, chère Œnone.
> Je ne me soutiens plus, ma force m'abandonne.
> Mes yeux sont éblouis du jour que je revoi,
> Et mes genoux tremblants se dérobent sous moi.
> Hélas!

In phrases that are broken, yet gentle, Racine conveys the weariness of a woman exhausted by her struggle against an unlawful love, and establishes the theme of light and darkness that will run through the play. Here she cannot stand the light of the day. In Act V, after precipitating a series of disasters, she dies and describes her death in terms of restoring purity to the sunlight:

> Et la mort, à mes yeux dérobant la clarté,
> Rend au jour, qu'ils souillaient, toute sa pureté.

Racine's plays are miracles of compression, depth, intensity and poetry. Quite unlike the vast range of Shakespearean theatre, they appeal through their apparent simplicity and hidden depths, through their psychological penetration expressed in inimitable verse, and through the impression of total inevitability, the awareness that every line is essential to the tense unfolding of the tragic plot.

Further reading

E. Vinaver, *Racine and Poetic Tragedy* (1955); J. Lapp, *Aspects of Racinian Tragedy* (1956); P. France, *Racine's Rhetoric* (1965); O. de Mourgues, *Racine or The Triumph of Relevance* (1967); R. Knight (ed.), *Racine: Modern Judgements* (1969); P. Butler, *Racine* (1974). Editions: *Athalie*, ed. P. France (1966); *Britannicus*, ed. P. Butler (1967); *Phèdre*, ed. and transl. by R. Knight (1971). Studies of individual plays: W. Moore, *Racine: 'Britannicus'*

(1975); P. France, *Racine: 'Andromaque'* (1977); J. Short, *Racine: 'Phèdre'* (1983); J. Supple, *Racine: 'Bérénice'* (1986).

Workpoints

1   The nature of tragedy: 'Tragedy is for Racine the working out of an inexorable series of events leading to a foreseeable catastrophe' (*W. Howarth*).
    'Those the gods crush and destroy are not necessarily the wicked and the damned, and the harsh severity of their fate arouses distress and sympathy, compassion as well as awe and horror. This is an important aspect of Racinian tragedy, and it is, perhaps, the essence of tragedy' (*P. Butler*).

2   The hero: 'Instead of solitary and splendid figures, brought low through some error of judgement or character, Racine creates characters who carry within them the tares common to human nature. The standards whereby men live, which are often elaborate structures of conduct and manners, fail them in a crucial moment of their destiny, collapsing when the elemental forces of nature make their demands' (*J. Lapp*).
    'The opposition between the two dramatists (Racine and Corneille) according to which one, Racine, is nearer to psychological reality than the other, is erroneous. In both of them we find the reality of human nature; in neither, a realistic transcript of it' (*O. de Mourgues*).

3   Dramatic conventions: 'Dramatic conventions play a positive part in his tragedies: they are precious tools used to create tragic intensity' (*O. de Mourgues*).

4   Language: 'Racine's poetry differs as much from Shakespeare's as some calm-flowing river of the plain from a turbulent mountain torrent. To the dwellers in the mountain the smooth river may at first seem unimpressive. But still waters run deep; and the proverb applies with particular truth to the poetry of Racine' (*L. Strachey*).

3

The eighteenth century

The eighteenth century has been described as the Age of Elegance and as the Age of Enlightenment. Both labels are accurate, so long as it is remembered that neither applies to four-fifths of the nation, in 1700 some 16 million peasants, who were struggling to survive famine, poverty and sickness.

The elegance is captured in the paintings of Watteau and Fragonard; it was the elegance of those who continued to enjoy a life of wealth, privilege and spendthrift indolence; the name of Louis XIV's successor is a byword for distinctive styles of footwear and furniture. At the same time, the ideas of Descartes began to be more widely known and fully understood by an educated and increasingly dissatisfied middle class, who examined and questioned the basis of the country's institutions. Once the touchstone of reason was applied to traditional values and attitudes, the result was a period of intellectual fermentation stimulated by the work of powerful minds like those of Diderot and d'Alembert, of Rousseau and Voltaire. The elegance looked back to the spirit of feudalism and Versailles. The enlightenment was situated elsewhere. These two tendencies could not be reconciled and, by the Revolution of 1789, the old order (*l'ancien régime*) was overthrown in the name of 'Liberty, Equality and Fraternity'. It is tempting to suggest that the eighteenth century, which began with the divine right of kings, was to end with the Declaration of the Rights of Man (1789). In fact, one form of absolute rule replaced another for, after ten years of violence and political instability, Napoleon Bonaparte expelled the Assembly (18 brumaire 1799) and subsequently became emperor. These developments can be traced in four stages: the Regency, the long reign of Louis XV, the far shorter one of Louis XVI, and finally the French Revolution.

The France inherited in 1715 by Louis XIV's great grandson was already in decline. The Sun King's final years, scarred by famine and distress, by injustice and crippling taxation, already contained clear indications of the intellectual and social upheavals which would mark the next seventy-five years. The work of Pierre Bayle at the end of the seventeenth century had stressed the potential of the scientific method when applied to human and social problems. His motto 'Tout connaître pour tout critiquer' was a foretaste of the work undertaken by the *philosophes* some fifty years later, when a group of thinkers produced an encyclo-paedia ostensibly comprising the sum total of human knowledge, but in reality containing also forthright or veiled attacks upon established beliefs and traditional values. Similarly, the revolt of the Camisards at the very start of the eighteenth century was one violent manifestation of the reactions to religious oppression; it also foreshadowed the more widespread violence which destroyed the monarchy and killed the Sun King's descendants.

These dangers were not apparent when Louis XV became king at the age of 5. For eight years, under the Regency of the Duke of Orleans, the court devoted itself almost singlemindedly to frivolity and debauchery. Gone were the restraints of Madame de Maintenon's austerity and the corrective influences of Jansenism. There was a period of moral decadence. The unscrupulous Abbé Dubois controlled the affairs of state. The Regent believed that he had found a solution to the country's serious economic problems as well as a method of paying for the pleasures and excitements of the court which had moved again to Paris: he followed the advice of a Scottish financier, John Law. However, Law's system, based on credit rather than industrial development, provided no lasting solution. It served only to defer the ultimate economic and financial disaster.

In 1723 Louis XV took personal control. The country welcomed the boy king. He was dubbed 'le bien aimé'; but the affection soon waned. He preferred hunting to ruling; he lacked the Sun King's administrative skill and his authority; he was more successful at translating his mistresses into court favourites than at transforming the failing economy, or resolving the conflict between central and provincial government, or regulating the abuse of privilege. Moreover, during his reign, France was involved in two costly wars: the War of the Austrian Succession (1741–8) and the Seven Years War (1756–63). In the first, the king gained some personal prestige by gallantly appearing on the battlefield and, when taken ill, by renouncing his current mistress and returning to his queen, the Polish princess (Maria Leszcynska) he had married unenthusi-astically at the age of 15. However, any advantage was short-lived: by the Peace of Aix-la-Chapelle (1749) France gained nothing. The second was even more disastrous. By the time of the Peace of Paris (1763), France had lost its colonies in Canada and India; Louis XV had returned to the arms of Madame de Pompadour; and there was an increasingly public ventilation of dissatisfactions

– intellectual, political and religious – through the *Encyclopédie* which was already making its appearance, volume by volume, under the general editorship of Diderot and d'Alembert.

When Louis XVI came to the throne in 1774, the problems were too deep-rooted for any process of gradual change to be either possible or acceptable. Whatever reforms were attempted were thwarted by privilege, for to modify taxation was to modify the very basis of French society. Even France's participation on the winning side in the American War of Independence (1778–83) had counter-productive results at home: for one thing it was costly, and for another it was seen as a fight for a republican, and therefore anti-monarchist, cause. To the background of discontent, of poverty, of increasing numbers of vagabonds and of grain riots, the court and aristocracy seemed insensitive or resolutely indifferent. Marie-Antoinette may or may not have suggested that the mob, deprived of bread, should eat cake. She was certainly involved in the notorious extravagance at court; she was unacceptably foreign by birth; she was disastrously implicated in the scandal surrounding the theft of a necklace. The extent of aristocratic insensitivity can be judged by an edict published in 1781 that required any candidate for a commission in the army or navy or for high office in the church to belong to a family of established nobility. On top of all other reasons for discontent, this reinforcement of privilege at the expense of middle-class ambitions was particularly ill-timed.

The *ancien régime* was bankrupt, politically and financially. Privilege was enjoyed by, at most, 2 per cent of the population. The government was forced to capitulate and, in the hasty Convocation of the States General on 5 May 1789, there was public acknowledgement of its failure. There followed the Tennis Court Oath by which the commoners (the 600 deputies of the *tiers état*) refused to leave until they had established an acceptable constitution. However, the Paris mob did not wait for constitutional change: on 14 July 1789, it stormed the Bastille.

Then came ten years of violence, death and disorder in which the highest of principles expressed in the Declaration of the Rights of Man were often ignored or betrayed. By the time the mob had invaded the Tuileries palace in 1792 the protest could no longer be considered liberal or moderate. Clearly it had ceased to be legal. The king attempted to escape; he was recaptured and in 1793 he was beheaded. Some of the aristocrats were more fortunate: those who had once dallied in the celebrated rose gardens of Marie-Antoinette were sometimes lucky enough in the early 1790s to come across a modest scarlet pimpernel; others delighted the *tricoteuses* by demonstrating the clinical efficiency of the guillotine.

There was a reign of terror presided over by Robespierre during which the Committee of Public Safety dealt ferociously with all enemies, real and imaginary. There is, no doubt, in the royalist uprising of 1795, some hint of the persistent sympathy for the traditional form of government which was to lead to a temporary restoration of the monarchy in the following century, but that uprising could only be unsuccessful. For one thing, the opposing forces were commanded by one of the world's greatest generals. Having dealt with the monarchists, Napoleon's next move was to expel the revolutionary government in 1799 and to establish his own constitution. France was soon to become an empire.

*   *   *

The conflict between traditional attitudes and established values, like the increasingly cogent arguments for change, was not confined to the political or constitutional scene. The cultural life of France was similarly marked by stresses and divisions, visible in the literature and thought of the entire century. One important contributory factor to the development of new ideas occurred when, at the end of the Regency, the young Louis XV moved the court back to Versailles: much of the social life remained in Paris, centred around the fashionable and influential salons, with the result that courtiers were increasingly and even geographically isolated from the intellectual movements and the changing spirit.

The Enlightenment, or whatever name is given to the new intellectual climate of eighteenth-century France, was not an abrupt, but a gradual, change of direction and of emphasis. As the ideas of Descartes and Pierre Bayle became more fully appreciated, there was increased mistrust of traditional beliefs and principles, and there was a gradual substitution of new authorities: human reason and scientific method were to challenge both church and state. The new spirit is most clearly seen in the work of a group of intellectuals (the *philosophes*) whose combined attacks upon despotism, privilege, injustice and superstition were for a time concentrated upon the production of a vast compilation of human knowledge known as the *Encyclopédie*. This work, with all that it represents, stands as a monument to the intellectual force and courage which characterized the Enlightenment, even though its content is now hopelessly out-dated. There was, towards the end of the century, a reaction against cold rationalism, against the mood of materialism which had largely replaced metaphysical speculation. The resurgence of a more lyrical mode with an enlarged place in literature for emotion and nature certainly heralds the spirit of Romanticism which emerged in nineteenth-century France, but it did not entirely supplant the more critical, detached and cerebral approach. The essential scepticism of the age is conveyed by the description of Pierre Bayle's *Dictionnaire historique et critique* (1697) as 'la Bible du XVIIIe siècle'. From the attacks upon superstition and unscientific credulity in his *Pensées sur la Comète de 1680* to the *Dictionnaire* with its application of a critical method to the realms of history and thought, Bayle's work forms a stepping-stone between Cartesianism and the spirit of independent investigation found in the writing of Montesquieu and the *philosophes*.

The legacy of the seventeenth century is also perceptible in much eighteenth-century literature, especially in the theatre and the novel (for until André Chénier's work appeared on the eve of the French Revolution lyric poetry continued to be a neglected form).

There was much activity in the theatre, but drama ceased to be the dominant genre. Voltaire and others attempted for a time to maintain the Racinian tradition, but succeeded in retaining the form rather than the feeling. The dramatists whose work has kept its popularity are Marivaux and Beaumarchais, both writers of comedy. Moreover, Voltaire was quite prepared to use the stage as a platform for his philosophical preoccupations: his *Œdipe* (1718) contains attacks on absolute monarchies so blatant that he escaped a long term of imprisonment only by taking refuge in England. This period of exile was a rewarding experience for Voltaire personally in ways which extended far beyond the theatre. It was the first of his many journeys throughout Europe, and he was profoundly influenced by the work of English philosophers and scientists. This stay must be seen as an early example of the influence which English ideas were to exert throughout the whole century upon French thought and art. In purely theatrical terms, Voltaire returned to France with an increased respect for English drama, and particularly for Shakespeare. By the 1760s, when Garrick, the celebrated English actor, was reciting Shakespeare to enthusiastic audiences in Parisian salons, French dramatists were seeking alternatives to formal tragedy. Diderot, one of the most inventive of French minds, advocated a new genre situated between tragedy and comedy, and by this advocacy of the 'drame bourgeois', a serious form of play in which the central characters were no longer kings and emperors, he may well have introduced melodrama to the French stage. Diderot's own plays have been forgotten, but his work in the theatre is important because his analysis of drama shows a growing concern for man within the society of eighteenth-century France – the lawyers and judges, the noblemen and politicians – rather than for man in general presented customarily, in tragedy, as rulers in the myths, legends and history of antiquity. Eighteenth-century theatre placed a new emphasis upon realism in other ways: greater attention to costuming was one important development; another was the success of Voltaire and the comte de Lauraguais in removing spectators from the stage, where fops, dandies and wealthy exhibitionists had encroached so far as to impede the action and destroy all semblance of theatrical illusion.

Alongside the various modifications to the theatrical life of France, there was a development of fictional writing, remarkable for its variety and quantity, to satisfy the growing number of readers. The eighteenth century can claim to have established the novel as a genre which would fully flower in the following 200 years. Voltaire adopted the *conte*, more a short story than a novel, and one of these, *Candide*, is considered a masterpiece of French fiction. Other writers such as Diderot, Prévost, Rousseau and Laclos all favoured the longer, more sustained form of narrative.

Many of these novels are presented as memoirs; some are inserted in longer works. One example which illustrates both these tendencies is Prévost's *Manon Lescaut* (1731), which comprises Volume VII of his *Mémoires d'un homme de qualité*. Another common form, which comes to prominence in the second half of the century, is the novel written as letters between the principal characters: Rousseau's *La Nouvelle Héloïse* (1761) portrays the love of Julie d'Etanges and her young tutor, Saint-Preux, a passion remarkable for its purity and endurance despite all temptations, separations and even Julie's marriage. A very different novel using the epistolary mode is Laclos's *Les Liaisons dangereuses* (1782), in which Valmont, a cold and calculating rogue, plans the seduction of an honest married woman in an exchange of letters between himself and his amoral accomplice, Madame de Merteuil.

A comparison of Laclos's novel with another written at almost the same time highlights two major and divergent tendencies within the eighteenth century. *Paul et Virginie* (1787) by Bernardin de Saint-Pierre is a short romance describing the innocent love of two young people on the tropical Ile de France where they had been shipwrecked as children. There is a striking contrast between this somewhat sentimental tale of fidelity and integrity in an exotic setting and the cynical, cerebral behaviour of Laclos's main characters. The idealized love of Paul and Virginie portrayed against an idyllic background echoes Rousseau's dissatisfaction with the corruption and immorality of society, and marks an important stage in the development of French Romanticism.

Another feature apparent in this selection of novels is the increasingly international flavour of French fiction. The form of the epistolary novel is reminiscent of much early fiction brought to France from across the Channel. Important as the influence of England was on French thought and literature throughout the century, the foreign influences were not confined to an exchange between these two neighbouring countries. There was a growing interest in man's social behaviour which led to a curiosity about other societies with different standards, culture, beliefs and institutions. The hero and heroine of *Manon Lescaut* end their sad relationship on the far side of the Atlantic, where Chateaubriand was shortly to situate the action of his two pre-Romantic works, *Atala* (1801) and *René* (1802); and in *La Nouvelle Héloïse* the foreign travels of Saint-Preux after Julie's marriage are typical of those undertaken by Rousseau, Voltaire and many of their contemporaries. Some who did not themselves travel learned about distant civilizations from the reports of others: Diderot went as far as Russia, and his writings take in cultures from as far away as Tahiti.

Conversely, *Les Liaisons dangereuses*, a novel set firmly in France and one from which foreign travels and exotic settings are excluded, illustrates a different but equally significant feature of eighteenth-century France: rather than the emergent *sensibilité* with its concern for emotion and feeling, Laclos's novel depends upon a reasoned, analytical examination of human behaviour.

The application of a detached and dispassionate approach to worthier tasks than the seduction and corruption of a married woman explains the increasingly scientific manner adopted by writers of non-fictional works on subjects as varied as political history and natural history. Voltaire, describing the reigns of Louis XIV or Charles XII of Sweden, offers a very different type of history from the descriptions of a personal and anecdotal variety available in the memoirs and chronicles of his predecessors; and Buffon, as Keeper of the Jardin du Roi, devoted forty years of his life to the description and classification of insects, animals and birds, a task never before undertaken so thoroughly or so systematically. His patiently prepared and elegantly phrased descriptions differ considerably from the style of today's treatises on zoology, just as Voltaire's history may at times reveal prejudices to which modern historians would object. Nevertheless, they demonstrate a growing desire in the eighteenth century to examine the world of man and the world of nature in ways unfettered by tradition and convention. Moreover, like the majority of influential figures in the Age of Enlightenment, they were able to make their increasingly dispassionate assessments and scientific judgements on the basis of an amazingly broad general culture.

Attempts to understand and evaluate man's position in the universe inevitably led to judgements which were critical of established beliefs and authorities. Writers examined the present rather than the past; they considered man in contemporary society rather than, like La Rochefoucauld, man in a general, almost abstract, manner; they compared French forms of government with those

available in England and more distant countries. They found much
that failed to satisfy the growing desire for an improved society
based on reason, tolerance and humanitarian principles. The main
writers found various ways of voicing these widespread dissatisfactions, and much eighteenth-century literature can be interpreted
as a social, political and even economic commentary, expressed at
times with a gentle or concealed mockery, at other times with an
outspoken bluntness or ferocity. This tendency for literature to act
as social criticism can be traced from the beginning of the century
in works by Montesquieu or the dramatist Lesage, through the
activity in the middle of the century surrounding the publication
of the *Encyclopédie*, to the eve of the Revolution when the
performance of Beaumarchais's *Le Mariage de Figaro* (1784) was
delayed because the authorities could not fail to see in it an attack
upon injustices in the *ancien régime*.

One of the earliest writers to use humour as a weapon against
social abuse was Montesquieu (1689–1755). Long before the
appearance of his major work, *De l'Esprit des lois* (1748), Montesquieu had published an irreverent fictional commentary on
Parisian society, court life and other aspects of contemporary
France in the form of letters written by two tourists from Persia.
The *Lettres persanes* (1721) was a source of scandal or a source of
amusement depending upon the reader's personal reactions to
Montesquieu's witty and satirical observations upon customs,
political authority and religion during the Regency. Many of
Montesquieu's targets in the later work (slavery and political
abuse, the folly of war, religious intolerance) are already treated in
the exchange of letters between Rica and Usbek in Paris and their
friends in Persia. The serious purpose of the earlier work is
disguised; the irreverent humour and gentle satire throw a veil
over the landscape which softens both the abuses and Montesquieu's attacks; but the contours were still visible to his
contemporaries. Where the author's characters wrote about the
Koran or about despotism in the Middle East, the French readers
were not slow to substitute the Bible or the monarchy in France.
The *Lettres persanes* do more therefore than sketch the terrain to
be treated in a less flippant manner by Montesquieu in his later
work: they provide an early exploration of ground to be examined
exhaustively by the Encyclopédistes in the middle years of the
century. Two particularly well-known elements of his work are, in
the *Lettres persanes*, the imaginary social evolution of a primitive
people known as the Troglodytes; and in Book XIV of *De l'Esprit
des lois*, an attempt to demonstrate scientifically a relationship
between the climate and human behaviour. Montesquieu can
therefore be seen as a witty, charming and imaginative forerunner
of today's sociologists and political scientists.

Drama was also a vehicle for attacks upon particular social and political abuses throughout the eighteenth century; but whereas Montesquieu and other prose writers were able to publish abroad, the dramatist's audience was in France, where the authorities could prevent the performance of any dubious material. A play called *Turcaret* (1709) by Lesage was quickly suspended because of its devastatingly ironic attacks upon the world of French finance. At a time when France was involved in the War of the Spanish Succession, the moneylenders and tax-collectors were a particularly influential group. Lesage was not, like Molière in *L'Avare*, attacking some universal human foible: the scathing mockery of *Turcaret* was aimed at the emergent breed of high financier. His irony and his accusations of corruption were resented and suppressed – at least temporarily. A similar fate befell *Le Mariage de Figaro* in 1781.

Between the dates of these two plays, the attacks in the name of reason and humanity against social ills and political privilege continued unremittingly, mostly in works of prose. Of these, a number (like Voltaire's *contes*) employed the same weapons of satire, irony, mockery, flippancy and other deftly manipulated forms of humour. Others were more serious and more consciously constructive in manner. In *Emile* (1762), for example, Rousseau highlighted defects in the educational system by his programme for a more natural and a more stimulating form of upbringing. However utopian and visionary the theories may be, both in this work on education and in *Du contrat social* (1762), where Rousseau advocates the replacement of a corrupt system by a more just form of government based upon equality and liberty, there is an earnest and explicit attempt to suggest improvements. These works have endured, not merely as literary monuments, but as eloquent examples of the best endeavours to find a solution for problems which, under the *ancien régime*, were becoming intolerable.

The most notable of all such endeavours must be the *Encyclopédie*, published in over twenty volumes between 1751 and 1766, under the editorship of Diderot. The original intention was to provide a translation of Chambers's *Cyclopædia*, but Diderot was more audacious: rather than a dictionary, the French encyclopædia was to be a compendium of all human knowledge. To that end, Diderot enlisted the support of numerous specialists, including d'Alembert (1717–83), who was to supervise the scientific contributions. It was a huge undertaking, requiring the collaboration of men of immense energy, breadth of vision, intellectual courage and inventiveness. Diderot had the necessary power, and it is largely through his energies that, despite the vast range of subjects, the final work has shape and unity. The explanation for this rather surprising homogeneity lies in the principles common to all the *encyclopédistes* and *philosophes*: however varied the contributors may have been as individuals, there was a common belief in the power of reason to combat superstition and prejudice ('Il faudra renverser les barrières que la raison n'aura point posées'), and a common desire to overthrow all forms of injustice and inhumanity. It was this critical spirit which, infusing the entire work, turned the publication of the *Encyclopédie* into one long battle against the authorities.

The object, as stated by Diderot in the *Prospectus* and by d'Alembert in the *Discours préliminaire*, was reasonable and anodine: to provide a methodical and comprehensive study of all human knowledge, 'un dictionnaire raisonné des arts, des sciences et des métiers'. However, the independent outlook of the *philosophes*, together with their reliance upon the rational rather than the conventional, and their insistence upon observation and experiment, led to conclusions which could only be seen as challenges to established thought and accepted views. The authorities, largely the religious leaders and the politicians, contrived to interfere with the publication: in 1752, soon after the appearance of the first two volumes, opposition from Jesuits and Jansenists led to an interruption in the sale and distribution of the work; and later, in 1759, there was a further interruption on the grounds that the subsequent volumes were subversive. Such fears were entirely valid. The pervading spirit behind the work of the *philosophes*, within and outside the covers of these volumes, sprang from a desire for liberty and justice. Their attacks upon church and state were sometimes blatant and flagrant; and, when the censors objected, the same effect was obtained by presenting this critical message in a more veiled and insidious manner. The reader would be referred to counter-arguments in footnotes or other articles; the editorial comments would reveal the true intention; and the elaborate or extravagant praise of some abuse would satisfy the authorities, while simultaneously encouraging the reader to concentrate more upon what was implied between the lines than upon what was expressed literally in the text.

There may be a temptation to overemphasize the revolutionary flavour of the *Encyclopédie*. In fact, the prolonged onslaught upon established authority throughout the century is also discernible in other works by the most influential of the *philosophes*. Voltaire's account of England in his *Lettres philosophiques* (1734) has been described as 'la première bombe lancée contre l'Ancien Régime'; and the opening words of Rousseau's *Du contrat social*, 'L'homme est né libre et partout il est dans les fers', have served as an inspiration to many revolutionary socialists.

In reality, the aim of the *philosophes* was to modify patiently rather than to overthrow violently. It was not their hope that philosophers should become kings, but that kings would become philosophers, with all that such a label conveyed in the way of humanitarian principles. It has been calculated that, until Louis XVI attempted to escape, only a very small percentage of the population was anti-monarchist. Nevertheless, the *Encyclopédie* was a powerful expression of intellectual discontent which contributed to the growing mood of political and economic dissatisfaction. The official response was invariably repressive. The productions of *Turcaret* and *Le Mariage de Figaro* were delayed; the views of Diderot and Voltaire resulted in terms of imprisonment; both Voltaire and Rousseau considered it prudent at times to take refuge abroad in England or Switzerland. Ultimately, however, the efforts of the authorities were counter-productive: they could defer or delay, but not destroy. Indeed, the burning of a book added to its notoriety and encouraged its clandestine sale.

If there was a real threat to the rationalism and materialism of the philosophical outlook, it came from within. The term 'philosophes' is a valid label, so long as it is remembered that the powerful intellects to which it is applied did not constitute a unified and uniform body. The celebrated and bitter quarrel between Voltaire and Rousseau illustrates the great divergence of opinions. Curiously enough, Voltaire is seen as the archetype of the eighteenth-century *philosophe*, but he was merely on the fringes of the *Encyclopédie*, to which his direct contributions were relatively slight. To say that is in no way to minimize the contribution he made, from his retreat on the Swiss border, to the general movement of European thought. Put simply, his view was that twenty volumes were less effective than one well-aimed pamphlet. Rousseau's involvement was more considerable, as the expert upon subjects as varied as music and political economy; but the principal difference lay in the nature of these two writers. The author of *La Nouvelle Héloïse* and *Emile* displays a reaction to the purely rational and excessively intellectual attitudes of many of the *encyclopédistes*. There is within Rousseau's work a passionate love of nature and a place for human emotion, a sensitivity and a belief in the natural goodness of mankind which distinguish him from other *philosophes*. For Rousseau, society is a corrupting influence and, throughout his entire work, from his first essay on the adverse effects of culture and scientific progress to his later autobiographical writings, there is a *sensibilité* which marks him out as a forerunner of French Romanticism. According to a contemporary: 'avec Voltaire, c'est un monde qui finit; avec Rousseau, c'est un monde qui commence'.

The change was, of course, neither entire nor abrupt. Cartesian reason would persist into the currents of positivism and scientism which were influential in nineteenth-century philosophy. Nevertheless, the re-emergence of a more emotional literature was visible before the storming of the Bastille. With the arrival of the more personal style and the renewed taste for a melancholy state of mind comes the reappearance of a more lyrical form of poetry, notably in the works of André Chénier. The literature of the eighteenth century acts as a transition between Classicism and Romanticism, just as contemporary political activity marks the shift from autocratic rulers to a more democratic style of government. The major figures, in a century where there is no predominant genre, tended to be giants and all-rounders whose strong views on the need for human liberty inclined them to favour a literature of propaganda. As Diderot put it in a letter to Princesse Dashkoff in 1771: 'Chaque siècle a son esprit qui le caractérise. L'esprit du nôtre semble être celui de la liberté.' It is also a century notable for its increasingly cosmopolitan flavour. The visits of the *philosophes* to countries such as Prussia, Russia and England, and the voluminous correspondence between Voltaire or Diderot and the rulers of European countries were particularly important: they helped to establish the cultural influence of France and, with that, the influence of the French language, which was never greater; and they marked a shift of focus from the Mediterranean cultures of antiquity towards more northerly countries from which Romanticism was to draw much of its inspiration.

Further reading

C. Behrens, *The Ancien Régime* (1967); J. Brumfitt, *The French Enlightenment* (1972); E. Cassirer, *The Philosophy of the Enlightenment* (1951); A. Cobban, *Aspects of the French Revolution* (1968); L. Crocker, *The Age of Crisis* (1959); A. Goodwin, *The French Revolution* (1970); N. Hampson, *The Enlightenment* (1968); P. Hazard, *The European Mind 1680–1715* (1953) and *European Thought in the Eighteenth Century* (1954); J. Lough, *An Introduction to Eighteenth-Century France* (1960); J. Thompson, *The French Revolution* (1943).

R. Grimsley (ed.), *The Age of Enlightenment (1715–1789)* (1979); H. Mason, *French Writers and their Society, 1715–1800* (1982); G. May, *Le Dilemme du roman au XVIIIe siècle* (1963); V. Mylne, *The Eighteenth-Century French Novel* (1965, 1981).

Pierre Augustin Caron de BEAUMARCHAIS (1731–99)

Beaumarchais is best remembered as the creator of Figaro, the central character in two of the liveliest comedies in the French theatre, *Le Barbier de Séville* (1775) and *Le Mariage de Figaro* (written in 1781 and first performed in 1784). There is an undeniable family likeness between creator and character: like the playwright himself, Figaro is quick-witted and clever, entertaining and impertinent, crafty and resourceful, immensely talented and resilient in adversity. The consequence of placing such a sparkling and ingenious character at the hub of the dramatic action is two comedies remarkable for the intricacy of their plots, the dancing humour of the dialogue, the pace and inventiveness of the episodes – in other words, for sheer vitality and comic verve. As one famous actress in the Comédie Française observed: 'If it was the custom to signal the mood of a play as it is for a musical score, the one word for Beaumarchais' drama would be *andante*.'

Much is known about Beaumarchais's life; far more is unknown, half-known or strongly suspected. The confusion is hardly surprising, since his career included numerous activities which, by their very nature, require confidentiality and even secrecy: some very dubious commercial activities, a few missions as ambassador or envoy to foreign countries, a bit of smuggling, and at least two instances of gun-running, first selling arms to the Americans during the War of Independence, and later buying weapons for the revolutionary government in France. It is certainly proof of his irrepressible vitality, his opportunism and his ambitions that he should start life as a clockmaker, become *horloger du roi* in 1753 and then be appointed music master to Louis XV's daughters; it is proof of his ability to survive adversity that he bounced back into social prominence after two periods of imprisonment and finally contrived not to die by the guillotine. For the intervening years, the best description of his career was written by Professor T. Lawrenson: 'His life defies summary.' The same could be said of his plays.

In both *Le Barbier* and *Le Mariage*, with Figaro's inventiveness in control of proceedings and his brightness setting the tone, we have two outstanding examples of the comedy of intrigue, based on a bewildering complexity of schemes, stratagems and subterfuges. The first play deals with a collaboration between Figaro and his former master, the Count of Almaviva, as the latter attempts to woo, win and marry the lovely young Rosine in spite of all the obstacles with which her guardian, Bartholo, surrounds her. In the second play, Figaro is no longer a collaborator but an opponent, for Almaviva, bored by the countess after a few years of marriage, now intends to seduce Figaro's fiancée. Whatever similarities there are between the characters, the mood of the two plays is at times quite different. Whereas, in *Le Barbier*, Figaro's impudent comments about society and his impertinence towards Almaviva were deft but light-hearted, the attacks in *Le Mariage* are more flagrant and more determined (but fortunately without destroying the essential humour). Criticisms of the *noblesse d'épée*, in the person of the count, and of the *noblesse de robe*, in the form of an inept and foolish lawyer, account for the hostility of Louis XVI, the intervention of censorship, and the long delay before *Le Mariage* was performed.

It is easy to exaggerate Beaumarchais's contribution to the revolutionary tendencies in France at the time: by his attacks on the *ancien régime*, he was a reflection of the philosophical attitudes with which society was, by the second half of the century, imbued or at least familiar. If Beaumarchais's personal sympathies lay with the middle class and the man in the street, Figaro's manoeuvres are less a catalyst of social upheaval than a display of widely held views. His flair caught the public imagination, his popularity has endured, and his immortality is assured not only by the continuing presence of the two plays in the repertory of the Comédie Française but also by their translation into the operas of Rossini and Mozart.

Although none of his other plays enjoyed a comparable success, Beaumarchais made a valuable contribution to theatre in other ways: his essay on 'le genre dramatique sérieux' reinforced Diderot's attacks upon conventional tragedy; and in Paris to this day, his portrait occupies a place of honour at the Société des Auteurs et Compositeurs Dramatiques in recognition of his efforts to protect playwrights from unscrupulous theatre managers.

Further reading

R. Niklaus, *Beaumarchais: 'Le Barbier de Séville'* (1968); R. Niklaus, *Beaumarchais: 'Le Mariage de Figaro'* (1983).

Workpoints

1 Try, without losing any of the sense, to summarize *Le Barbier de Séville*, Act III Scene 11, using less words than Beaumarchais.
   or
   Try to summarize the plot of *Le Mariage de Figaro* on one side of a sheet of file paper.
   (Both endeavours are doomed to failure, but the exercise is rewarding because of what can be learned about Beaumarchais's skill.)

2 Estimate how much of the laughter provoked by Figaro depends upon wit, pun, irony, satire, slapstick and spectacle, mockery, playfulness, sarcasm, quickness of thought and rejoinder, cynicism, impudence and sheer good humour.

3 'As an observer of human nature Beaumarchais is superficial;

as a manipulator of plot and character he is incomparable.' Do you agree?

Denis DIDEROT (1713–84)

Diderot was educated by the Jesuits in his home town of Langres, then in Paris, where he obtained the degree of 'maître-ès-arts' in 1734. He subsequently spent four years avoiding poverty by teaching, literary hack-work and various financial expedients. During this time he made friends with Rousseau and from here onwards most of his life was caught up with the world of ideas, literature and the arts. By the mid 1740s he was involved with the *Encyclopédie*. As director and main contributor Diderot was to be heavily committed for twenty years, and during this time the authorities interrupted publication more than once. Nor was this Diderot's only problem with officialdom: he was imprisoned for three months because of his other writings, especially the apparently materialist treatise *Lettre sur les aveugles* (1749). He wrote prolifically in other forms, both while continuing the *Encyclopédie* and after its completion in 1765. At this point he made safe his financial future by selling his library to an admirer, the Czarina Catherine the Great, but he continued to write until his death.

Diderot is now considered on a par with his contemporaries Voltaire and Rousseau, but his reputation has been hard to come by. For one thing, many of his major works (for example *Le Neveu de Rameau* and *Paradoxe sur le comédien*) were published only long after his death; for another, he worked in a wide variety of forms and genres, including the philosophical dialogue, and has never been safely pigeonholed as, say, 'novelist', 'satirist' or 'dramatist'. Further, no one work stands out as a masterpiece representative of Diderot as a whole. Yet as a thinker who conveyed ideas on every subject to his reader, and as a writer who was always attentive to his literary and artistic responsibilities, Diderot has a unique position. Before, during and after his work on the *Encyclopédie*, he reflected the impact scientific knowledge was making on philosophical and moral issues. Thus *Lettre sur les aveugles* shows how human beings' ideas depend on their sense-impressions, and disputes the existence of God; *Le Rêve de d'Alembert* (published 1830) excludes the notion of spirit from the universe, argues that matter is the basis of all reality, and speculates on the cellular structure of organisms. The insights into human nature provided by contemporary travel writing are also grist to Diderot's mill, as when Bougainville's *Voyage autour du monde* (1771) inspires the *Supplément au voyage de Bougainville* (published 1796). Here Europe's civilization, in the person of the chaplain, is shown to be confused and unhappy whereas Tahitian society is innocent, uninhibited and based on natural virtue and morality.

Perhaps the most memorable example of Diderot's handling of ideas comes in *Le Neveu de Rameau* (1821), like so many of Diderot's texts a dialogue, offering the reader a confrontation of opposites. One afternoon in a café in the Palais-Royal, surrounded by chess players, Moi and Lui have their own contest. Moi, who introduces the conversation, spars with Lui, a character based on Jean-François Rameau, an unpredictable eccentric, minor musician and nephew of the great eighteenth-century composer. The work is headed 'Satire', and accordingly lambasts Palissot, author of *Les Philosophes*, a play attacking Diderot and his circle; other philosophical writers, untalented actresses and reactionary financiers are also among the victims. Diderot did not publish the text in his lifetime, and several times reworked it; its interest then goes beyond the merely topical. Discussion ranges over the value of sycophancy (of which Lui is a past master), the importance of money and pleasure (Lui dismisses conventional morality as 'vanité'), and the notion of genius (considered socially disruptive as well as innovative, and while both sides argue their cases forcefully, the disreputable Lui often comes across as more effective than the upright Moi. And the whole debate is heightened not only by the brilliance of the words exchanged, but also by Lui's extraordinary powers of mime and mimicry. The debate is also explicitly concerned with the aesthetics of music – which links it with other major areas of Diderot's work, such as the *Salons* (1759–81), pioneering studies in art criticism, and another dialogue, the *Paradoxe sur le comédien* (published 1830), which argues that the most effective acting derives from the greatest degree of emotional detachment on the part of the actor. Diderot's other major contribution to the theatre was the theory of the *drame bourgeois*, a form lying between conventional tragedy and comedy, giving a serious and realistic treatment to ordinary social life; in practice his own plays were too overtly moralizing to be fully convincing.

The mainsream literary genre in which he succeeded best was fiction. In *contes* such as *Les Deux Amis de Bourbonne*, and especially in his full-scale novels, Diderot found the scope to combine his intellectual and aesthetic concerns with his talent as a story-teller. His *Eloge de Richardson* (1762) gives some useful clues as to his attitude towards the novel in the 1760s. While admitting the generally low status of the form (as compared with, say, drama or history), Diderot argues that the English novelist convinces the reader of the reality of his situations, and succeeds in conveying moral truths. *La Religieuse* (mostly written in 1760, though not published until 1796) likewise aims at a realistic presentation of serious issues. Suzanne Simonin is made a novice because she is illegitimate and, despite her lack of a vocation, has to remain in a series of convents until her eventual escape. Although the book is not an attack on Christianity as such, it graphically illustrates the cruelty and unnaturalness of celibate life in the eighteenth century ('Dieu qui a créé l'homme sociable, approuve-t-il qu'il se renferme?'). The story was based on the case of Marguerite Delamarre, a nun who tried to have her vows annulled, and Diderot took care to establish credibility through realistic detail. The text also embodies the two most popular fictional forms of the time: as Suzanne is recounting her own experiences, it follows the conventions of the memoir novel; and as her story is at the centre of an exchange of letters involving Diderot's friend the Marquis de Croismare, it also belongs to the epistolary tradition. Unusually for eighteenth-century novels, but typical of Diderot, La Religieuse contains a large proportion of dialogue.

Dialogue is also at the heart of Diderot's other major novel, Jacques le fataliste (written 1778, published 1796). On one level Jacques consists of a series of constantly interrupted conversations in which the hero tells his master of his life and loves. But on another, and more originally, it is a dialogue between the narrator and an imagined reader, who is presented with a series of questions in the first paragraph, addressed regularly and even drawn into arguments. Clearly Diderot is not aiming here at the illusion of reality he achieved in La Religieuse. And yet he is aiming at a reality of sorts; as the reader is told: 'Je ne fais pas un roman. . . . Celui qui prendrait ce que j'écris pour la vérité serait peut-être moins dans l'erreur que celui qui le prendrait pour une fable.' While there are references to contemporary society – the class structure of the ancien régime, or the depopulation of the countryside – the reality the reader encounters is more to do with the confusing, fragmentary character of day-to-day experience. A key influence here is not the plausible Richardson but the freewheeling Sterne, whose Tristram Shandy Diderot explicitly mentions. But the self-referring world of the text is also a perfect arena for the play of ideas on the theme of destiny and determinism. As the title suggests, Jacques is a spokesman for 'fatalism', claiming that 'Tout ce qui nous arrive de bien et de mal ici-bas est écrit là-haut'; yet often, despite his beliefs, Jacques acts as if he were free, and uses his own initiative, whereas his master still claims to be free, even when, say, it is Jacques who causes him to fall from his horse. Early on the question is asked: 'Est-ce que nous menons le destin, ou bien est-ce le destin qui nous mène?', and in a true spirit of dialogue Diderot offers no neat answer.

There is no certainty even as to what happens to Jacques and his master, as alternative endings to the novel are offered. To the end of his career then, Diderot kept faith with what he wrote in one of his earliest works, the *Pensées philosophiques*: 'On doit exiger de moi que je cherche la vérité, mais non que je la trouve.'

Further reading

A. Wilson, *Diderot* (1972); J. Mason, *The Irresistible Diderot* (1982); G. Bremner, *Order and Chance* (1983); P. France, *Diderot* (1983); V. Mylne, *Diderot: 'La Religieuse'* (1981); G. Bremner, *Diderot: 'Jacques le fataliste'* (1985); J. Falvey, *Diderot: 'Le Neveu de Rameau'* (1985).

Workpoints

1 Diderot the thinker: What is the basis for Diderot's ideas? 'His approach was undogmatic, empirical and dialectical' (*R. Niklaus*). 'Neither a rationalist nor an empiricist, but a realist' (*P. France*). Which description suits him best? Do any others suggest themselves?

2 On *Le Neveu de Rameau*: 'The one thing that has been revealed totally, honestly and unhypocritically is the character and energy of Lui, this instructive specimen, exploiter and victim of cultural mankind' (*J. Falvey*). Consider the central figure of the dialogue in the light of this remark.

3 On *La Religieuse*: How wide is the appeal of the novel outside its own time? 'Indépendamment de toute institution religieuse, le roman de Diderot peut se lire comme une "fable" de la liberté et continuer à émouvoir ceux qui ont en partage ce goût de la liberté' (*R. Desne*). Discuss this judgement.

4 On *Jacques le fataliste*: How far – and how successfully – is *Jacques* a 'novel about the novel'? Assess Jean Fabre's contention that '*Jacques* est un récit où l'esthétique du récit intervient constamment dans la conduite du récit.'

Pierre Choderlos de LACLOS (1741–1803)

An artillery officer with a *petit bourgeois* background and a talent for mathematics, Laclos spent his early career in the obscurity of provincial garrisons; he died, under the Consulate, as one of Napoleon's generals. With one exception, his writings did little to distinguish him, even if his pre-feminist essays are a telling indication of his concerns. But at the age of 40, according to a contemporary, he set out to write 'un ouvrage qui sortît de la route ordinaire, qui fît du bruit, et qui retentît encore sur la terre quand j'y aurais passé'. *Les Liaisons dangereuses* (1782) amply fulfilled this aim, in terms both of immediate shock and later repercussions.

The novel, consisting of 175 letters exchanged over a five-month period, is an outstanding example of the epistolary form. All the letters are properly motivated, instead of being mere excuses for story-telling or emotional outpourings – which is often the case in cruder models. And there is great economy of means, so that nothing irrelevant to the plot is included. At the same time, the variety of correspondents (seven major contributors plus half-a-dozen minor ones, instead of one or two, as often) allows a brilliant juxtaposition of points of view, and even variations on the same event, as with the seduction of Cécile (the Vicomte de Valmont's account in letter 85 and Cécile's own in 87). This diversity also makes for striking contrasts of style and tone, for instance between the incisiveness of the Marquise de Merteuil and the vague sentimentality of Danceny. The letters perform many tasks, notably recording past events and anticipating future ones, exposing the writer's feelings and probing those of others. Moreover, it is never forgotten that the correspondence has a material existence: the details of composition and delivery are often mentioned; more important, letters, once read, are kept or passed on, rather than destroyed. Valmont and Merteuil in particular obtain letters not intended for them. They also supervise some of the correspondence of the naive Cécile and Danceny. More than simply a plausible vehicle, letters are, in one critic's words, 'l'étoffe même du roman'.

The story traces Merteuil's plan to have the notorious Valmont, her former lover, debauch the young *ingénue* Cécile; the pair are thus to take revenge on one Gercourt, Cécile's intended husband, who has offended them both. The plan eventually succeeds, destroying in the process the simple love of Cécile and Danceny. But Valmont's long drawn-out seduction of the pious Présidente de Tourvel – and his increasing feeling for her – arouse the Marquise's jealousy. The novel ends with Valmont dying after a duel with Danceny instigated by Merteuil – but not before he has ruined her reputation, by making public her private correspondence with him. The plot is beautifully constructed, with delicate symmetries and parallelisms, and crowned with the irony of the two leading protagonists, who aspire to control others' destinies, finally losing control of their own.

The social context is of a leisured *ancien régime* aristocratic circle apparently losing its traditional warfaring role – a point neatly made by the frequent use of military imagery to describe the sexual activity which seems now to be the main preoccupation. However, as with all the major letter–novels, attention focuses on moral issues. According to the 'Préface du rédacteur' the text proves that any woman should flee a known libertine, and that a mother should be her daughter's only *confidante*. Yet this may well be understood as merely Laclos's version of the conventional eighteenth-century preface designed to forestall moral criticism, and it gains little from being echoed almost word for word in the final letter, written by Madame de Volanges, Cécile's pompous and self-deceiving mother. Merteuil and Valmont, as in the former's autobiographical letter 81, represent the values of libertinism in its sense of erotic gratification. For Merteuil, 'l'amour que l'on nous vante comme la cause de nos plaisirs, n'en est au plus que le prétexte'. Both deploy a formidable armoury of intellect and will to achieve these 'plaisirs', and both have a grandiose view of their powers; Valmont, prophesying his conquest of the Présidente, boasts: 'Je serai vraiment le Dieu qu'elle aura préféré'; while Merteuil, manipulating Cécile and her mother, declares: 'Me voilà comme la Divinité'. However impressive their wit and energy, Merteuil and Valmont fail in the end by overrating their intelligence and underestimating their own capacity for love and jealousy. The Présidente, passive where the main protagonists are active, and living by emotion where they believe in reason, stands for *sensibilité*, and if she dies a helpless victim, her self-sacrificial declaration of love for Valmont (letter 128) arguably gives her great stature. The *dénouement*, where the punishment does not always fit the crime, heightens the ambiguities. It is difficult, if not impossible, to find any clear lesson in the text, and tempting, perhaps, to see a kind of tragedy adapted to the artistic and moral climate of the time. Throughout the nineteenth century *Les Liaisons dangereuses* impressed only a few perceptive readers, such as Baudelaire. Since then, however, it has been held in the highest regard: Gide placed it second among all French novels, and many subsequent judges would concur.

Further reading

D. Thelander, *Laclos and the Epistolary Novel* (1963); P. Thody, *Laclos: 'Les Liaisons dangereuses'* (1970, 1975); R. Rosbottom, *Choderlos de Laclos* (1978); S. Davies, *Laclos: 'Les Liasions dangereuses'* (1987).

Workpoints

1 *The novel as a picture of society*
   How valid is the novel's epigraph (taken from Rousseau's *La Nouvelle Héloïse*): 'J'ai vu les mœurs de mon temps et j'ai publié ces lettres'?
   How far would you agree with the Marxist critic Roger Vailland, who sees in it the 'peinture réaliste d'une classe sociale à la veille de sa chute'?

2 *Morality and values*
'*Les Liaisons dangereuses* restent un roman prestigieux dans la mesure même où Laclos n'a pas réussi à en faire un roman moral' (*J. Fabre*). Discuss.

3 *Psychology*
'*Les Liaisons dangereuses* is not a psychological novel in the usual sense of the term. It does not take us into the minds of its characters and this is exactly its fascination. . . . We have to get there ourselves' (*D. Thelander*). Discuss.

4 *Technique and style*
'L'originalité de Laclos, c'est d'avoir donné une valeur dramatique à la composition par lettres . . . et d'avoir réalisé ainsi entre le sujet du livre et le mode de narration un accord si étroit que ce mode en devient non seulement vraisemblable mais nécessaire' (*J.-L. Seylaz*). Discuss.

Pierre Carlet de Chamblain de MARIVAUX (1688–1763)

Journalist, novelist and, above all, dramatist, Marivaux is particularly remembered for a handful of the thirty comedies he wrote: those in which he concentrated upon young and innocent love at the stage of encounter and courtship. Unlike Molière, half a century earlier, in whose plays love was a largely static element (the affection of Molière's young lovers was not questioned, but merely impeded by external forces such as unsympathetic parents or guardians), Marivaux focuses on the discovery of love made by two young, often inexperienced, people. His most enduring plays are remarkable for the delicate and subtle analysis of emotions conveyed in a dialogue that has a deceptively simple, conversational flavour and rhythm. This choice of material involved a careful analysis of the feminine character, and Marivaux has been dubbed a 'Racine en miniature' because of the psychological penetration and skill with which he portrays the heroine's nature. Instead, however, of passion and violence, the birth of love in Marivaux's plays is a largely pleasurable event, presented with grace and urbanity, usually in a setting that recalls the idyllic country estates found in Watteau's landscapes or the rarefied atmosphere of the elegant salons which Marivaux frequented; for although, by 1722, he had lost all his money in unsuccessful financial speculations based on Law's system, Marivaux belonged to the *noblesse de robe* and was welcomed by such leaders of Parisian society as Madame du Deffand, Madame de Tencin, Madame de Lambert and Madame Geoffrin.

Marivaux's theatre was particularly popular between 1720 and 1740, when plays like *La Surprise de l'amour* (1722), *La Double*

Inconstance (1723), *Les Fausses Confidences* (1737), and *L'Epreuve* (1740) were performed by the *Théâtre Italien*. These companies of visiting actors, banished by Louis XIV for their mockery of Madame de Maintenon, but back in Paris at the start of the Regency, had an expressive style of performance well suited to convey the subtlety and charm of Marivaux's texts. His masterpiece is considered to be *Le Jeu de l'amour et du hasard* (1730), an entertaining play based upon the encounter between Silvia, who has disguised herself as her maid Lisette, and Dorante, who, by coincidence, has decided on a similar tactic and arrives wearing the livery of Arlequin, his lackey or manservant. As hero and heroine struggle behind self-imposed disguises to assess their own and their partner's emotions, the servants also fall in love, a device which allows Marivaux to provide a blunt and forthright counterpoint to the more refined and delicate melody at the centre of the play.

To describe Marivaux's idiosyncratic treatment of love, its intricate developments as well as the finely chiselled style of dialogue, the word *marivaudage* has been coined. Some use the term affectionately to convey the witty, elegant and somewhat affected manner the playwright adopts to portray a new and innocent emotional attraction; for others, *le marivaudage* implies a criticism of the dramatist's lightness, frivolity and artificiality. Marivaux claimed that: 'J'ai guetté dans le cœur humain toutes les niches différentes où peut se cacher l'amour lorsqu'il craint de se montrer.' Voltaire's rejoinder was that Marivaux 'connaît tous les sentiers du cœur humain, mais il en ignore la grande route'.

Marivaux's theatre is certainly notable more for its skill than its depth, but concentration upon a few of the more charmingly presented encounters between young lovers has misled some critics into believing that Marivaux merely wrote variations upon one play. In fact, there are some shorter, frequently neglected plays dealing with a social rather than an amorous problem. *La Colonie* is an early, none too serious examination of feminism, and *L'Ile des esclaves* (1725) toys with social reconstruction when masters and servants are shipwrecked on a desert island. Like many of his contemporaries, Marivaux was inclined to examine social changes with the detachment enjoyed in a fashionable and elegant drawing room, and it is in such surroundings that he observed and portrayed the amorous adventures for which he is best remembered. Echoes of his style can be detected in the plays of Musset in the nineteenth and Giraudoux in the twentieth centuries.

Further reading

Le Jeu de l'amour et du hasard, ed. M. Shackleton (1954); G. Rodmell, *Marivaux: 'Le Jeu de l'amour et du hasard' and 'Les Fausses Confidences'* (1982); D. Coward, *Marivaux: 'La Vie de Marianne' and 'Le Paysan parvenu'* (1982).

Workpoints

1 Using the following comments as starting-points, examine Marivaux's treatment of love, his use of disguise, his portrayal of contemporary society and his style: 'Marivaux's comedy is charming and original though with familiarity it is inclined to cloy' (*L. Bisson*). 'Marivaux est le peintre de l'amour. L'amour n'est plus chez lui un accessoire de la comédie comme chez Molière. C'est le sujet essentiel de ses pièces' (*R. and D. Ledésert*). 'Marivaux places greater value on character than birth' (*K. McKee*).

2 According to Voltaire, Marivaux spent his time weighing flies' eggs using a spider's web as scales. Two other views are: 'A style which may be mannered and affected, but is full of psychological penetration' (*D. Charlton*). 'A la finesse de l'analyse correspond une extrême subtilité du langage' (*Lagarde et Michard*).

3 Having read *Le Jeu de l'amour et du hasard*, can you explain the title?

Abbé PREVOST (1697–1763)

After a Jesuit education in his home town of Hesdin in northern France, Prévost switched more than once between religious and military life and – as has been neatly observed – experienced in his turbulent youth all the ups and downs of a picaresque novel, such as scandals, flights from justice, and exile. He was eventually ordained into a Benedictine order, but thereafter devoted himself increasingly to writing and finally settled to a largely secular, literary existence.

His prolific output relates closely to the tastes and interests of his time: he produced works of travel, *Pour et contre* (1733–40) – a literary and intellectual review (serving as a forum for contemporary ideas) – and, later in his career, translations of Richardson. He also wrote a dozen novels, nearly all in the *mémoire* form, including *Cleveland* (1731–9), the most popular of them in his own age. His early success, *Mémoires d'un homme de qualité* (1728–31), had as its seventh and last volume the *Histoire du chevalier des Grieux et de Manon Lescaut*, a controversial text in its time and the only one by Prévost which is widely read today. It traces the couple's love-affair from the *coup de foudre* of their first meeting in Amiens, when he is an aristocrat of 17 about to embark on a career, and she, younger and of lower rank, is being sent to a convent to check her already apparent 'penchant au plaisir'. There follows a series of separations, when the beautiful Manon – despite her affection for Des Grieux – yields to richer and more influential rivals; but each separation ends in reunion, even when imprisonment and, eventually, Manon's deportation put still greater obstacles between them. Her death in the New World when – not for the first time – they are both forced to flee from their enemies, brings the novel to an end. Renoncour, the 'homme de qualité', simply records Des Grieux's words as he hears the story one evening in an inn; thus the protagonist is also the narrator – one deeply absorbed in his own subjective feelings and correspondingly vague about those of others, including Manon, who therefore remains elusive for the reader as well as for the Chevalier. The style reflects the informality of oral delivery but also the correct speech of an educated man. The narrative falls into two parts (one recounted before supper, the other after), but its essential characteristic is the swift, if not always credible, progress from one episode to the next. As Des Grieux puts it, with typical hyperbole: 'La Fortune ne me délivra d'un précipice que pour me faire tomber dans un autre.' There is much of documentary and social interest: the setting of Regency Paris is often evoked, especially in its more sordid aspects – gaming-houses, street crime and prisons; money features as a vital necessity; and an important factor in the hero's predicament is the tension between his own, insecure noble caste and an increasingly powerful middle class. As in other novels of the period, fiction is supposed to serve a serious purpose by giving the reader instructive experiences: the prefatory 'Avis de l'auteur' describes *Manon* as 'un traité de morale, réduit agréablement en exercice' – an illustration of the dangers of unbridled passion. Within the story Des Grieux's conduct is criticized – from both the viewpoint of the Church (by Tiberge, his long-suffering friend) and that of the aristocratic code of honour (by his father). He certainly remains sensitive to the latter, but for all his admissions of guilt and weakness, and all his misdeeds, including lying, cheating, and killing a prison guard (albeit accidentally), Des Grieux continues to champion love as an innocent, natural and ennobling emotion, and thereby to vindicate himself. More generally he rejects the values of reason and the social system of the real world, favouring instead a hierarchy based on *sensibilité*, or the capacity to feel: 'Le commun des hommes n'est sensible qu'à cinq ou six passions. . . . Mais les personnes d'un caractère plus noble peuvent être remuées de mille façons différentes.' His frequent references to supernatural powers, notably 'le Ciel', both stress his status as a helpless victim and associate him with the tragic heroes of half a century earlier. If *Manon Lescaut* does not necessarily stand comparison with the greatest works (Flaubert said it was perhaps 'le meilleur des livres secondaires'), it nevertheless occupies a special place in the development of the French novel. Its fusion of opposites – purity and corruption, hard-headed realism and lyrical effusion, tragic grandeur and picaresque baseness – makes it something quite unique.

Further reading

Manon Lescaut, ed. F. Deloffre and R. Picard (1965); V. Mylne, *Prévost: 'Manon Lescaut'* (1972).

Workpoints

1   What sort of novel is it? The 'Avis de l'auteur' describes it as 'un traité de morale, réduit agréablement en exercice'. How far is this double claim justified? How is interest in the story maintained, and how are moral issues raised?

2   What is Des Grieux's role as narrator? How successful is he in winning over his reader? The novel has been called 'an exercise in literary persuasion' (*G. Jones*). Can this be reconciled with the argument that 'le roman tout entier est l'histoire, toujours recommencée, de la faiblesse de des Grieux' (*Deloffre and Picard*)?

3   How big a part does realism play? Discuss the assertion that 'in *Manon Lescaut* . . . the situation of the lovers . . . inevitably brings us into the everyday world of practical affairs' (*V. Mylne*).

4   Characterization and psychology: to what extent is it true that 'Des Grieux and Manon come to life for us as we read'? (*V. Mylne*).

5   The balance of opposites: 'Dans *Manon Lescaut*, réalité vulgaire et noblesse tragique coexistent, sans que la vulgarité se dissimule ni que la tragédie se fêle' (*Deloffre and Picard*). How far does this statement capture the essential nature of the text?

Jean-Jacques ROUSSEAU (1712–78)

From his neglected childhood in Geneva to his lonely death in Ermenonville, Rousseau led a sad and tormented life. At the age of 16 he cut loose from his uncaring father and set off on a lifetime of travels which were to take him to many European countries, where he found a variety of wealthy, influential patrons and many occupations unusual for one who was to become a giant in French literature. A rather inaccurate and frequently idealized account of his early life is given in the *Confessions* (which were published after his death).

From 1728 to 1742, he benefited from the patronage of Madame de Warens at Annecy and Chambéry. During this important, formative period he was able to compensate, by vast and energetic reading, for the unsystematic education he had received as a child, and to indulge his passion for the countryside and natural beauties of France and Switzerland; but his frequent departures – to work, for example, as a private tutor in another household or as a music master in Switzerland – reveal, even at this early stage, the instability and mistrust which were, throughout his entire career, to prevent him from enjoying more than briefly any sort of lasting friendship, any peaceful and regulated form of social existence.

Rousseau left for Paris, confident that his newly-invented scheme of musical notation would earn him a fortune. It was an important time, not because of any financial success, but because of the opportunity to meet writers such as Marivaux, Fontenelle and Diderot, and to make a number of influential acquaintances such as Madame d'Epinay, in whose country estates he was to live during the most productive period of his literary career (1750–62). His celebrity began with the first of two important essays, the *Discours sur les sciences et les arts* (1750); it was reinforced by the *Discours sur l'inégalité* (1754); it has endured to the present day, exerting in the intervening years a very considerable influence upon literature, education and political thought.

In broad terms, Rousseau's writing can be classified in three groups: first, these two essays in which he points out what is wrong with human behaviour, with society and human endeavours generally, and within that group could also be included the *Lettre à d'Alembert* (1758); the second group consists of three major works (in many ways Rousseau's solutions to the problems identified in the essays) which he produced in an amazing burst of creative activity: *La Nouvelle Héloïse* (1761), *Emile* (1762) and *Du contrat social* (1762); and finally there are his more strictly autobiographical writings, with the *Confessions* complemented by *Les Rêveries du promeneur solitaire*.

It was with the encouragement of Diderot that Rousseau became acquainted with the *encyclopédistes* and wrote his first important essay. His reply to the question 'Si le rétablissement des sciences et des arts a contribué à épurer les mœurs' was awarded first prize by the Académie de Dijon, a particularly surprising result since the essay was a vehement attack upon civilization and, like so much of his work and behaviour, ran contrary to the spirit of the day. According to Rousseau, civilization has served only to corrupt man and to destroy his natural happiness. However forced or false the arguments may be, the judges were doubtless swayed by Rousseau's unexpected approach and by his eloquence. Having demonstrated in the first essay that science introduces luxury which in turn weakens man's moral fibre, Rousseau concentrates in the *Discours sur l'inégalité* upon the development of modern man and contemporary society more by a hypothetical reconstruction of human evolution than by reference to historical evidence. Whereas in nature there is scarcely any inequality, human society is entirely based upon the creation and formalization of various inequalities. The notion of private property is the fundamental flaw: 'Le premier qui ayant enclos un terrain s'avisa de dire "Ceci est à moi" et trouva des gens assez simples pour le croire, fut le vrai fondateur de la société civile.' Then, according to Rousseau, the will to protect property leads to laws and a judicial system. The final and inevitable stage is the transformation of what is legally permissible into rights based on heredity and on force. Property is presented as the forerunner of despotism. Rousseau's third essay, his *Lettre à d'Alembert sur les spectacles*, was written partly because he resented Voltaire's influence in his native Switzerland, but principally because he wished to preserve his country from the depravity and moral laxity which theatre, in his opinion, brings to society. This hastily written and unconvincingly argued work is a further example of Rousseau's distaste for social corruption. It is also an illustration of his prickly, unyielding behaviour towards friends and colleagues; whereas his association with Diderot had led to an involvement in the preparation of the *Encyclopédie*, the attack on d'Alembert wounded many who had befriended him. It crystallized Voltaire's attitude into one of enduring and savage enmity.

Rousseau then withdrew from Paris, and the positive side of his thesis becomes more apparent in the three major works to which he devoted himself in his retreat at L'Ermitage, a modest cottage on Madame d'Epinay's estate. There, in the company of Thérèse Levasseur, an uneducated servant girl who was to be his constant companion until he died, he took pleasure in the natural surroundings uncontaminated by social contacts and falseness, and gave free rein to his imagination:

L'impossibilité d'atteindre aux êtres réels me jeta dans le pays des chimères; et ne voyant rien d'existant qui fût digne de mon délire, je le nourris dans un monde idéal, que mon imagination créatrice eut bientôt peuplé d'êtres de mon cœur.

La Nouvelle Héloïse is the passionate love story which emerged from Rousseau's dreams and imagination, the pure and tender relationship which the author yearned to enjoy. The hero, Saint-Preux, is a private tutor at the Château de Wolmar, where the attachment between himself and the heroine Julie develops into a totally virtuous, but overwhelmingly violent love, which persists even beyond her marriage. The sensitivity and fervour with which Rousseau described their love responded so perfectly to the interest of a wide reading public that this is the novel that survives when hundreds of others written by his contemporaries have been forgotten. There is an undeniably idealized element of autobiography; Rousseau said: 'Ce n'est pas tout à fait ce que j'ai été, mais ce que j'aurais voulu être.' Along with its morally appealing descriptions of intense joy and the lovers' struggles to resist temptation at a time of libertinage and corruption, Rousseau's novel brings a freshness based upon his own genuine experience: his fondness for country life and rustic pleasures presented with an enthusiasm and verve which captivated his readers and provided a sometimes pantheistic model for later novelists and poets in the eighteenth and early nineteenth centuries.

This passion for nature reappears in *Emile*, a treatise on education which has acted as an inspiration for such notable educationists as Froebel and Pestalozzi. In the course of four of the five books in this work, a young boy, the exclusive charge of his private tutor, is systematically formed into a healthy, well-adjusted and happy adult by a process of physical, then intellectual and finally moral development under conditions which make the entire endeavour utterly utopian. As Rousseau admits in the introduction, *Emile* consists of the 'rêveries d'un visionnaire'. This is the upbringing, removed from society and based almost entirely upon the lessons of nature, that Rousseau himself would like to have enjoyed. The final part, Book V, deals far more briefly with the education of girls, principally for the purpose of providing Emile with a suitable partner. Such inequality would, in today's feminist climate, provoke an outcry; in fact, the work was attacked with an official vigour that persuaded Rousseau to take refuge in Switzerland largely on account of the religious views expressed by Julie and in the 'Profession de foi du Vicaire Savoyard'. The religious authorities objected to such unorthodox and deistic theories. The Paris Parlement ordered *Emile* to be burnt in 1762.

No really precise line should be drawn between these longer works and the earlier essays. When, in *Du contrat social*, Rousseau broadens the scope of his theories from the individual to mankind in general, many of the ideas – on equality, on man's natural goodness and on society's imperfections – were already implicit in the earlier, shorter essays. Moreover, all his work has the same highly subjective and personal flavour, placing a greater stress

upon emotion and intuition than upon reason, and expressing his
views in a prose that is energetic and eloquent. The autobiographical works provide an intimately revealing portrait and,
not surprisingly, one that is embellished. Indeed, with *Les
Rêveries du promeneur solitaire*, the title alone contains much of
the author: his penchant for day-dreaming and idealization, his
restless wanderings, and his decidedly moody, anti-social, even
misanthropic tendencies.

Whatever real or imaginary unpopularity isolated Rousseau for
long periods of his life from friends, colleagues, patrons and
indeed every lasting human contact, his work was widely,
sometimes wildly, popular and influential. As political theorist, he
portrayed the poorer sections of the community and pleaded for
'la douce égalité' in a way that attracted revolutionary thinkers. As
writer, he marks a reaction against the arid, reasoned and
unemotional tone of much classical and post-classical literature,
bringing instead a vibrancy and passion which form a transition to
Romantic literature.

Further reading

J. Broome, *Rousseau: a Study of his Thought* (1963); R. Grimsley,
Jean-Jacques Rousseau (1983); P. Jimack, *Rousseau: 'Emile'*
(1983); D. Williams, *Rousseau: 'Les Rêveries du promeneur
solitaire'* (1984); R. Howells, *Rousseau: 'Julie ou la Nouvelle
Héloïse'* (1986); P. France, *Rousseau: 'Confessions'* (1987).

Workpoints

1   *Some comments by Rousseau*:
    'Trop souvent la raison nous trompe.'
    'Conscience! conscience! instinct divin.'
    'La vie ambulante est celle qu'il me faut.'
    'L'homme est né libre, et partout il est dans les fers.'
    'Le pays des chimères est en ce monde le seul digne d'être
    habité.'

2   *Some comments on Rousseau*:
    'A style remarkable for its terse rigour, its cogent rhetoric and,
    often, its poetical beauty' (*D. Charlton*).
    'Rousseau is the first great Romantic, in whom we find the
    Romantic experience in its purest, undiluted form – its
    melancholy, its love of solitude, its unsatisfied yearning, its
    religiosity, its fondness for communion with nature' (*L.
    Bisson*).
    'A la peinture des mœurs de la ville il a substitué celle des
    mœurs rustiques' (*M. Morel*).

'Les idées sociales de J.-J. Rousseau forment un système cohérent, dont le point de départ est ce grand principe que l'homme, bon et heureux à l'état de la nature, est rendu méchant et malheureux par la société' (*M. Braunschvig*).

'Rousseau is able to fascinate and disturb in a way that very few writers in the eighteenth century manage to do' (*D. Williams*).

'A very bad man' (*Dr Johnson*).

François-Marie Arouet VOLTAIRE (1694–1778)

Voltaire became a legendary figure in his own lifetime. He was, and has remained, the figurehead of the philosophical movement in France and throughout Europe. In an age of astonishingly gifted all-rounders, he can be seen as the outstanding example. It would be impossible in the few pages available even to list the complete works of Voltaire the philosopher, Voltaire the historian, the dramatist, the poet, the writer of fiction and the critic.

His literary career virtually spans the entire century: it began during the Regency and ended just before the Revolution; the repertoire of his theatrical work alone, stretching from *Œdipe* (1718) to *Irène* (1778) and including tragedies, comedies and operas, brought him more fame than is enjoyed by most dramatists; and his place in literary history would have been justified by the prodigious quantity of letters (some 21,000 at least) which reinforce his views and reveal the man himself in a more intimate way than his public writings, of which paradoxically very few are now read.

Voltaire, although only on the fringe of the *Encyclopédie*, was seen as representative of the *philosophes*, and certainly there are in his work three facets by which his influence on the modern world can be traced: the political, the intellectual and the philosophical. In reality, however, Voltaire's fame in the Age of Enlightenment and his reputation for succeeding generations depend less on his power as a philosopher, and more upon his bold and vigorous work as a social reformer. An outspoken critic of the established institutions of pre-Revolutionary France, he was perfectly atuned to the sympathies and aspirations of his contemporaries. His attacks upon church and monarchy led to imprisonment and exile; but the public appreciated what the authorities disliked; and when his ideas formed a basis for revolutionary legislation, his post-humous reputation acquired a 'mystique républicaine'. In fact, he was not a revolutionary, and his hatred of war and violence would have made him the enemy of many zealous and fanatical figures who gained power in the Revolution. Expressed positively, Voltaire was, in an age of oppression, the champion of liberty; he advocated freedom of speech and conscience, freedom from slavery and unjust arrest, freedom to work and to own property. It is therefore wrong to exaggerate the destructive side of his career: his work was also constructive both in theory and in practice, for unlike some eighteenth-century thinkers he was a man of action who applied his principles in a realistic and productive way.

François-Marie Arouet was the son of a notary. After schooling at the Lycée Louis-le-Grand, he escaped from the intended career in law and found his way into Parisian society. Soon his talent for poetry and his quick, sometimes vitriolic, wit became notorious in an unfortunate way: he was blamed for every lampoon and every scurrilous verse at court, so the Regent decided to provide young Arouet (or Voltaire, as he was now calling himself) with an opportunity to examine the architecture of the Bastille – from the inside looking out. With characteristic resourcefulness and resilience, Voltaire used his time well: he wrote his first play (*Œdipe*) for which, already back in favour, he received a medal and a pension. This event marks the beginning not only of his theatrical and literary career, but also of his commercial career. Rather than become a hack writer at the mercy of unscrupulous publishers, Voltaire made very sound financial arrangements, investing various pensions and building a personal fortune as supplier to the army and as moneylender. Consequently, Voltaire is doubly representative of his century: as philosopher and as financier. Indeed, without this buttress of financial independence, the philosopher's ideas could well have been more vulnerable and less influential.

Voltaire was rarely out of trouble: his wit and the epigrammatic brilliance of his conversation opened the doors of society and, once inside, offended his adversaries. A quarrel with the Chevalier de Rohan ended with Voltaire receiving a beating on the streets and making a second visit to the Bastille. Released on condition that he keep away from Paris and the court, Voltaire went to England. The two-year stay from 1726 to 1728 was to have a particularly important influence on his thought and his writing. He found much to praise in the philosophy of John Locke, in the religious toleration enjoyed by the Quakers and other sects, and in the constitutional arrangements of England as compared with the oppressive absolutism of government in France. Voltaire's reactions are conveyed in one of his best-known and most accessible works, the *Lettres philosophiques* or *Lettres sur les Anglais*.

Ostensibly, all but one of the twenty-five letters deal in a few pages with some aspect of life in England. In reality, every one contains praise for whatever Voltaire saw as preferable in English attitudes towards society, government and religion, and so, by implication, every one constitutes a penetrating criticism of

France. From the letters on the Quakers and the Presbyterians there emerges a plea for religious toleration; from the letters on the English parliamentary system, the reader could infer criticism of malpractices in the French system; and through Voltaire's attempt to prove that Monsieur Locke was the wisest man in Europe, the French reader was introduced to a doctrine that placed the emphasis upon the empirical as opposed to the metaphysical. In Locke's philosophy and in the science of Isaac Newton, Voltaire was to find powerful weapons against religious credulity and the political abuses which marred his own country. The *Lettres philosophiques* fuelled the growing dissatisfactions in France, by claiming that life in England was based on a principle of liberty. It is rather an overstatement for Lanson to claim that these letters contain 'tout un programme révolutionnaire'; but whether one fully accepts the French view that the *Lettres* were 'la première bombe lancée contre l'Ancien Régime' or the English view that 'Voltaire bowled the first dangerous ball', the message was clear. Voltaire found it prudent to write them abroad and to live for ten years in relative seclusion at Cirey, the country home of the Marquise du Châtelet.

This was a time of solitude, study and considerable literary activity. As well as writing a number of tragedies, he undertook some scientific experiments and almost won an Academy prize for his work on *La nature du feu*. However, he missed the glamour and excitement of court, and ventured back to Versailles for a few years, with Madame de Pompadour's protection. These years form a period of literary inactivity, although one notable event was the publication of *Zadig* (1748), the first important example of the short stories or *contes* for which he is particularly remembered. More were written during his three years (1750–53) at the court of Frederick the Great of Prussia, with whom he had already been in regular correspondence for fourteen years; and he added to the collection on his return to France, then while in Geneva, and finally at Ferney where he settled on the Swiss–French border for the last eighteen years of his life.

The best-known of these short works of fiction are *Micromégas* (1752), *Candide* (1759) and *L'Ingénu* (1767). They all demonstrate Voltaire's skill as a story-teller; they also provide an opportunity for the author to support or undermine some philosophical, social, political or moral thesis. Voltaire's *contes* are always illustrations of the author's thought, and the reader should not be gulled by the fantasy or the frivolity: within and behind the entertainment there is always a serious and, at times, a devastating attack.

The main target in *Candide* is the philosophy of optimism propounded by, among others, Leibniz. Episode by episode, the story challenges the view that 'Tout est bien', that all is for the best in the best of possible worlds, or, as Pope expressed it, 'Whatever is, is right.' The pace and verve of the narrative style, the deftly chosen and revealing incidents, the humour and irony of the descriptions, all prevent the short story from degenerating into a philosophical tract. The central character, Candide, could be described as an accident looking for somewhere to happen. This young, ingenuous hero scuds from country to country, from calamity to calamity, with amazing rapidity. He arrives at the time of some national disaster, such as the Lisbon earthquake, or falls into some misfortune such as war, imprisonment or torture. At every stage, Voltaire is able to criticize local institutions, social injustices, religious fanaticism, political oppression and legal corruption, indeed every flaw and defect which interfere with individual liberty.

Voltaire had come to place a high price on his own freedom, given the bitter experiences of imprisonment, exile and even of feeling trapped in Frederick's court at Potsdam. The Swiss border provided him with a safe refuge from the age of 59 until his death, and the opportunity for great literary and social activity. In spite of sickness or hypochondria ('My dear friend, I am sick for eighteen hours of the day and none too good for the other six'), he continued to write for the theatre; he produced two of his most important works of philosophy – the *Traité sur la tolérance* (1763) and the *Dictionnaire philosophique* (1764); he added to his collection of short stories and he published two major works of history – *Le Siècle de Louis XIV* (1768) and *Essai sur les mœurs* (1769) – which mark a transition to a more scientific mode of historical writing.

Thanks to his vast personal fortune and his geographical immunity, Voltaire was able to live like a prince and simultaneously attack other princes – those of church and state. With his own private theatre, some sixty servants and twelve horses, he was on the local level established as an opulent and enterprising man of property who stimulated industry and commerce, while conducting attacks which resounded throughout France and Europe on all forms of injustice. He became a sort of self-appointed ombudsman who championed victims of religious intolerance and judicial corruption, such as Calas, a Protestant unjustly convicted in 1762 of murdering his son, or La Barre, convicted in 1765 for singing impious songs.

Whatever Voltaire's faults, he was rarely out of the news ('Voltaire fut le grelot le plus sonore de l'Europe' said Lanson). Indeed, as one of the first to spot the power of public opinion and to mould it by his writings, he was more than an eighteenth-century giant: he was a forerunner of the twentieth-century journalist. His fame drew so many visitors to Ferney that he saw himself as the 'innkeeper of Europe'. Ultimately the authorities were conquered by his popularity and reputation: in 1778, Voltaire was able to return in triumph to Paris. The fatigues of the journey and the excitements of his receptions were too great, and Voltaire died on 30 May. The revenge of the Church was to deny him a Christian burial, but his remains were transferred to the Panthéon where – the final irony – they lie beside those of Rousseau, his arch-enemy.

Further reading

T. Besterman, *Voltaire* (1976); H. Mason, *Voltaire* (1975); *Candide*, ed. O. Taylor (1942); *Candide*, ed. J. Brumfitt (1968); *Lettres philosophiques*, ed. F. Taylor (1946); *L'Ingénu*, ed. J. Brumfitt (1970); W. Barber, *Voltaire: 'Candide'* (1960); C. Todd, *Voltaire: 'Dictionnaire philosophique'* (1981); D. Fletcher, *Voltaire: 'Lettres philosophiques'* (1986).

Workpoints

On Voltaire, the man

1 'There are two Voltaires: a Voltaire of clear intelligence, brilliant wit and fine taste, sensible, essentially serious, possessed by a passion for justice, for truth, and a Voltaire childish, prejudiced, mean, jealous, violent, rapacious and conceited, scandalously untruthful, a man, in the phrase of Frederick II, with all the tricks of a monkey' (*H. Preston*).

2 'Few would choose him as a permanent companion, to soothe or to sustain, but as an occasional stimulus, amusing and vital, he is without equal' (*L. Bisson*).

On Candide

1 'A satire – provoked by the Lisbon earthquake of 1755 – on the optimism of Leibniz and J.-J. Rousseau' (*J. Reid*).

2 '*Candide* epitomizes Voltaire because it compresses into a small space two basic aspects of his personality – his "realistic" philosophical pessimism and his fundamental personal optimism' (*J. Brumfitt*).

On the Lettres philosophiques

1 'The keynote of the whole book is liberty' (*F. Taylor*).

2 'Voltaire proposes a new set of social values, with emphasis not on the vainglorious right of war and conquest, but on peace and the untrammeled cultivation of the human mind' (*F. Taylor*).

3   'One of the corner stones of the French Revolution. . . .
    Readers, when they had shut the book, found that they were
    looking out upon a new world; that a process of disintegration
    had begun among their most intimate beings and feelings'
    (*L. Strachey*).

Overall assessments

1   'Un chaos d'idées claires' (*Faguet*).

2   'Voltaire a soutenu éternellement le pour et le contre'
    (*Chateaubriand*).

3   'Voltaire ne s'occupe guère qu' à détruire' (*B. de Saint-Pierre*).

4   'Toute son intelligence était une machine de guerre' (*Flaubert*).

5   'Despite certain imperfect sympathies and defects of temper,
    he was one of the greatest cosmopolitan figures in the age of
    enlightenment' (*F. Taylor*).

4

The nineteenth century

The nineteenth century, for France, was the age of revolution: political, social, industrial and literary revolution. Politically, the pattern of 1789 was repeated with variations throughout the century, as the hopes raised by rebellion were continually dashed by a return to monarchy or imperial rule – until 1871, when the Third Republic was established. 1830, 1848, 1871: these are the dates when barricades were set up in Paris and bloody street battles were fought in the name of revolution; 1804, 1814, 1830 and 1852 are the dates when monarchy or empire was re-established. And these momentous events were reflected in the literature of the time, in many cases by writers like Chateaubriand, Lamartine, Hugo and Zola, who became deeply involved in the politics and social aspirations of the age.

Memories of the French Revolution of 1789 dominated the early nineteenth century, although the century properly starts with Bonaparte becoming First Consul, then Consul for life in May 1802 and finally Emperor in May 1804. The republic had been turned into an empire. Imperial rule meant stability after the excesses of the Revolution, as many administrative reforms were carried out, laying the foundation of much of modern France: the formation of a centralized secondary school system free from clerical influence, the establishment of the Bank of France, the creation of a new hierarchy of merit with the *Légion d'honneur*, the clear formulation of law in the *Code Civil* and the stabilizing of religious enthusiasms in the agreement between Rome and Napoleon, the Concordat of 1804. Under this regime scientific research developed – rather later than in other European countries and the industrial revolution began to make an impact, as machines for spinning and weaving were imported or developed, and the iron industry flourished. However, there was a negative side to this stability in the form of censorship and the creation of something very like the old court. Little of literary value was produced at this time under the patronage of the Emperor, whose tastes lay in the direction of a revival of classical art, and who discouraged anything remotely innovatory or subversive.

Outside France, Napoleon continued the wars of expansion which were to form a magnificent memory and source of myth for the rest of the century; indeed this myth-making had already started with, for example, the splendidly dramatic painting of David, *Napoléon au Saint-Bernard* (1801), depicting Napoleon crossing the Alps, not on a mule as in reality, but on a magnificent rearing charger. Egypt had been invaded by an army of scholars as well as soldiers in 1798, starting a great wave of enthusiasm for all things exotic and oriental, which were to form another rich source of images for poets and for Romantic painters like Delacroix. In spite of the defeat of the French navy by Nelson at Trafalgar in 1805, victory at Austerlitz, followed by various treaties, gave Napoleon domination over most of continental Europe by 1810. Then in 1812 came the beginning of the end, as Napoleon invaded Russia and lost vast numbers of men in the retreat from Moscow across the frozen land, a scene vividly evoked by Hugo in 'L'Expiation': 'Il neigeait. On était vaincu par sa conquête. / Pour la première fois l'aigle baissait la tête. / Sombres jours! l'Empereur revenait lentement, / Laissant derrière lui brûler Moscou fumant.' In spite of heroic efforts he was forced to abdicate in April 1814 and exiled to the island of Elba, while Louis XVIII, returning from *his* exile, was proclaimed king. This, however, was not the end of Napoleon who, in 1815, began a hundred day return to power, the *Cent Jours*, by leaving Elba and marching triumphantly on Paris, acclaimed by all as he went. But the armies of England and Prussia advanced, and Napoleon was finally defeated on 18 June 1815 at the battle of Waterloo. 'Waterloo! Waterloo! Waterloo! morne plaine' wrote Hugo in 'L'Expiation'; Stendhal's account at the beginning of *La Chartreuse de Parme* was the most modern and realistic description of a battle before *War and Peace*. Napoleon was now sent to St Helena, where he died in 1821. This Napoleonic saga is constantly evoked by the writers of the first half of the nineteenth century, forming a heroic contrast to the more humdrum life of monarchy, materialism and peace.

1815 saw the return of a king, and the period known as the Restoration, but now it was a constitutional monarchy, with two legislative chambers, the *Chambre des Pairs* and the *Chambre des Députés*, trying to find a compromise between the ideas behind the French Revolution and the principles of monarchy. However, the wish to recreate the old France of the *ancien régime* constantly resurfaced, especially when Charles X, 68 years old and extremely reactionary, ascended the throne on his brother's death in 1824. The control of the Church spread to many aspects of life, censorship was increased, the influence of the old aristocratic families reasserted itself. This is the period described by Stendhal in *Le Rouge et le Noir* as a time of hypocrisy and boredom, when the aristocracy and the bourgeoisie went in fear of a new revolution, remembering the bloodshed of the old, and any deviation from conventional mediocrity was regarded with suspicion. Writers looked back nostalgically to the military glory of the age of Napoleon and saw no prospect for the young people of the day other than the Church. This is the case with Julien Sorel, the hero of *Le Rouge et le Noir*, and is repeated by Musset in *La Confession d'un enfant du siècle* (1836): 'Quand les enfants parlaient de gloire, on leur disait: "Faites-vous prêtres"; d'espérance, d'amour, de force, de vie: "Faites-vous prêtres".' Eventually even the supporters of the regime protested, a liberal majority was elected and, when Charles X tried to impose a right-wing government by force, the people rose against him in the streets of Paris and he fled to England.

This revolution of 1830 did not, however, lead to the establishment of a republic, but to a period known simply as the July Monarchy. The Bourbon branch of the royal family was out, but in came a different branch with the Orleanist middle-class king, Louis-Philippe, carrying his umbrella under his arm and caricatured as a pear. In spite of the literary bent of some members of the royal family – the duc d'Orléans and his wife were patrons of Hugo – and in spite of some military success abroad with the conquest and colonization of Algeria, the main image of the regime is of repression, as the middle classes flourished and the poor became poorer. It was a materialistic era lacking in idealism and compassion and devoted to money-making, a time of corruption scathingly exposed in Stendhal's *Lucien Leuwen*. The country as a whole did not prosper, lagging behind the rest of Europe in industrial development. Writers and intellectuals as well as republicans turned against the social injustice and mediocrity of the regime, until an organized campaign led to barricades once more in the streets of Paris and the proclamation of a republic in February 1848.

1848 began on a wave of idealism; universal suffrage was proclaimed, slavery in the colonies was abolished, national workshops were set up to reduce unemployment. But divisions between moderates and revolutionaries, together with the failure of these measures really to improve the lot of the poor, gave rise to more street fighting, the June Days, in which hundreds were killed. A new constitution called for the election of a president by universal suffrage. Lamartine was one of the candidates, but the man chosen was the one with the powerfully evocative name of Napoleon: Louis-Napoléon, nephew of the great Napoleon I, the man whom Hugo was later to call 'Napoléon-le-Petit' in contemptuous comparison with 'le *grand* Napoléon'. For Louis-Napoléon, not content with remaining President, dissolved the government by a *coup d'état* on 2 December 1851, bloodily suppressed the subsequent revolt on the boulevards of Paris and was proclaimed Emperor with the title Napoléon III. Fear of unrest and political instability had once more destroyed the republic; the Second Empire had begun.

In spite of criticism from within and without – Hugo, for example, producing bitingly satirical poems from his exile in the Channel Islands – the regime thrived in an atmosphere of economic prosperity and peace, partly thanks to Napoleon III's enthusiasm for the vision of a new society based on production, put forward earlier in the century by Saint-Simon (1760–1825). Paris was transformed by the baron Haussmann, continuing the work of the First Empire, as vast straight boulevards were driven through the city. 'Le vieux Paris n'est plus (la forme d'une ville / Change plus vite, hélas! que le cœur d'un mortel)', lamented Baudelaire in his poem 'Le Cygne'. Railways were greatly extended, industry and agriculture flourished. France was seen as the fashionable capital of the world. But this period was to come to a violent end when foreign entanglements led ultimately to the siege of Paris and the overthrow of empire. Peace was first broken by the Crimean War in 1854; then in July 1870, provoked by Bismarck, France declared war on Prussia. Ill-prepared and badly led, the French troops were no match for the Prussians and surrendered at Sedan, leaving the Emperor himself a prisoner. When news of this humiliation reached Paris the mob came out on the streets and Gambetta proclaimed a republic. Prussian troops surrounded Paris and a bitter winter siege began with all the suffering of cold, starvation and bombardment. Peace was negotiated in February, involving the loss of Alsace-Lorraine.

The newly elected National Assembly with Thiers at its head moved out of Paris to govern from Versailles. More Royalists and Bonapartists than Republicans had been voted into this National Assembly by a moderate French population, but in Paris the old revolutionary spirit was at work. Infuriated by the humiliating peace terms, by the government moving to Versailles and by continuing poverty, the people of Paris, isolated from the rest of the country, elected a Commune to power. Paris was subjected to a second siege as the Versailles forces surrounded it in April and May 1871. The siege came to an end in appalling violence and reprisals with nearly 20,000 insurgents killed within the city. Thiers had won, but the Third Republic was still not firmly established.

For a long time the very idea of a republic continued to be associated with violence and terror. The Republicans were divided among themselves and under threat from the new Right of church and army. Conflict between, on the one hand, those who had inherited the rationalism of the Enlightenment and were, broadly speaking, anti-clerical, republican and often freemason and, on the other hand, those who supported the church and the monarchy, had grumbled on for most of the nineteenth century. At the end of the century it was the Dreyfus case which brought all these tensions to the surface.

The facts of the case are extremely complex but the main lines are clear. In 1894 a young Jewish officer called Alfred Dreyfus was arrested and accused of passing secret documents to Germany. Evidence was fabricated to incriminate him and he was convicted and condemned to solitary confinement on Devil's Island. As the efforts of the army to suppress all evidence of his innocence continued, public interest was aroused and fuelled by a famous letter by Zola headed 'J'accuse!', in which he accused the army command of injustice. Zola was put on trial and convicted; ordinary citizens, writers and intellectuals became more and more passionately involved, polarized between those who saw the Dreyfus case as a massive anti-semitic conspiracy backed by church and army, and those who thought it necessary to defend their country at all costs and regarded the supporters of Dreyfus as traitors. Eventually there was a retrial; Dreyfus was again found guilty though with extenuating circumstances, and in 1899 a presidential pardon was issued; this was not the victory for justice that the *Dreyfusards* had fought for and which was to come later, but was more or less the end of the affair. Subsequent elections brought the Republicans firmly into power and the threat from the church and army was averted. An episode which had split France in two was over and, instead of destroying the Republic, had consolidated it.

However, not everything was political controversy in the Third Republic. This was also the period in which the Impressionist painters flourished, with their paintings full of light and colour, using techniques which find their literary counterparts in the impressionistic scenes of Zola's novels and Verlaine's poetry.

The nineteenth century saw not only the progression from monarchy or empire to republic and the gradual democratization of the political process, but also a dramatic change brought about in ordinary people's lives by the advance of science and its application in the industrial revolution. Writers like Hugo and Zola could have an optimistic vision of the century progressing steadily towards perfection through science; they could also see the darker side of industrialization, the exploitation and misery of the urban poor. Others, like Gautier, preferred to remain aloof from social and political matters and to see art and beauty in isolation. Indeed, art became in some cases a replacement for religion as the old certainties crumbled; and strange pseudo-religions grew up to fill the spiritual gap which science and the new critical spirit had widened.

*   *   *

Romanticism was the first great artistic movement of nineteenth-century France. It can be seen as a revolution in both feeling and form. The change in feeling, in the way of looking at the world, goes back to the eighteenth century and Jean-Jacques Rousseau. In his writings we find that preoccupation with the self as a uniquely interesting object, that vague religiosity, that love of nature and projection of emotions onto nature, that lyrical prose so characteristic of early Romanticism. In Bernardin de Saint-Pierre the additional ingredient of an exotic location is added in *Paul et Virginie* (1787), and with Chateaubriand's *René* of 1802 we find the melancholy of tormented adolescence and unsatisfied longing, the *mal du siècle*. These three writers can be seen as the indigenous roots of Romanticism: grandfather, uncle and father, the critic Sainte-Beuve would later call them. However there was also considerable input from abroad, especially from Germany and England where Romanticism had been a force for a long time. Exiled from Napoleonic France, Mme de Staël, in 1810, wrote *De l'Allemagne*, praising German writers and calling for a renewal of French literature which could also leave the classical model and find its national roots in medieval and Christian France. Art was not to be judged by some universally applicable classical criterion but would vary according to climate and country. From England came the vague, misty epic verse of the 'Nordic bard' Ossian; later the poems of Byron and the novels of Walter Scott and the vital inspiration of unexpurgated Shakespeare. Gradually the dead weight of tradition was being removed, helped by a relaxation of censorship in the early days of the Restoration and a more open attitude towards the literature of France's old enemies, Germany and England.

Romantic poetry found its first exponent of genius in Lamartine. The staggering success of his musical, lyrical laments when they appeared in 1820 showed how timely was this versification of the feelings so far only expressed satisfactorily in prose. His language, however, was still marked with the artificiality of eighteenth-century verse, in which a spade could never be called a spade: *eau* was *onde*, *vent* was *zéphyr*. It was Victor Hugo who, with justification, claimed to have revolutionized and reinvigorated French poetry with a seemingly inexhaustible supply of words, images, rhythms. *Les Orientales* (1829) is a firework display of technical virtuosity as well as a vivid exploitation of the new exotic orientalism. Other poets make their individual contributions to this poetic revolution: Vigny with his more sober, thoughtful approach; Musset, carrying the concept of poetry as pure emotion to its limit with his tearful melancholy ('Les plus désespérés sont les chants les plus beaux / Et j'en sais d'immortels qui sont de purs sanglots'); Nerval, finding a vein of symbolic, mysterious poetry akin to that of the German Romantic poets.

Liberated from conventions, by 1830 poetry was beginning to develop in two different directions: one towards the poet as leader, speaking to the people and involved in social issues; the other seeing poetry as completely self-sufficient: art for the sake of beauty. Lamartine and Hugo both became involved in politics and wrote about social issues; Lamartine in his long poem *Jocelyn*, with its theme of charity and socialism, Hugo clearly asserting the role of poet as leader in 'Fonction du poète' (*Les Rayons et les ombres*, 1840): 'Le poète en des jours impies / Vient préparer des jours meilleurs. / Il est l'homme des utopies; / Les pieds ici, les yeux ailleurs.' However Hugo is far too wide-ranging to be confined to one tendency. The origin of the Art for Art's sake movement can also be traced back to him with *Les Orientales*, although it finds its most craftsmanlike exponent in Gautier. Reacting against the effusive facility of some early Romantic poetry and against the social turn poetry was taking after 1830, Gautier aspired to capture the evanescent in a permanent form. The very title of his *Emaux et camées* of 1852, and his comparison of poetry with sculpture, clearly indicate a wish to produce small, exquisitely crafted objects and to avoid any involvement with contemporary issues.

This emphasis on form and artistry is continued with Leconte de Lisle and the Parnassian poets. Disillusioned by the failure of the 1848 Revolution, Leconte de Lisle turned to the careful construction of the distant past with *Poèmes antiques* (1852), and distant lands with *Poèmes barbares* (1862).

However there gradually emerged a third view of poetry which was eventually to triumph, the view of poetry as a way of understanding the mystery behind creation and the relationships between this hidden world and the visible, tangible world we inhabit. The poet, with special access to this realm, becomes a kind of priest – a 'mage' – and his language that of symbolism. This is the kind of poetry produced by Nerval and also by Hugo, especially in exile: *Les Contemplations*, *La Fin de Satan*, *Dieu*; but the poems of Baudelaire demonstrate it most clearly.

In *Les Fleurs du mal* (1857) the personal poetry of Romanticism is transformed from pure sentiment by a consummate artistry;

compassion for the poor appears in the poems on Paris dedicated
to Hugo, but it is a compassion totally without sentimentality; and
we also find Gautier's search for artistic perfection – it is no
accident that Baudelaire favoured the sonnet, neglected for so
long, rather than the long, wandering poem, without any clear
shape or form. But what emerges above all is a stress on
imagination, on poetry as a way of reaching beyond the visible
world, on nature as a dictionary in which imagination can discover
hidden *correspondances*. Poetry is not just emotional effusion nor
technical perfection but *magie suggestive*. At the same time
Baudelaire's tormented consciousness produced searing poems
which are far from the comparatively simple outpourings of the
early Romantics. Modern civilization seems to make its harsh
entry into poetry with all the vices and miseries of the industrial
city.

The idea of poetry as a kind of magic is continued and
developed by three great poets – Rimbaud, Verlaine and Mallarmé
– and by the Symbolist school. Rimbaud, violent and rebellious,
breaks all the bounds of poetry, revealing correspondences more
extraordinary than those of Baudelaire, breaking through the
rationality of the world and creating a magical universe of poetic
prose in the *Illuminations* before abandoning poetry altogether.
Verlaine, with the musicality and personal lyricism of Lamartine,
but with Baudelaire's haunting use of symbol and suggestion,
creates a wistful, impressionistic poetry. However it is Mallarmé
who develops the Baudelairean idea of poetry to an extreme degree.
His exquisite but difficult poems make no concession to the
ordinary reader. With verbal magic he tries to express the very
essence of reality behind its transitory and individual manifestations. With Mallarmé we have left far behind the idea of the poet as
leader of the masses and arrived at the poet as high priest of an
esoteric cult. A group of minor poets cluster round Mallarmé to
pursue this ideal of poetry, and the so-called 'decadent' poets, with
their disabused, cynical view of life maintain a parallel movement
against the complacency and stultification of much traditional
verse. Among them, Jules Laforgue, with his ironic, parodic style
and experimentation with free verse, was to have a considerable
influence on both English and French poets of the twentieth
century.

In spite of the tendency to associate Romanticism with poetry,
the public battle was fought in the theatre. This was, after all, the
arena in which Classical French literature had excelled, with
Racine, Corneille and Molière, and where the new movement
should flourish in its turn. The Empire had produced nothing
new, favouring classical revivals for the educated, and popular,
moralizing melodrama for the people. Several young writers –

Dumas, Vigny, Stendhal with his significantly named pamphlet *Racine et Shakespeare*, and Hugo – felt that French theatre needed to be rejuvenated; a modern drama was needed for a modern age. It was Hugo who produced the most influential manifesto for the new movement with the *Préface de Cromwell* of 1827, where, in the name of *vérité*, he calls for freedom from restricting rules and particularly for a mixture of comedy and tragedy, until now rigorously separated. The time was ripe to take the theatre by storm, and this happened in 1830 with the performance of *Hernani*. Hugo's supporters lined up in the theatre to applaud and shout down opponents. It is difficult for those brought up in a different tradition to understand what a furore could be caused by an alexandrine line which ran on into the next line, but chaos was caused in the theatre by the opening words:

> Serait-ce déjà lui? C'est bien à l'escalier
> Dérobé.

1830, the year of the July revolution, also marks the triumph of Romantic drama. Hugo subsequently poured out a series of highly coloured plays, while Vigny produced the more sober *Chatterton* (1835), but the success of the movement was relatively short-lived. By 1843 we see the failure of a rambling, epic play, Hugo's *Les Burgraves*, and the success of classical imitations and revivals. Hugo abandons the theatre and later writes plays to be read rather than performed: *Théâtre en liberté*. Musset's plays were also written without any care for staging, and the subtle and poetic *Lorenzaccio*, probably the most truly historical drama to emerge from the Romantic period, was not performed until after his death, and then only with modifications. Romantic theatre had opened the way for future experiment, but the Romantic spirit was not at its best in the theatre and tends too much towards melodrama for modern taste. The well-made plays of Scribe, classical revivals and light-weight operettas took over for the rest of the century, though Edmond Rostand was enormously popular with the neo-Romantic *Cyrano de Bergerac* in 1897, and symbolic drama, with its Romantic roots, appeared at the end of the century with Maeterlinck and Claudel.

The novel, in the first half of the nineteenth century, was developing into a highly successful genre with a group of significant landmarks appearing around 1830. At the beginning of the century, first-person novels, ideally suited to the lyrical outpourings of tormented youth, proliferated: Chateaubriand's *René* in 1802; Senancour's *Obermann* in 1804; and the masterpiece of the genre, with its combination of the analytical and the confessional, Constant's *Adolphe* in 1816. Other writers were moving away from the first-person novel towards a realistic representation of society. In *Le Rouge et le Noir* (1830) Stendhal combined an ironic, analytical view of the world and a cool, unsentimental style with the depiction of a complex but undeniably Romantic hero. His great novel *La Chartreuse de Parme* (1839), is more lyrical in inspiration, but continues the ironic mode. However Stendhal, with his elusive irony and ambiguous morality, was not appreciated by his contemporaries. They preferred another development: the rise of the historical novel under the inspiration of Walter Scott, stimulated by the fascination with historical processes after the watershed of the Revolution, as well as by the new interest in the Christian Middle Ages. Drama and even poetry were inspired by this need to organize material into a coherent historical pattern, but it was clearly the novel which was going to take the place of the old epic. Hugo's *Notre-Dame de Paris* (1831), with its evocation of the Middle Ages and its hunchback, immortalized by Hollywood, is probably the best-known of the colourful revivals of the past, followed in the 1840s by Alexandre Dumas's *Les Trois Mousquetaires*. Mérimée, like Hugo, brought an antiquarian interest in the past to bear on the writing of historical novels, but is better known for his short stories, with their combination of imagination and precision, of passion and realistic detail.

The desire to see society in perspective was not, however, confined to the past. More popular than Stendhal, Balzac, from 1829 to 1848, completely revolutionized the novel with his vast *Comédie humaine*, in which the whole of contemporary society was to be depicted, covering both Paris and the provinces, and using the new device of recurring characters. Balzac aimed to be the secretary of his age and also to reveal the underlying categories of human beings in the way that scientists had categorized animals.

This scientific spirit became stronger in the second half of the century. With *Madame Bovary* (1857) Flaubert, who had begun by writing Romantic semi-autobiographical works and lurid gothic tales, represents a new stage in the development of the novel, both in content and in form. The writer was to exclude the overt expression of personal feelings and opinions and thereby reach the objectivity of science. Unlike Stendhal or Balzac, Flaubert does not intervene to comment on his characters or give his opinion on general matters; events are mainly seen through the eyes of his characters. Flaubert also, again unlike his predecessors, took enormous care over his style, endlessly polishing and refining so that the phrases would flow like poetry. The novel had reached a peak of artistic perfection.

Madame Bovary and *L'Education sentimentale* (1869) were seen as creating a new way of depicting ordinary life, different from the larger-than-life characters of Balzac or the noble-spirited heroes and heroines of Stendhal, and poles apart from Hugo's grand, epic and immensely popular novel of social injustice, *Les Misérables* (1862). About 1850 the term *realism* was applied to this new way of representing the world, first to the painting of Courbet and then to novels, though Flaubert always rejected the label and indeed, like most labels, it could hardly serve to define a great writer. The Goncourt brothers conformed more closely to the kind of painstaking documentation that one associates with realism, as in *Sœur Philomène* (1861) and *Germinie Lacerteux* (1865). They also favoured the depiction of the lower classes, a subject which was taken up with enormous panache by Zola in his novels of peasant and working-class life.

Novel-writing in this second half of the nineteenth century was greatly influenced by the new scientific spirit apparent in Comte's positivist philosophy and the works of Taine and Bernard. Comte, a disciple of Saint-Simon, is considered to be the founder of sociology. Human societies, he maintained, should be studied scientifically, and the laws which lay beneath them revealed. According to him the age of theological or metaphysical speculation was past. Taine applied a form of positivist thinking to literary criticism, considering that each work could be scientifically analysed by reference to the conditions in which it was produced: *race, milieu, moment*. The same criteria, he thought, would enable us to understand scientifically the historical process. Bernard's *Introduction à l'étude de la médecine expérimentale* (1865) led Zola to write his *Le Roman expérimental* (1880), in which he envisages the novel as being a scientific experiment, with characters subjected to various influences and their reactions recorded.

Zola coined the term *naturalism* to describe his kind of novel. He aimed to chronicle life under the Second Empire just as Balzac had chronicled the Restoration and the July Monarchy, but, inspired by the theories of Taine and Bernard, he also wanted to create a work that would be a scientific study of the influence of heredity and environment on human beings. For this reason he took a single family as his subject and investigated it through several generations as well as in several *milieux*. However, his work, especially *L'Assommoir* (1877), *Germinal* (1885), *La Terre* (1887) and *La Bête humaine* (1890), has a vigour and visionary quality which far outstrip the scientific framework. Indeed, it could be said that, in spite of the apparent contradiction between this kind of writing and the Romantic movement, in another way Romanticism lived on, in the sense of social concern and a glorious, sweeping, colourful style.

Among the writers of the 'naturalist' school, meeting at Zola's

villa in Médan, one of the most prolific and technically assured
was Maupassant, with his deeply pessimistic tales, notably *Boule
de Suif* (1880). Daudet, belonging to the same generation and also
author of realist novels, differs from the Médan group in his more
optimistic and poetic view of life, seen especially in the collection
of short stories, *Lettres de mon moulin* (1868).

In the last years of the nineteenth century a reaction set in
against the overwhelming insistence on realism and naturalism and
against the whole positivist, scientific, materialistic philosophy
that lay behind it. Bergson in the *Essai sur les données immédiates
de la conscience* (1889) tackled the prevailing positivist view that
there was no such thing as free will, that human beings were simply
bundles of molecules conditioned by external circumstances, by
showing that the philosophers were mistakenly treating people as
if they were objects in space instead of creatively developing in
time. He reasserted the individuality of the self, man's creativity
and free will. In *Matière et mémoire* (1896), he developed a theory
of memory prefiguring that of Proust, and brought back the idea
that the human mind was much more than just the physical brain.
This reassertion of the traditional values of the individual, creative,
free human being came as an invigorating breath of fresh air,
particularly to young people who felt oppressed and stifled by the
deadness of positivism.

Side by side with Naturalism, the personal narrative took on a
new lease of life. Fromentin's *Dominique*, a semi-autobiographical
story of lost love, was published in 1862, and Pierre Loti, a
melancholy wanderer particularly fascinated by Turkey, wrote
nostalgically of his lost romance in *Aziyadé* (1879). Gide began his
literary career with a personal work, *Les Cahiers d'André Walter*
(1891) and Proust also, with *Jean Santeuil*. Huysmans began by
adhering to the tenets of the naturalist school but turned against it
to create an artificial, decadent, hot-house world (*A Rebours*,
1884). A preoccupation with a refined literary style brought the
novel close to Symbolist poetry.

Some novels explicitly criticize the atheistic society of the day.
Bourget, in *Le Disciple* (1889), depicts the disastrous influence of a
determinist philosopher upon his pupil, who, feeling free from all
personal responsibility, first seduces a young girl and then causes
her death. Some writers look towards religion to rescue them from
the dead hand of positivism – Huysmans in *La Cathédrale* (1898),
Léon Bloy in *Le Désespéré* (1886). There is a strong Catholic
revival at the turn of the century, seen in novels, poetry and plays.
Other writers stress *patrie*, family and tradition. Barrès, after a
celebration of the self, le *culte du moi* (1888–91), writes *Les
Déracinés* (1897), in which he emphasizes the need for people to be
anchored in their inherited background. Gide, on the other hand,

in the same year celebrates the joyful liberation of the self from all constraints in *Les Nourritures terrestres*.

The nineteenth century is enormously rich in literature. Romanticism, though in one sense a historical movement limited to the first half of the century and followed by other movements was, in another sense, a profound and lasting change in the way that writers, painters and musicians reacted to the world. The preoccupation with the self, *le moi*, through all its permutations, constantly appears in poems, novels and plays. The hero, alone in a dull world, serious in the dramas of Hugo, treated ironically in the novels of Stendhal and Flaubert, can still be recognized in another transformation in Camus's twentieth-century *L'Etranger*. The creative artist becomes isolated, seeing himself as different and superior, outside or above society, poet–prophet or *poète maudit*, rebellious or resigned but always at odds with the world of the bourgeoisie, which becomes an object for vilification and satire. As the century wears on the poet becomes more and more estranged from his public. As poets push back the boundaries of normal, rational experience and experiment with structures more and more different from prose, so they appeal to a small élite only. Even some novelists, like Stendhal, apparently renounce any attempt to communicate with the masses and appeal to a future band of noble souls. Others, like Flaubert, offend current morality and suffer at the hand of the censors. At the same time a much wider potential readership opens up with the spread of literacy and proliferation of reading matter. One of the best-sellers was George Sand, who was particularly renowned for her novels of provincial life. Novelists like Hugo and Zola also became extremely popular.

The language available to the artist had also changed in the course of the century. From the view of poetry as the conventionally restricted ornamentation of essentially rational discourse, we move to poetry which, through its imaginative use of imagery and rhythm, seeks to take us into a dream world, a visionary universe which otherwise would remain closed. The theatre breaks out of its classical mould. The novel develops into the most important *genre* of the century. It was, for literature as for politics, indeed a revolutionary era.

Further reading

D. Charlton (ed.), *The French Romantics* (1984); D. Evans, *Social Romanticism in France: 1830–1848* (1951); L. Furst, *Romanticism* (1976) and *Romanticism in Perspective* (1979); R. Griffiths, *The Reactionary Revolution: the Catholic Revival in French Literature* (1966); F. Hemmings, *Culture and Society in France: 1789–1848* (1987) and *Culture and Society in France: 1848–1898* (1971);

F. Hemmings (ed.), *The Age of Realism* (1978); E. Hobsbawm, *The Age of Revolution* (1962); M. Milner, *Le Romantisme* (1973); M. Praz, *The Romantic Agony* (1951); J.-P. Richard, *Etudes sur le romantisme* (1970); J. Smith Allen, *Popular French Romanticism* (1981); J.-Y. Tadié, *Introduction à la vie littéraire du XIXe siècle* (1984); J. Talmon, *Romanticism and Revolt: Europe 1815–1848* (1967); A. Thorlby, *The Romantic Movement* (1966); E. Wilson, *Axel's Castle* (1932).

L. Austin, *Poetic Principles and Practice. Occasional Papers on Baudelaire, Mallarmé and Valéry* (1986); M. Bowie, A. Fairlie and A. Finch (eds.), *Baudelaire, Mallarmé, Valéry. New Essays in Honour of Lloyd Austin* (1982); M. Gilman, *The Idea of Poetry in France* (1958); J. Houston, *The Demonic Imagination. Style and Theme in French Romantic Poetry* (1969); A. Lehmann, *The Symbolist Aesthetic in France* (1950); C. Scott, *A Question of Syllables: Essays in Nineteenth-Century French Verse* (1986); J.-P. Richard, *Poésie et profondeur* (1955); B. Weinberg, *The Limits of Symbolism* (1966).

W. Howarth, *Sublime and Grotesque. A Study of French Romantic Drama* (1975).

H. Gershman (ed.), *Anthology of Critical Prefaces to the Nineteenth-Century French Novel* (1962); R. Giraud, *The Unheroic Hero in the Novels of Stendhal, Balzac and Flaubert* (1957); M. Iknayan, *The Idea of the Novel in France: the Critical Reaction, 1815–1848* (1961); H. Levin, *The Gates of Horn: A Study of Five French Realists* (1963); C. Prendergast, *The Order of Mimesis: Balzac, Stendhal, Nerval, Flaubert* (1986).

Honoré (de) BALZAC (1799–1850)

Balzac's life, with his provincial origins (in Tours) and subsequent struggle for fame and fortune in the capital, follows a pattern typical of his generation – and of many Balzacian characters. At school in Vendôme he was a modest student but a voracious reader, absorbing all kinds of literature, philosophy and science, as he would continue to do in later life. Having studied law in Paris he aimed at a literary career and, by 1825, had produced a range of pseudonymous novels, some earnestly philosophical, others in fashionable idioms such as the sensationalist *roman noir*, all equally uncommercial. He now tried his hand at printing and publishing, but realized only debts, from which he would never be completely free. Then in 1829 came *Les Chouans*, based on the royalist insurrection in Brittany in the 1790s. This was the first novel published under his own name, and his first popular success.

From here on, his life was dominated by his immense literary output (nearly a hundred novels in the next twenty years), although his energies were also channelled into a series of love affairs, notably his liaison with the Polish countess, Eveline Hanska. Soon he conceived the ambitious idea of presenting his works in an organic whole, linked by recurring characters and treating the diverse aspects of post-Revolutionary France. Eventually, in 1842, he found a comprehensive title, *La Comédie humaine* (an echo of Dante), and wrote the famous 'Avant-propos' as a rationale. By the 1840s his health was undermined by his punishing work schedule (often involving unbroken stints of twelve hours or more), and in 1850 he died, having just married Mme Hanska, and leaving behind scores of uncompleted projects.

Inspired by the example of Sir Walter Scott, Balzac saw the novel as a vehicle for history – hence his claim in the 'Avant-propos': 'La société française allait être l'historien, je ne devais être que le secrétaire.' French history, from the upheavals of the Revolution, described in, say, the early pages of *Eugénie Grandet* (1833), to the coming of the railways in *La Cousine Bette* (1846), is thus a constant presence. Events are explicitly dated, and the characters' circumstances are always rooted in historical realities: Raphaël's despair in *La Peau de chagrin* (1831) stems from the stagnation of Charles X's France, which offers no opportunities to a young man of talent; Philippe Bridau of *La Rabouilleuse* (1841–2) dies on a colonial adventure in Algeria in 1839. Indeed, characters are often called by some title indicating the historical or social type to which they belong, as in *Le Père Goriot* (1835), where Goriot is sometimes 'l'ancien vermicellier', Rastignac 'l'aventureux Méridional' or 'le pauvre étudiant', and his elegant rival Maxime de Trailles, 'le dandy'. Balzac's social range embraces the aristocracy and the peasantry (though not the urban poor), while he specializes in the middle classes – financiers, journalists, doctors and the like. Within the social setting he identifies significant moving forces – intrigue, snobbery, ambition and, above all, the quest for money, seemingly the greatest force of all. In Goriot's words, 'l'argent, c'est la vie. Monnaie fait tout'. For the miser, Grandet, to go bankrupt is to commit 'l'action la plus déshonorante entre toutes celles qui peuvent déshonorer l'homme'. But Balzac is also meticulous in detailing material reality, which is so often a clue to deeper truths, as with the physiognomy of the master-criminal Vautrin, whose burning red hair and lined face betray prodigious psychological strength. Similarly the clothing of the drunkard Séchard in *Illusions perdues* (1837–43) 'exprimait si bien sa vie, que ce bonhomme semblait avoir été créé tout habillé'. The very environment interacts with the characters, not only in the familiar case of Madame Vauquer's establishment ('toute sa

personne explique la pension, comme la pension implique sa
personne') but in the gloomy, dank house owned by Félix
Grandet, and throughout the *Comédie humaine*. The heavy
emphasis on documenting physical detail, often of a sordid nature,
is vital to Balzac's role as a recorder of social realities; but it also
serves to counter lofty aspirations within the world of the novels.
The mud which spatters Rastignac on his way to the comtesse de
Restaud's prestigious residence in the faubourg Saint-Honoré is
also a rich metaphor for the grim truths idealists overlook;
learning from the cynical Vautrin, Rastignac eventually concludes:
'Votre Paris est donc un bourbier.' By the end of *Goriot*, the
narrator notes, the young man's 'education' is complete. *Illusions
perdues* describes the disenchantment of a youthful Angoulême
poet in Paris in the 1820s – but its title could equally well be given
to any number of Balzac's other novels.

The conflict between dream and reality is but one of a set of
dualities and contrasts into which Balzac organizes his world.
Paris is juxtaposed with the provinces, the godlike qualities of
Goriot with the diabolical nature of Vautrin, the striving Rastignac
with the unambitious medical student Bianchon. In the overtly
allegorical *La Peau de chagrin* the whole of life is presented as a
series of oppositions, such as nature and culture, science and
magic, asceticism and debauchery, between which choices have to
be made. The most crucial choice of all lies between the
conservation and dissipation of energy: the skin of the title,
symbolic of Raphaël's life, shrinks with his every expression of
desire; he is unable to conserve his life-force, and the novel ends
with his death. But *La Peau de chagrin* is merely a schematic
presentation of one of Balzac's profoundest concerns; for his
works are dominated by obsessives who expend their ration of
energy in an attempt to impose themselves on their world, and face
destruction as and when the supply is exhausted. Goriot sacrificing
all for his daughters, Grandet the miser, the vengeful cousin Bette
whose virginity is seen to concentrate her strength – all are
reflections of the same principle.

Vigour is a keynote of Balzac's narrative manner, which urges
the work on the reader – even to the point of direct appeals, as at
the beginning of *Goriot*: 'Ah! sachez-le . . . *All is true.*' In his texts
the narrator intervenes regularly, offering judgements on the
characters and generalizations of all kinds. And the style reveals a
constant effort to maximize the effect – humour, pathos or
excitement – from every situation; hence a pronounced tendency
to superlatives, and a profusion of metaphors and similes (over
1200 in *Goriot*, for example). The narrative structure of *Goriot* and
Eugénie Grandet, if not ubiquitous, is certainly representative of
Balzac's technique and his desire both to explain and to entertain.

A static opening, perhaps using the present tense, sets the physical scene, but then a summary of past events accounts for the current situation; thus, after the detailed information about Grandet's rise to wealth and reputation during and after the Revolution, the narrator comments, in a telling phrase: 'Il est maintenant facile de comprendre toute la valeur de ce mot: la maison à monsieur Grandet.' Once the causes of the initial situation have been established, the action proper can begin. Typically, this is with an unusual or unprecedented event: Rastignac's curiosity is aroused by the 'mystery' of Goriot's night-time activities (the theme of mysteries, discovered then solved, will run through the whole text); Eugénie experiences real excitement 'for the first time' when her cousin Charles arrives unexpectedly in Saumur. Then the drama can unfold. Balzac's widespread use of terms such as 'acteur', 'scène', 'drame' and 'tragédie' is seriously meant. The climaxes in his novels are the culmination of events dating far back into history, but coming to boiling point in a short, intense period of time – as generally happens in the theatre. It is curious that Balzac was never particularly successful as a dramatist, given that he had so thoroughly assimilated the spirit of drama in his fiction.

It is not difficult to find shortcomings in Balzac's writing: lapses into sentimentality or sensationalism, excesses of language, or awkwardness in plot-construction, to name some of the most obvious. It is easy, too, to point to the lack of balance in the *Comédie humaine* (the *Etudes de mœurs* make up three-quarters of the whole; the *Etudes philosophiques* and *Etudes analytiques* are never fully developed) or to question his consistency (can his admiration for strong-willed, disruptive individuals possibly square with his claims to favour social order and to write 'à la lueur de deux vérités éternelles, la Religion, la Monarchie'?). His aspiration to scientific accuracy is also open to doubt. But all this ignores the scope of Balzac's achievement. He used the novel form to create a world on a scale undreamed of before him and probably unmatched since. His work of art is the *Comédie humaine* as a totality; in his words, 'une génération est un drame à quatre ou cinq mille personnages saillants. Ce drame, c'est mon livre'.

Further reading

F. Hemmings, *Balzac: An Interpretation of 'La Comédie humaine'* (1967); H. Hunt, *Balzac's 'Comédie humaine'* (1959); S. Rogers, *Balzac and the Novel* (1953). On specific texts: P. Lock, *Balzac: 'Le Père Goriot'* (1967); D. Bellos, *Balzac: 'La Cousine Bette'* (1980); D. Adamson: *Balzac: 'Illusions perdues'* (1981); H. Hunt's edition of *Eugénie Grandet* (1967).

Workpoints

1 *Balzac as historian*: P.-G. Castex sees in *Eugénie Grandet* 'une réalité que les historiens n'hésitent pas à reconnaître'. To what extent does this hold for any of Balzac's novels?

2 *Characters*: In the 'Avant-propos' Balzac talks of the differences between various professions, and goes on 'il reste au romancier à incarner dans quelques individus représentatifs ces diverses espèces sociales'. How far are his characters stereotypes? How far, on the other hand, are they individualized?

3 *Neutral observer or visionary creator?* 'Balzac semble avoir moins observé la société de son époque qu'il n'a contribué à en former une' (*P. Bourget*). Discuss the pros and cons of this judgement.

4 *Optimism or pessimism?* 'Balzac is moved by a fundamentally Manichean vision of life in which the forces of evil, the demonic presences, are capable of triumphing over the good' (*S. John*). Is this a fair assessment?

5 *Narrative and style*: 'Whether we like it or not, the author's voice is a force to be reckoned with' (*P. Lock*). Discuss, with a range of textual illustrations.

6 *General technique*: 'One after another, the rarer, obscurer effects of fiction are all found in Balzac, behind his blatant front' (*P. Lubbock*). Give an account of the composition of Balzac's novels, showing both the obvious and the more subtle devices he uses.

Charles BAUDELAIRE (1821–67)

Baudelaire is, for many, the most representative French Poet, crystallizing all that is best in Romantic poetry, yet essentially modern, pointing forward to the developments of later poets but without their obscurity, immediately accessible yet full of richness. Unlike Hugo's prolific talent, his genius is principally contained within one structured collection of poems, *Les Fleurs du mal* (1857). He was also the first major writer to experiment with prose poems (the *Petits poèmes en prose*, also known as *Le Spleen de Paris*, published posthumously in 1869). He was a highly perceptive critic with articles on, among others, the writers Laclos, Flaubert and Hugo and the painters Delacroix and Ingres. The short story, *La Fanfarlo*, and the autobiographical fragments, *Fusées* and *Mon cœur mis à nu*, add to his relatively small output.

The poems of *Les Fleurs du mal* can be related to Baudelaire's life: his lack of financial security, his constant struggle to write, his

journey to the tropical island of Réunion, his love for the three
women who inspire many of his poems (the mulatress Jeanne
Duval, the actress Marie Daubrun and the idealized figure of
Madame Sabatier), his experiments with drugs and his final
debilitating illness. However, a much more rewarding approach
would be to look at the poems in themselves, for they are not an
autobiographical transcript of his life but an orchestration of
themes common to all humanity.

These themes can be simplified into an opposition between the
forces of degradation: *ennui* (that world-weariness so much
stronger than mere boredom), lethargy, remorse and sin on the
one hand, and the forces of expansion – joy, spiritual ecstasy,
serenity, calm – on the other. This opposition is indicated clearly
in the title of the first book: *Spleen et Idéal*. The first poem, 'Au
lecteur', characteristically draws the reader into complicity with
Baudelaire in a long list of vices, concluding with the most
dangerous of them all, the symbolic hookah-smoking figure of
ennui:

> C'est l'Ennui! – l'œil chargé d'un pleur involontaire,
> Il rêve d'échafauds en fumant son houka.
> Tu le connais, lecteur, ce monstre délicat,
> – Hypocrite lecteur, – mon semblable, – mon frère!

The poems entitled 'Spleen', through a series of telling images –
the blasé young king of a rainy country, the cluttered lumber
room of the heart, the tedium of long winter days – evoke again
this life-denying weariness:

> Rien n'égale en longueur les boiteuses journées,
> Quand sous les lourds flocons des neigeuses années
> L'ennui, fruit de la morne incuriosité,
> Prend les proportions de l'immortalité.

Other poems, in contrast, conjure up the delight of escape from
this meaningless tedium into a world of freedom and comprehen-
sion, symbolized in 'Elévation' by the spirit soaring above this
material world:

> – Qui plane sur la vie, et comprend sans effort
> Le langage des fleurs et des choses muettes!

In this realm the poet can penetrate the outer surface and grasp the
relationships, the *correspondances*, between different aspects of
creation, different sensations and feelings. Nature, as in the poem
'Correspondances', becomes a temple, a living and communicating
whole, a 'forêt de symboles'. The poet can experience these

moments of intense joy and, through the suggestive magic of
language, communicate them to the reader.

Poetry, for Baudelaire, distils beauty from an often ugly reality:
of paris he writes in a *Projet d'épilogue*: 'Tu m'as donné ta boue
et j'en ai fait de l'or.' It combines rhythms, words and images in
such a way that a rich complex of associations is evoked (for
example the many links between waves and dreams, exotic lands
and forests, perfume and music all conjured up by the woman's
hair in 'La Chevelure'). It aims to suggest rather than to give a
complete picture; it is 'quelque chose d'un peu vague laissant
carrière à la conjecture'. The poem 'Le Cygne' ends, not with a
rounded image, but with a trailing line inviting the reader to
imagine all those in exile:

> Je pense aux matelots oubliés dans une île,
> Aux captifs, aux vaincus! . . . à bien d'autres encore!

The classical figure of Andromaque, weeping in exile for her dead
husband Hector, becomes the focus for a web of associations all
conveying a sense of exile and loss: the changing face of Paris, the
escaped swan frantically and pathetically trying to bathe in the
dusty streets of the city, the negress wandering in the mud and fog
and vainly searching for 'les cocotiers absents de la superbe
Afrique'.

Rhythm plays a very important part in this art of suggestion.
Contrast the soaring first lines of 'La Musique':

> La musique souvent me prend comme une mer!
>   Vers ma pâle étoile,
> Sous un plafond de brume ou dans un vaste éther,
>   Je mets à la voile;

with the relentless, monotonous rhythm of 'L'Horloge', symbol
of the passing of time:

> Horloge! dieu sinistre, effrayant, impassible,
> Dont le doigt nous menace et nous dit: *Souviens-toi*!

or the prosaic, flat conclusion of 'Le Crépuscule du soir', moving
in its very lack of imagery after the densely complex description of
Paris at night:

> Encore la plupart n'ont-ils jamais connu
> La douceur du foyer et n'ont jamais vécu!

This last example shows us Baudelaire the poet of the modern
city. In poems dedicated to Victor Hugo, 'Le Cygne', 'Les Sept

Vieillards', 'Les Petites Vieilles', he describes without sentimentality – indeed with a sense of the grotesqueness and absurdity of modern civilization – the old, the poor, the outcast, and associates them with himself and his own sense of spiritual exile.

It is this lack of sentimentality, this ability to communicate directly yet hauntingly the dilemmas, the joys, the despair of modern man, in a context that is both eternal and localized, that make Baudelaire, in spite of certain melodramatic trappings of Romanticism, a poet for the late twentieth century as well as of his own age.

Further reading

E. Starkie, *Baudelaire* (1958); A. Fairlie, *Baudelaire: 'Les Fleurs du mal'* (1960); D. Mossop, *Baudelaire's Tragic Hero* (1961); H. Peyre (ed.), *Baudelaire. A Collection of Critical Essays* (1962); M. Ruff, *Baudelaire* (1966); B. Wright and D. Scott, *Baudelaire: 'La Fanfarlo' and 'Le Spleen de Paris'* (1984).

Workpoints

1 'If by some fearful accident French culture and poetry had been cut short soon after Baudelaire's death . . . there would be no difficulty whatever in seeing his work as the crown and epitome of the Romantic movement, and Baudelaire himself as the last and greatest of the French Romantics' (*G. Brereton*). What do you think Baudelaire's poetry has in common with other poets of the Romantic movement?

2 'The two great aspects of Baudelaire's life as manifested in his works are his religious sensibility and his loves, experienced, imagined and sublimated' (*H. Peyre*). Trace these themes and see how they are treated in *Les Fleurs du mal*.

3 Baudelaire wanted poetry to 'créer une magie suggestive'. Show how his poetry suggests and evokes feelings, thoughts and sensations rather than merely giving us an accurate picture of the world.

4 'It is not as the first poet ever to discover the life of the modern city, decay, perversity or the theory of the *Correspondances* that Baudelaire matters. He creates a new kind of poetry because of his particularly penetrating insight into central human struggles and his mastery of the art of suggestion' (*A. Fairlie*). Discuss this assessment of his poetry.

François-René de CHATEAUBRIAND (1768–1848)

Although best known to posterity for his writing, Chateaubriand
had a particularly varied career. A member of an aristocratic
Breton family, he served as an army officer, travelled to America,
returned home to fight for the monarchy of Louis XVI, and was
exiled in England. Rehabilitated by 1800, he entered the diplomatic
corps, and spent some time in government under the Restoration,
before devoting the end of his life to literary work – most notably
the *Mémoires d'outre-tombe* (1848–50), the massive, stylized
autobiography which he conceived as his lasting monument.

Among his many other writings, including travel literature and
the prose epic *les Martyrs* (1809) (an account of Christian martyrs
under the Roman Empire), the most substantial is doubtless *Le
Génie du christianisme* (1802). Here he seeks not really to justify
Christianity on philosophical grounds, but rather to prove how
vital it is to human civilization, as an inspiration for art, science
and literature. He was thus able to offer an appropriate defence
against the attacks of eighteenth-century rationalists, such as
Voltaire, and of revolutionary atheism. And by stressing the value
of new models of inspiration – the Old Testament, Dante and
Milton, the culture of the Middle Ages and Gothic architecture –
he weakens the hold of a tired Classical tradition and prepares the
way for Romanticism. Chateaubriand's account of his conversion
well reflects the general tone: 'Je n'ai pas cédé . . . à de grandes
lumières surnaturelles; ma conviction est sortie du cœur: j'ai
pleuré, et j'ai cru.' The texts by which he is best-known, however,
are short fictional works: *Atala* (1801), originally intended as part
of *Les Natchez* (another epic in prose, devoted to a tribe of
American Indians), and *René* (first published in 1802 as part of *Le
Génie du christianisme*). Both are interpolated first-person narratives – the one told by Chactas, an old Red Indian, to René; the
other being René's life story, recounted to Chactas and a
missionary. Written in a lush, resonant prose, they stand some
way from the mainstream of the novel's evolution: for its author
Atala is 'une sorte de poëme, moitié descriptif, moitié dramatique'.
But between them they crystallize many of Chateaubriand's most
salient features. *Atala*, according to its didactic epilogue, shows 'le
triomphe du christianisme sur le sentiment le plus fougueux et la
crainte la plus terrible, l'amour et la mort'; but in this story of love
between Chactas and the doomed heroine, a Christian convert,
Chactas can only resent a creed which leads Atala to suicide. On
the other hand, the description of their simple life together has a
lyrical conviction; and the magnificence of the exotic Mississippi
setting, with its mountains and forests, suggests that the real centre
of gravity lies in the importance of nature, a mystic cult seemingly

more impressive than Christian doctrine. Another text centring less on events than on 'les sentiments secrets de l'âme', *René* was ostensibly intended to denounce the 'vice' of introspection which Chateaubriand detected among his contemporaries; père Souël's rejection of the hero's 'inutiles rêveries' points in the same direction. But the creator seems to identify with the hero more than this would suggest. Chateaubriand and René – described as 'une grande âme' – share a similar gloomy solitary adolescence and a similar intense relationship with an older sister. Above all they suffer the same sense of the hopelessness of their lives; in René's words, 'je cherche seulement un bien inconnu, dont l'instinct me poursuit. Est-ce ma faute, si je trouve partout les bornes, si ce qui est fini n'a pour moi aucune valeur?' Beyond the individual case, René expresses a general sense of the fragmentation of human existence, especially the division created by passing time. 'Le passé et le présent sont deux statues incomplètes: l'une a été retirée toute mutilée du débris des âges, l'autre n'a pas encore reçu sa perfection de l'avenir.' Some of Chateaubriand's postures may seem implausible and extreme, but his re-creation of 'le mal du siècle' vividly captured the individualism and pessimism of the time, as countless witnesses such as Sainte-Beuve have noted; in addition his use of a 'confessional' style of fiction will find successors from Constant to Gide to Camus. The subsequent progress of Romanticism would have been unimaginable without him.

Further reading

Atala and *René* ed. P. Crump (1951); G. Painter, *Chateaubriand, a biography*, vol. 1 (1977).

Workpoints

1 *Religion*
How far was Chateaubriand's Christianity intellectual, how far emotional? Consider Sainte-Beuve's view that 'Chateaubriand avait la sensation chrétienne, il n'avait pas le sens chrétien'.

2 *Nature*
Why is nature so important to Chateaubriand? What aspects of it does he most emphasize?

3 *The cult of the individual*
'Dans *René*, j'avais exposé une infirmité de mon siècle' (*Chateaubriand*). Analyse the main character's shortcomings.

4 *Present interest*
Pierre Barbéris talks of the power of *René* to interest the reader above and beyond its historical and biographical qualities, and asks '*René* possède-t-il encore un tel pouvoir?' What does the

text have to say to the modern reader psychologically, socially, politically?

Benjamin CONSTANT (1767–1830)

Although his reputation rests mainly on one short piece of fiction, drawing on various of his well-known love affairs, Constant's many talents have led to comparisons with such a gifted contemporary as Goethe. He was by turns a major liberal politician, a historian of religion, a brilliant diarist, a lively literary critic. His life took him from his Swiss origins to a cosmopolitan education, deep involvement in French politics over thirty-five years, and periods of travel and exile outside France. His first published writings – in the 1790s – were political: pamphlets on revolutionary politics, to be followed by others, such as the anti-Napoleonic *De l'esprit de conquête* in 1814. *De la religion* (1824–31) is an outstanding study of the evolution of religious ideas. But it is the personal, autobiographically-based narratives which have reflected the most fascinating sides of his work. His diaries (published 1952) are telling documents of self-revelation; and *Le Cahier rouge* (1907) relates the story of his first twenty years – his voracious reading of eighteenth-century *philosophes*, his friendships, his early love affairs. *Cécile*, never completed and published only in 1951, draws on his experiences with Charlotte von Hardenberg, whom he married secretly in 1808, and Mme de Staël, with whom he was involved intermittently from 1794 to 1811. But here he takes care to stylize characters and events, and adds episodes derived from other literary texts, such as Mme de Staël's *Delphine*. The first-person narrator, looking back over fifteen years of his life, effectively conveys his weakness in terms both of his hesitations between Cécile and Mme de Malbée and of his general reluctance to take responsibility for his own affairs, and his vacillation governs the plot. But well written though *Cécile* is, the suspicion lingers that Constant remains too close to real life to create a fully satisfying work of art. This objection cannot be made about *Adolphe*, started, like *Cécile*, in 1806, but brought to completion, and published some ten years later. Much inconclusive effort has gone into tracing the models for the heroine (probably including Julie Talma and Anna Lindsay as well as Charlotte and Mme de Staël), but this entirely misses the point that *Adolphe* goes far beyond autobiography; simple identifications of sources do no justice to its complexity. Adolphe's story is presented as a manuscript left by its mysterious author in an Italian inn; but this device, so popular as a superficial way of authenticating eighteenth-century fiction, is here a crucial part of the whole. It allows an outside observer to describe Adolphe after his affair with Ellénore is complete – even more morose and alienated than ever; and the exchange of letters at the end involving the 'éditeur' offers another dimension of judgement on Adolphe's conduct and character. The narrative itself is not the casual picaresque that might be expected, but a taut unified structure that has been compared with Racinian tragedy, leading to inevitable disaster. The sense of formal control is enhanced by the use of parallels and contrasts – as between the passage describing Adolphe's love for Ellénore in chapter 3 ('L'air que je respirais était à lui seul une jouissance . . .') and the one just before her death, as she loses her hold on him ('L'air que je respirais me paraissait plus rude . . .'). The recurrent strands of imagery, emphasizing, say, conflict ('Ellénore me parut une *conquête* digne de moi') or restriction ('Elle n'était plus un but: elle était devenue un lien') further demonstrate the patterning of the text. Yet for all Constant's linguistic skill, he is always mistrustful of language – even when, as so often, he expresses himself via maxims; at one point he notes the confusion of men's feelings and adds: 'La parole, toujours trop grossière et trop générale, peut bien servir à les désigner, mais ne sert jamais à les définir.' In such an economical work, amounting to barely 100 pages in some editions, there is limited space for local colour and realistic detail; the social background of mediocrity and hypocrisy, and the secondary characters – Adolphe's remote father, the vulnerable comte de P—— and the shrewd baron de T—— – are treated deftly but briefly. The focus is concentrated on the central couple, who are delineated with the greatest finesse. Ellénore can be seen as a masterpiece of characterization, developing from the repressed mistress of the comte de P—— to the vital, passionate lover of Adolphe, able even to understand in the end why the affair is doomed ('L'amour était toute ma vie. Il ne pouvait être la vôtre'). Adolphe himself is subtle enough to reveal the desire for love which initiates the crisis, the weakness and fear of commitment which propel it, and the emptiness which it leaves behind. But a still greater subtlety lies in the shifting perspective of the narrator as he changes from the detached observer of the early chapters to an increasingly involved commentator, moving ever closer to the 'étranger' who appears in the 'Avis de l'éditeur'. In such a sophisticated work there is no simple moral lesson – but Constant's many-sided portrayal of a quest for truth offers something far more valuable.

Further reading

D. Lowe, *Benjamin Constant: an Annotated Bibliography of Critical Editions and Studies* (1979); J. Cruickshank, *Benjamin Constant* (1974); W. Holdheim, *Benjamin Constant* (1961); I. Alexander, *Benjamin Constant: 'Adolphe'* (1973); A. Fairlie,

Imagination and Language (1981); T. Unwin, *Constant: 'Adolphe'* (1986).

Workpoints

1 *Position in literary history*: Constant is frequently seen as a pivotal figure, located between Classicism and Romanticism. What evidence is there to support this view? Does he incline more one way or the other?

2 Adolphe *as tragedy*: 'The novel is a tragedy of character rooted in the strengths and weaknesses of the two protagonists' (*J. Cruickshank*).

3 Adolphe *as a character*: To what extent is Adolphe at fault? What is the role of 'une société si facile et si travaillée'? On the other hand, how far is it possible to accept this judgement: 'Despite protests to the contrary, Adolphe tells his story in a manner that frequently confuses explanation with justification' (*J. Cruickshank*)?

4 *Technique*: 'To study *Adolphe* is to discover how the text operates as an organic entity, full of echoes, reversals, structural symmetries and counterpoints' (*T. Unwin*). Discuss the language and the composition of the novel in the light of this remark.

Gustave FLAUBERT (1821–80)

Flaubert is an extremely important figure in the development of the novel. Not only did he produce one of the finest novels of the century in *Madame Bovary*, but he also theorized a great deal about the art of writing in his correspondence. His work is also more varied than an examination of just *Madame Bovary*, *L'Education sentimentale* and *Trois Contes* would suggest, and is constantly open to reinterpretation.

In a way there are two Flauberts: the Romantic, loving to write exotic or lyrical tales; and the painstaking literary 'scientist', carefully dissecting the humdrum characters and failures of this world. His early work was mainly Romantic, with confessional semi-autobiographical narratives and violent gothic tales, though even here we find a comical pseudo-scientific dissection of a social type with *Une Leçon d'histoire naturelle, genre commis* (1837). By the time he began *Madame Bovary* (published 1857, the same year as Baudelaire's *Les Fleurs du mal*), he was developing a different view of the novel and one more in tune with the times. As his friends apparently told him when he subjected them to a continuous four-day reading of a philosophical extravaganza, the first *Tentation de Saint-Antoine* (1849), it was time to stop indulging in Romantic fantasies and treat a down-to-earth subject in modern France. So with *Madame Bovary* we have the story of a woman buried in the provinces, nurtured on Romantic novels, expecting excitement and romance, and repeatedly meeting disappointment. It was also time for the writer to remove his own intrusive voice from the novel and let the characters and situations speak for themselves, for this was the age of science and objectivity: 'Est-ce qu'il n'est pas temps de faire entrer la justice dans l'art? L'impartialité de la peinture atteindrait alors à la majesté de la loi, et à la précision de la science.'

In one sense, of course, a novel can never be totally impartial, just as a photograph can never be totally objective. The author chooses the characters, the situations, the words on the page. What Flaubert intended to avoid were the obvious intrusions of the author. In a famous phrase he said that the author should be like God in the universe, 'présent partout, et visible nulle part'. The writer would certainly have an opinion, but this should never be expressed directly: 'Il peut la communiquer, mais je n'aime pas qu'il la dise.'

This combination – keeping the authorial voice out of the novel as much as possible and yet making the author's view pervade the work – leads to the perfection of a variety of stylistic devices. Most important is the sophisticated use of *style indirect libre*, whereby the characters' thoughts, emotions or points of view can be expressed without an intervening 'she thought that . . .' or 'she felt that . . .'. This gives an ambiguity and richness to the text, where the reader is never quite sure at what point he is leaving the character's views for the author's or vice versa. 'La conversation de Charles était plate comme un trottoir de rue, et les idées de tout le monde y défilaient . . .': is this Emma Bovary's opinion of Charles or the author's? We also see an extensive use of clichés, often italicized. When a character starts to speak in clichés, whether the Romantic platitudes of Emma, or those of Rodolphe bent on seduction, or the Voltairean rationalist commonplaces of the archetypal bourgeois Homais, we can usually sense the hidden criticism, although there are also a few occasions when these hackneyed phrases are the inadequate expression of genuine feeling. At other times a simple juxtaposition will bring out the irony of the situation: the shout of 'fumiers' at the agricultural show, for example, just as Rodolphe is mouthing totally insincere romantic phrases at Emma. Sometimes simple description is enough: 'Disséquer est une vengeance', wrote Flaubert.

There is also a complex network of symbols in the novel, some of which serve as an ironic and ambiguous replacement for direct comment: 'la crotte des rendezvous' on Emma's boots, for example, or the blind man at the end – is he a figure of fate symbolizing Emma's punishment or yet another example of Emma's Romantic distortion of reality? Emma's boring environment is conveyed through a rich weave of descriptions, similes and metaphors indicating flatness and decay, and a routine of sleeping and eating; her aspirations emerge through images of escape (ships, exotic countries, windows onto another world). Her dreams repeatedly dissolve and decay like the environment in which she lives and as her own body does by arsenic poisoning. This network of references was the result of the painstaking elimination of excess images by Flaubert; nothing was to be superfluous or gratuitously poetic. The same care went into the construction of each phrase, declaimed by Flaubert aloud to ensure its harmony and appropriateness. Flaubert constantly complained in his letters of the trouble it was causing him: 'Vouloir donner à la prose le rythme du vers (en la laissant prose et très prose) et écrire la vie ordinaire comme on écrit l'histoire ou l'épopée (sans dénaturer le sujet) est peut-être une absurdité.'

With *Madame Bovary* Flaubert had succeeded in writing a 'realist' novel, in the sense that it is set in an ordinary town with ordinary, relatively inarticulate people – but he has transmuted that reality, through his language, into a work of art. Standing, like Baudelaire, at a crucial turning point in the century between a dying Romanticism and a new cult of realism, he could echo Baudelaire's 'Tu m'as donné ta boue et j'en ai fait de l'or.' But he has also chosen a heroine steeped in Romantic attitudes and has therefore given both a critique of Romanticism and a sympathetic, though ironic, treatment of the search for the ideal which he found in his more Romantic self: 'Madame Bovary, c'est moi.'

The same search for stylistic perfection and the same pattern of hope followed by disillusionment can be found in Flaubert's other works. *Salammbô* (1862) inhabits a completely different world from the bourgeois tedium of *Madame Bovary*: 'Je vais pendant quelques années peut-être vivre dans un sujet splendide et loin du monde moderne dont j'ai plein le dos,' wrote Flaubert. By means of a great deal of research, Flaubert recreated a barbaric, violent Carthage, with extravagant banquets, strange gods and ruthless revenge, but the central figure, like Emma Bovary, is never satisfied when she reaches her ideal: 'Elle restait mélancolique devant son rêve accompli.'

With *L'Education sentimentale* (1869), Flaubert returned to contemporary France, reworking the first version of 1845, which was already a substantial novel. The later version contains the transposed love and dreams of Flaubert but was also intended to be 'l'histoire morale de ma génération' and to incorporate the political upheavals of 1848 and 1851. Even more than *Madame Bovary* it is a story of disillusionment and inaction as the hero fails in both life and love. A whole generation slowly disintegrates as one ideal after another is betrayed.

Trois Contes (1877), after the poor reception of *L'Education sentimentale* and of the final version of *La Tentation de Saint Antoine* (1874), represents a moment of success in Flaubert's life. Apparently so different, the stories are linked in theme and style to each other and to the rest of Flaubert's work. They are miniature masterpieces. *Un Cœur simple*, like *Madame Bovary*, deals with a humble life in the provinces and, though tinged with irony, is full of tenderness for the old servant whose life is spent in devotion to a series of people who leave her, or die. Each new love fills the gap left by the other until eventually the parrot Loulou assumes the characteristics of all and, gradually confused with the Holy Ghost, seems to hover in splendour over her deathbed. After the story of someone so patient and good that she is a kind of saint, Flaubert placed his version of the legend of a medieval saint, Saint Julien l'Hospitalier. Finally he went back to antiquity, as he had with *Salammbô*, and told the tale of Hérodias and John the Baptist, not in any traditionally biblical way, but recreating the barbaric splendour of a decadent age. All three stories depict a different world and focus on a saintly figure.

The treatment of failure is resumed with *Bouvard et Pécuchet* (published after his death in 1881). Two clerks decide to take early retirement and devote themselves to the systematic pursuit of knowledge. In every branch of knowledge they fail as their agricultural, educational and scientific experiments lead them to more and more ridiculous excesses and their indiscriminate attempts to understand and digest in their entirety subjects like history, philosophy and religion founder in a wealth of contradictory opinions. However, failure in one field is always followed enthusiastically by entry into another. So the cycle continues until, at last, they abandon their search and decide to devote themselves to copying once more.

Flaubert is a very self-conscious writer and a perfectionist. His works have given rise to an enormous volume of criticism. Taken at one time as a 'realist' only concerned to dissect the mundane world, or as the supreme artist, author of the novelist's novel in its technical perfection, he now appears as an eminently 'modern' underminer of meaning, subversively whisking the carpet of interpretation and certainty from under the reader's feet. This power to polarize critical opinion and make readers strongly like or dislike him is obviously a testimony to his greatness and an invitation to plunge into his work and make a personal judgement.

Further reading

M. Tillett, *On Reading Flaubert* (1961); R. Giraud (ed.), *Flaubert: A Collection of Critical Essays* (1964); V. Brombert, *The Novels of Flaubert. A Study of Themes and Techniques* (1966); P. Cortland, *A Reader's Guide to Flaubert* (1968); R.Sherrington, *Three Novels by Flaubert* (1970); J. Culler, *Flaubert* (1974); D. Knight, *Flaubert's Characters. The Language of Illusion* (1985).

On individual texts: A. Fairlie, *Flaubert: 'Madame Bovary'* (1962); J. Fletcher, *A Critical Commentary on Flaubert's 'Trois Contes'* (1968).

Workpoints

1   Alison Fairlie writes that Flaubert 'is most successful in creating moods through the tiny details of the physical world'. Can you apply this to the works you have read?

2   'There lingers some coldness and probably an excess of self-awareness on the part of the novelist, too relentless a control of his inspiration in *Madame Bovary*' (*H. Peyre*). Do you agree with this criticism?

3   'Flaubert is the great novelist of inaction, of boredom and immobility' (*J. Rousset*). How does he portray these in his novels? Look at theme, structure, style, imagery.

4   'Si la *Bovary* vaut quelque chose, ce livre ne manquera pas de cœur. L'ironie pourtant me semble dominer la vie' (*Flaubert*). Look at Flaubert's use of irony.

5   'We tend to see order, control, and repression of emotional involvement in all that Flaubert wrote after 1849. Yet, with the possible exception of *Trois Contes*, his mature writings are characterized by anger, fury, and even madness' (*R. Giraud*).

6   Diana Knight writes of 'the influential view of Flaubert as not only elusive ironist but also supreme dismantler of all stable values'. Discuss this view.

7   Flaubert wrote about *Salammbô*: 'Il n'y a point dans mon livre une description isolée, gratuite; toutes *servent* à mes personnages et ont une influence lointaine ou immédiate sur l'action.' Does this apply to his other works as well?

Victor HUGO (1802–85)

Hugo is found at every crossroads of the nineteenth century: poetry, novels, dramas, social tracts – wherever one looks one cannot avoid the name of Victor Hugo. His life begins virtually with the century: 'Ce siècle avait deux ans! Rome remplaçait Sparte, / Déjà Napoléon perçait sous Bonaparte,' he wrote in the autobiographical opening poem of *Les Feuilles d'automne*. It ends in 1885, marked by a massively-attended national funeral. 'Echo sonore', poet–prophet, popular writer, he dominates the century.

His poetry began in a fairly derivative way with *Odes et Ballades* (1822–8), but his extraordinary skill with rhythm and imagery was already evident. After playing expertly with picturesque medieval themes in the *Ballades*, he transferred this virtuosity to an eastern setting in *Les Orientales* (1829), prefaced by a defiant claim that it is 'un livre inutile de pure poésie', a theme taken up later by Gautier and the Art for Art's Sake school. From 1831 to 1837 three more collections of lyric poetry appeared, first *Les Feuilles d'automne* (1831), mainly peaceful verses about the family, of which 'Lorsque l'enfant paraît' is a typical example. This was, however, the time when Hugo's old religious and monarchist convictions were crumbling and among these quiet, domestic verses is a foretaste of the visionary poet to come. 'La Pente de la rêverie', with its progress from gentle reverie to awesome contemplation of the mystery of existence, points in this direction.

Les Chants du crépuscule (1835), contains poems of doubt and distress about the outcome of the July Revolution ('De quel nom te nommer, heure trouble où nous sommes?'), but also poems of love. In 1833 Hugo's liaison with the actress Juliette Drouet, who was to remain his lifelong companion, had renewed the sources of poetic inspiration. His love for her, associated with an idyllic natural setting and a classical spirit, permeates 'A Virgile' in *Les Voix intérieures* (1837). With *Les Rayons et les ombres* (1840) Hugo is apparently continuing the themes of the previous collections: love, nature, children. However, in the poem 'Tristesse d'Olympio', he finds that nature has changed: 'Que peu de temps suffit pour changer toutes choses! / Nature au front serein, comme vous oubliez!' Permanence must rather be sought inside man's heart, in memory. The poet's deeper experience is reflected in these poems, and the public, social role of the poet as leader and reformer is outlined: 'Le poète en des jours impies / Vient préparer des jours meilleurs.' He cannot just sing about nature and beauty.

In 1839–40 Hugo had travelled to the Rhine where the more sombre and fantastic side of his imagination had been stirred by ruined castles and magical legends. Before this could be expressed in poetry, however, a series of shattering events were to take place in his life. In 1843, on 4 September, his eldest and most beloved child Léopoldine was drowned, with her husband, just after their marriage, in a boating accident at Villequier. Hugo turned to politics, became a *pair de France*, spoke frequently on

social issues, but, deeply disappointed by what he saw as the
betrayal of France by Napoleon III, and with his life in danger,
went into exile, first to Brussels, then in 1852 to Jersey, and in
1855 to Guernsey. He was to remain in exile for a total of nineteen
years, returning only in 1870 with the proclamation of the Third
Republic.

This period in exile was to be the most fruitful in poetry for
Hugo. First in *Châtiments* (1853), he fulminated against the
regime of Napoleon III, who is compared derisively with 'le grand
Napoléon' and indeed in 'L'Expiation' is seen as a punishment for
Napoleon I's own usurpation of the republic. In 'Souvenir de la
nuit du 4' he creates a vivid and moving tableau of the suffering
brought to an ordinary family by the futile killings of the *coup
d'état* and exposes the vain ambition behind the bloodletting:

> Il veut avoir Saint-Cloud plein de roses l'été,
> Où viendront l'adorer les préfets et les maires;
> C'est pour cela qu'il faut que les vieilles grand-mères,
> De leurs pauvres doigts gris que fait trembler le temps,
> Cousent dans le linceul des enfants de sept ans.

However, what many consider Hugo's best collection of
poetry, *Les Contemplations* (1856), was produced under a quite
different inspiration. The pivot on which the book rests is the
death of Léopoldine. The death of Juliette Drouet's daughter
Claire in 1846 had released a flood of poems about Léopoldine –
among them 'A Villequies', 'Elle avait pris cepli', and 'Demain dès
l'aube' – which later appear in *Les Contemplations*. The whole
book is described as the 'mémoires d'une âme'. In it Hugo
transposes his life by rearranging the dates of the poems into a
stylized pattern: *Autrefois* and *Aujourd'hui*, before and after that
fateful 4 September 1843. And with Léopoldine's death he
associates his own exile, also a kind of death. The book leads us
from youth and happiness to the contemplation of the infinite; the
'regardeur' becomes the 'contemplateur'. The poet becomes, not
just a leader, but a priest, the isolated thinker doomed to
contemplation of the abyss, of the eternal questions of life and
death. The final poem, 'A Celle qui est restée en France', ends with
this vision of the poet:

> Pâle, ivre d'ignorance, ébloui de ténèbres,
> Voyant dans l'infini s'écrire des algèbres,
> Le contemplateur, triste et meurtri, mais serein,
> Mesure le problème aux murailles d'airain.

The kind of poetry adumbrated in 'La Pente de la rêverie'
flourishes in this last book of *Les Contemplations*, creating a
visionary world of enormous power as Hugo attempts to convey

the unknowable with striking images of *abîme* and *gouffre*, darkness and light ('Un affreux soleil noir d'où rayonne la nuit'); vague and disturbing swirls of aimless movement ('Nous sommes les passants, les foules et les races. / Nous sentons, frissonnants, des souffles sur nos faces. / Nous sommes le gouffre agité'); combinations of abstract and concrete in compressed metaphors ('le tas de cendre Néant', 'O sombre fosse Eternité!').

Many of these visionary poems were not originally separate entities at all but part of a long meditation on the problems of existence, poured out by Hugo in the years 1853 and 1854 when he was dabbling with table-tapping and living a haunted life. The same preoccupations – questions about the purpose of life and death, of good and evil – dominate two unfinished epics started at the same time: *La Fin de Satan* and *Dieu*. The figure of scepticism, the *hibou* of *Dieu* speaks just like the poet:

> Je suis le regardeur formidable du puits;
> Je suis celui qui veut savoir pourquoi; je suis
> L'œil que le torturé dans la torture entr'ouvre.

His dark universe is conveyed in the same image as that of the poet, a vague, sinister space brought out of the abstract by geographical or architectural features: 'Et, sur le seuil du vide aux vagues entonnoirs, / L'âpre frémissement des escarpements noirs.' Satan also, in his fall from Heaven, inhabits this space with its 'porches monstrueux de l'infini profond'. By 1855 however, the crisis was over and Hugo regained his serenity. *La Fin de Satan* was to conclude with the pardoning of Satan and the end of evil; *Les Contemplations* ends with a call for peace throughout the whole of creation.

This new confidence is expressed in *La Légende des siècles* (1859), which comes closest to fulfilling the nineteenth-century ambition to produce an epic. A series of vivid tableaux trace the history of mankind from Adam and Eve to a vision of the future with 'Pleine mer' and 'Plein ciel'. Several of Hugo's best known poems including 'Booz endormi' and 'Le Satyre' come from this collection.

Even when Hugo seemed uniquely preoccupied with the great themes of existence, he could write light, amusing verses, full of fantasy and imagination. These can be found in the first three books of *Les Contemplations* and at the beginning of 'Le Satyre', and they predominate in *Les Chansons des rues et des bois* (1865). More poetic works follow: *L'Art d'être grand-père* (1877), inspired by his grandchildren, and *Les Quatre Vents de l'esprit* (1881), containing the enigmatic 'Je suis fait d'ombre et de marbre'. Others were published after his death, notably *Toute la lyre.* There are many neglected jewels to be found in all these later miscellaneous collections.

More time has been spent on Hugo as a poet because this is where his real genius lay. It is arguably as a *poetic* dramatist and a *poetic* novelist that he is successful. His dramatic career started in 1827 with the unplayable *Cromwell* and its resounding preface, which forcefully expressed the ideas behind Romantic drama in its break with classical theatre: the abandoning of the unities of time and place, the use of local colour, the mixing of comedy and tragedy, the concept of the grotesque. *Cromwell* was followed by a veritable deluge of plays, both in prose and in verse: *Hernani* (1830), where Romantic drama visibly and noisily triumphed; *Marion Delorme* (1831); *Le Roi s'amuse* (1832), banned by the regime for its unfavourable portrayal of royal behaviour and from which Verdi took the magnificent *Rigoletto*; *Lucrèce Borgia* (1833); *Marie Tudor* (1833); *Ruy Blas* (1838); and finally his failure with *Les Burgraves* in 1843. Of all these plays, which have a panache and an operatic quality which makes them enjoyable on the level of poetic melodrama, *Ruy Blas* is probably the most acceptable nowadays. Written after the first enthusiastic flush of Romanticism, based on a typically Hugolian opposition, the valet in love with a queen, the 'ver de terre amoureux d'une étoile', it carries the spectator or reader along in a great wave of poetry, from lyrical love scenes to the comic alexandrines of Don César. This is also the play in which Hugo combines most successfully tragedy and comedy, in the grotesque figure of Don César, the joyful rogue, the aristocrat turned bandit. Hugo's aim to create a genuinely popular theatre, however, was not achieved and he turned to plays written to be read, the *Théâtre en liberté*.

As a novelist, Hugo achieved a style of his own with *Notre-Dame de Paris* in 1831 – a historical novel, but one drawing on Hugo's real concern for the preservation of old monuments, which brings medieval Paris to life and creates a galaxy of picturesque characters and symbolic types: the hunchback, ugly but good at heart, the innocent gypsy girl Esmeralda, the sinister priest Frollo. However, a vein of sober, realistic writing on social matters had also been tapped with *Le Dernier Jour d'un condamné* (1829), a first-person narrative against capital punishment which is, in many ways, a forerunner of Camus's *L'Etranger*. This concern for the criminal, seen also as the victim of society, reappears in *Les Misérables* (1862), where it takes on a visionary quality like that of the exile poetry. Hugo described it as 'le poème de la conscience humaine', 'poème d'ailleurs plus que roman'. This vast story of good and evil, of justice and forgiveness, traces the development of Jean Valjean from convict to saint. The pattern of fall and redemption is there just as it is in *La Fin de Satan*, making it much more than a novel of social concern. Hugo's vast symbolic novels continued with *Les Travailleurs de la mer* (1866), *L'Homme qui rit* (1869) and *Quatre-vingt-treize* (1874).

As well as excelling in all these fields, Hugo wrote lively travel letters and diaries. After 1839, and especially in exile, he developed from a competent draughtsman into an artist of remarkable power, conveying his visions through drawings as well as poems. Throughout his work we see an immensely forceful personality, shown most graphically in his initials or signature carved into giant patterns on drawings and illustrations for his books. Some have been irritated by this self-glorification, by the claim to be a prophet-like poet and leader of the people and by the way in which Hugo turns his own life into a myth. But Hugo's poetry and novels, especially after exile, go much deeper than any facile self-confidence and introduce the reader into a visionary, dark, and deeply unsettling world.

Further reading

C. Affron, *A Stage for Poets. Studies in the Theatre of Hugo and Musset* (1971); J. Houston, *Victor Hugo* (1974); 'Châtiments', ed. P. Yarrow (1975); J. Richardson, *Victor Hugo* (1976); S. Nash, *'Les Contemplations' of Victor Hugo; an Allegory of the Creative Process* (1976); H. Peyre, *Victor Hugo, Philosophy and Poetry* (1980); Victor Hugo, *The Distance, the Shadows*, selected poems translated by H. Guest (1981); P. Cogman, *Hugo: 'Les Contemplations'* (1984); K. Wren, *Hugo: 'Hernani' and 'Ruy Blas'* (1984); V. Brombert, *Victor Hugo and the Visionary Novel* (1984).

Workpoints

1 'The visionary thrust of his work is always controlled by a will to lucidity, by a longing for order' (*V. Brombert*). Find examples of this in Hugo's poetry and/or novels.

2 Baudelaire wrote: 'L'excessif, l'immense, sont le domaine naturel de Victor Hugo.' Elaborate this statement.

3 'He was able to convert personal experiences into a destiny, and then relate this destiny to the disturbing configurations of contemporary history' (*V. Brombert*). Can you apply this to individual poems, to structured collections like *Les Contemplations* and *La Légende des siècles*, or to novels?

4 Harry Guest has written of Hugo's 'intense feeling for dramatic contrast, light and shade, the clash and reverberation of opposites'. On the other hand Jean Gaudon has stressed 'la ténébreuse et profonde unité d'un monde moins rassurant que

la forêt baudelairienne'. Look for these two distinct qualities in
Hugo's poetry.

5 'Hugo is as far removed from Stendhal's self-conscious and
ironic lyricism as he is from Flaubert's obsessive concern for
tight constructions and technical mastery. The dramatic and
psychological power of Hugo's novels depends in large part on
the creation of archetypal figures' (V. Brombert). Discuss this
analysis of the novels. Could it also apply to the theatre?

6 'All the worst tendencies of the Romantic Movement may be
seen completely displayed in the dramas of Victor Hugo' (L.
Strachey). What tendencies do you think Strachey had in
mind, and what do you think of this judgement?

Alphonse de LAMARTINE (1790–1869)

Lamartine's literary output was considerable, both in poetry and
prose, but he is read now principally for a handful of poems which
evoke in delicately musical verse the sadness of the passing of time
and love, and the beauty of nature.

The *Méditations poétiques* were immensely popular when they
appeared in 1820. They contained no great innovations in verse
form or vocabulary. Indeed Lamartine was described as an
eighteenth-century poet with genius added as an extra. The poems
are full of the stylized poetic vocabulary of the previous century:
the moon, for example, is 'l'astre du mystère' or, in the beautiful
line of 'L'Isolement', 'le char vaporeux de la reine des ombres'.
Standard adjectives are applied in a conventional fashion: 'la flèche
gothique', 'le volage zéphyr', 'les saints flambeaux'; and the verse –
form does not differ from that of the Classical age. So where did
the popularity of the *Méditations* lie and why does it continue?
The answer is partly in the musicality of the verse and partly in the
content, which corresponded so perfectly to an age which had
been moved by the sentiments of Rousseau, Chateaubriand and
Bernardin de Saint-Pierre in prose, and was just waiting for a poet
who could express these same feelings in verse.

The sentiments are firstly marked by sincerity, by the impression
at least that the poet is pouring out his heart without reserve or
artifice. 'Le public entendit une âme sans la voir, et vit un homme
au lieu d'un livre,' wrote Lamartine. Of course he corrected his
work like any other poet but the emphasis was on unchecked
inspiration, on poetry as 'la respiration de l'âme'. The mood is one
of sadness as life passes by, and this sadness is closely related to
nature. Nature is not described for its own sake but as a reflection
of the mood of the poet, a landscape of lake, valley, mountain and
meandering stream imposed by Lamartine's personality, a *paysage*

d'âme rather than a precise and picturesque description; and for this, imprecise vocabulary is highly effective:

Souvent sur la montagne, à l'ombre du vieux chêne,
Au coucher du soleil, tristement je m'assieds;
Je promène au hasard mes regards sur la plaine,
Dont le tableau changeant se déroule à mes pieds.

This opening verse of 'L'Isolement' does not identify the mountain or the plain; the old oak tree evokes a sense of age and permanence rather than a picturesque scene; the sunset corresponds to the poet's mood rather than giving us a picture. The emphasis of the verse falls upon the adverb 'tristement' and therefore upon the poet himself, not the landscape: '*je* m'assieds'; '*je* promène'.

This verse also demonstrates Lamartine's gentle musicality. The words flow harmoniously with a pause symmetrically in the middle of each twelve-syllable line. Each line is a complete unit with no dramatic *enjambement*. The rhyme at the end of each line is reinforced with internal assonance and alliteration. The effect is that of effortless verse which can almost be murmured rather than declaimed and which therefore corresponds perfectly to the mood of gentle melancholy evoked by Lamartine. An even more striking example, where words as well as sounds are repeated to give this musical and plaintive effect, is the last verse of 'Le Golfe de Baya':

Ainsi tout change, ainsi tout passe;
Ainsi nous-mêmes nous passons,
Hélas! sans laisser plus de trace
Que cette barque où nous glissons
Sur cette mer où tout s'efface.

This water imagery is characteristic of Lamartine. The opening verse of 'Le Lac' uses the image of the ocean to convey the vastness of life, where we are cast adrift, without control and unable to halt even for a moment the passing of time. The second verse moves to the image of the lake, this time an enclosed and comforting stretch of water which Lamartine addresses as a friend who will remember the time he spent there with his beloved; then the song of his beloved laments the passage of time in the image of flowing water or sand through an hour-glass: 'Assez de malheureux ici-bas vous implorent, / Coulez, coulez pour eux.' And the poem ends with a plea to nature to retain the memory of their love.

The combination of images conveying the transitory, fleeting nature of life with the desire to fix, to hold the moment for ever is characteristic of Lamartine's poetry. In 'L'Isolement' he asks for death in order to reach the reality behind the transitory external world; in 'Le Lac' he asks nature to retain the memory of their love; in 'Le Vallon' he asks his soul to see the permanence of God behind nature. A more specifically Christian poem like 'Le Crucifix' gives to the crucifix kissed by his beloved on her death-bed the function of providing the continuous link in a moving world. The characteristic tension is between the unstable, dissolving, disappearing world of seas, rivers and distant horizons and the stability of enclosed valleys and lakes, refuges and comforting maternal protection. The later poem, 'La Vigne et la maison' (1856), explores the same theme, but in a rather different poetic style. Instead of the vague adjectives so typical of Lamartine's earlier work we have a much more vivid and detailed picture of the old house, now decaying and symbolizing the inevitable passing of time:

> Le mur est gris, la tuile est rousse,
> L'hiver a rongé le ciment;
> Des pierres disjointes la mousse
> Verdit l'humide fondement.

Although these are the writings for which Lamartine is remembered, he himself considered his other work much more important. In the long epic poems *Jocelyn* (1836) and *La Chute d'un ange* (1838) he, like so many other Romantic poets, aspired to give France the modern epic which would rival those of the Middle Ages. In his historical works he aimed at contributing as poet–philosopher to the great political issues of the age and he was actively involved in politics from 1830 to 1851. However his fame now rests on those early poems which, inspired by love and sorrow, he claimed, in typically Romantic manner, to have poured out from his heart in moments of idleness.

Further reading

J. Ireson, *Lamartine. A Revaluation* (1969); C. Lombard, *Lamartine* (1973); M. Birkett, *Lamartine and the Poetics of Landscape* (1982).

Workpoints

1 Lamartine said of his poetry: 'Ce n'était pas un art, c'était un soulagement de mon propre cœur qui se berçait de ses propres sanglots.' Do you find that this adequately defines the poems you know? Are they entirely lacking in art or craftsmanship? Do they give the impression of being the unconstrained expression of personal and sad emotion? If so, which features of the poetry give this impression?

2 Georges Poulet described Lamartine as: 'le poète d'une réalité qui se dissout'. Can you find descriptions of nature in his

poetry which evoke this fading, dissolving, transitory nature of
things? What aspects of nature does Lamartine describe to
bring stability and comfort?

3 Musicality in a poet is very difficult to analyse, but depends on
   such features as rhyme, assonance, alliteration, repetition and
   refrain as well as on the rhythmical balance of the lines. See if
   you can pin down what makes some of Lamartine's verses
   seem particularly musical.

Stéphane MALLARME (1842–98)

In contrast with many nineteenth-century French poets, Mallarmé
led an uneventful life (as a teacher of English, first in Tournon and
eventually in Paris). After early poems strongly influenced by
Baudelaire, published in 1866 in *Le Parnasse contemporain*, he
worked on two longer poems, 'Hérodiade' and the dream-like
'L'Après-midi d'un faune'. By 1867 Mallarmé's style was changing
to his later, more obscure manner, and in Paris, at his famous
mardis (Tuesday evening gatherings), he became the revered leader
of a group of Symbolists, later joined by Gide and Valéry.
Musicians, Impressionist painters and poets all interacted in the
last quarter of the century: 'L'Après-midi d'un faune' was
illustrated by Manet and set to music by Debussy; Mallarmé's
portrait was painted by Manet and Whistler.

Mallarmé appears a difficult writer, but his work lingers in
the mind even if the reader feels he cannot quite grasp its meaning.
It is essentially a suggestive poetry, trying to communicate what
lies behind the obvious, physical presence of the world. It therefore works with symbols and allusions, letting the reader's
imagination develop simultaneously in many directions. The
reverse of ample, rhetorical poetry, it usually compresses a
multitude of ideas and images into a very small space: a sonnet or
four verses of eight-syllable lines. It is both intellectual and
sensuous, extremely serious and sometimes lightly humorous at
the same time. 'Toute l'âme résumée . . .', which is a kind of 'art
poétique', demonstrates some of these qualities.

The apparent subject of the poem is trivial, as it is for many of
Mallarmé's poems: someone smoking a cigar. The deeper subject,
again as so often with Mallarmé, is the nature of art. The first line:
'Toute l'âme résumée', expresses immediately the spiritual subject
('l'âme'), the absolute quality ('toute'), the idea of a concentrated
essence of the spirit ('résumée'). Then the poem moves into a long
sentence in which the various stages of smoking a cigar are evoked:
the slow exhalation of rings of smoke dispelled by other rings, the
skill needed to separate the ash from the bright fire so that the

cigar is smoked well. The verses wind in convoluted syntax like the smoke from the cigar, but the connection between the soul and the cigar is clear: the ash of reality must be shaken off if poetic inspiration is to burn with a bright light and produce these perfect yet evanescent poetic forms – evanescent because constantly leading to other forms, other images, equally perfect, but never stabilizing in absolute perfection. These perfect forms will contain the essence of the whole soul; the material object that caused them is secondary, in the background. In the next two verses Mallarmé makes his message plain, perhaps too plain to be taken altogether seriously as an illustration:

> Exclus-en si tu commences
> Le réel parce que vil
> Le sens trop précis rature
> Ta vague littérature.

This poem corroborates what Mallarmé in his theoretical statements said he was trying to do: depict objects at one remove: 'Peindre non la chose mais l'effet qu'il produit'; suggest rather than name: '*nommer* un objet, c'est supprimer les trois quarts de la jouissance du poème qui est faite de deviner peu à peu: le *suggérer*, voilà le rêve'; and evoke, not precise objects but some spiritualized ideal: 'Je dis: une fleur! et hors de l'oubli où ma voix relègue aucun contour, en tant que quelque chose d'autre que les calices sus, musicalement se lève, idée même et suave, l'absente de tous bouquets.' The role of the poet is to work with words so that they lose their ordinary, flat connotations and become a source of Baudelaire's 'magie suggestive': 'Donner un sens plus pur aux mots de la tribu', as he writes in 'Le Tombeau d'Edgar Poe'. In this way he will achieve man's highest purpose on earth: 'La poésie est l'expression, par le langage humain ramené à son rythme essentiel, du sens mystérieux des aspects de l'existence: elle doue ainsi d'authenticité notre séjour et constitue la seule tâche spirituelle.'

Baudelaire was a great influence on Mallarmé in both subject-matter and ideas on poetry. The richness of a woman's hair is celebrated in 'La Chevelure'; the early 'Brise marine' pursues the theme of the voyage to exotic lands to escape from *ennui*:

> La chair est triste, hélas! et j'ai lu tous les livres.
> Fuir! là-bas fuir! Je sens que des oiseaux sont ivres
> D'être parmi l'écume inconnue et les cieux!

The same theme appears in the later poem 'Au seul souci de voyager . . .', but there all personal references are removed as Mallarmé aspires to an impersonal, anonymous poetry that would reach behind immediate experience to an ideal, universal beauty.

Like 'Brise marine', this poem reflects a desire to escape, a sense of danger as well as exhilaration in the 'Nuit désespoir et pierrerie', and a vision of the poet/explorer determined in his quest.

Mallarmé's aim was ultimately to create 'Le Livre', which would be the essence of all poetry. His poems are therefore often expressions of the difficulties of creation, the fear of sterility as well as the fascinating potential that there is in the as yet unsullied page. This theme appears in 'Brise marine': 'Sur le vide papier que la blancheur défend,' and in 'Le vierge, le vivace et le bel aujourd'hui' with its image of the swan trapped beneath the ice, its flights remaining always potential, unrealized: 'Le transparent glacier des vols qui n'ont pas fui.' Mallarmé's last poem, 'Un coup de dés jamais n'abolira le hasard', with its typographical use of blank spaces on the page, traces this attempt to convey absolute reality.

In many ways Mallarmé can be linked with previous poets: with Baudelaire in his vision of poetry and use of symbols, with Gautier in his search for an impersonal perfection. He takes these ideas, however, to a much more rarefied sphere and creates a poetry so dense, so full of allusions, so ambiguous in its imagery and syntax, that the reader must work hard to benefit from it. But these poems are not mere intellectual exercises, giving the same kind of satisfaction as a crossword puzzle. In their images of birds, sea, flowers, wings and waves, in their exquisite, musical rhythms, Mallarmé's poems convey a joyful invitation to the appreciation of beauty.

Further reading

W. Fowlie, *Mallarmé* (1953); R. Cohn, *Towards the Poems of Mallarmé* (1965); M. Bowie, *Mallarmé and the Art of Being Difficult* (1978); A. Gill, *The Early Mallarmé* (1979); L. Bersani, *The Death of Stéphane Mallarmé* (1982); R. Lloyd, *Mallarmé: 'Poésies'* (1984).

Workpoints

1 'Mallarmé's poems focus on a limited number of universally recognised themes: love, death, man's fears and longings, the beauty of the external world, nostalgia for a lost paradise, the celebration of artistic genius. Above all, however, they concern art and the image of the artist' (*R. Lloyd*). Examine these themes.

2 'Mallarmé porte en lui une mystérieuse fascination de l'absence' (*G. Clancier*). How does this appear in the poems?

3 Broome and Chesters write of Mallarmé's poetry: 'It is an art

of the ethereal, volatizing objects of physical experience into a state of "presque disparation vibratoire", so that all that remains is their aura, their spirit, their suggestive charge or symbolic life.' Show by what means Mallarmé achieves this end. How does he transform objects like the fan, the vase, the swan?

Guy de MAUPASSANT (1850–93)

Maupassant has been called the inventor of the commercial short story. He also wrote some poetry, a number of forgotten plays and sketches, and he was the author of seven novels; but his real claim to fame rests above all on his 300 or so short stories, the first of which was published in Zola's *Les Soirées de Médan* in 1880, followed by regular, often weekly, contributions to magazines and reviews such as *Le Gaulois* and *Gil Blas*, and ending with a number of grim and macabre tales as he neared his death from a form of madness brought on by syphilis.

Maupassant was born in Normandy, and many of his tales are, like *Le Baptême*, set in the Normandy countryside and, like *La Ficelle*, portray the simple peasant mentality of its inhabitants. A brief period of military service at the time of the Franco-Prussian war provided experiences recreated in, for example, *Mademoiselle Fifi*; and although he was not personally involved in the hostilities, his very first short story, *Boule de suif*, gives an amazingly succinct description of the collapse and rout of the French forces. Thereafter, for ten years, he was an unenthusiastic civil servant, working – like the father in *A Cheval* – at the naval ministry, a humdrum and boring occupation from which he took refuge in vigorous outdoor sports. He was an excellent oarsman, which accounts for the frequency with which he sets his stories on the banks of the Seine: *Deux amis* and *Le Trou* are both based on fishing incidents.

It was at this time that Maupassant's literary apprenticeship began. One of his uncles, Alfred le Poittevin, was a very close friend of Flaubert, and it was from the supreme exponent of the French novel that Maupassant learned much of his craftsmanship. He is not, however, a mere imitator, a sort of minor Flaubert; and Flaubert's death in 1880 left Maupassant free to develop his own individual talents. In all he produced eighteen volumes of short stories, including important collections such as *Le Maison Tellier* (1881), *Mademoiselle Fifi* (1883) and *Miss Harriet* (1884). Together they form a telling picture of everyday life in a variety of settings, forms and episodes: the colour and drabness of village life, the comedy and pettiness of small peasant-farmer communities; malicious cameos of petty officialdom and Prussian invaders; shabby gentility and sham respectability. There are the farcical and frivolous, like the story of the peasant with – literally – a flea in his ear; there are the sad and touching, like *Madame Perle*, a tale of love that did not reveal itself until too late, and *La Parure*, describing the grim effects of poverty; and in the later 1880s with *Le Horla* and *Lui?* there are the anguished worlds of horror and madness, of death and suicide.

Many academic critics find Maupassant unappealing, perhaps because he is a writer with no intellectual pretensions, no 'literary' frills; but no-one denies his outstanding technical skill and his matchless style as a writer of short stories. His prose is simple, direct and economical in the extreme. Maupassant stresses the need for precision: 'Quelle que soit la chose qu'on veut dire, il n'y a qu'un mot pour l'exprimer, qu'un verbe pour l'animer et qu'un adjectif pour la qualifier. Il faut donc chercher jusqu'à ce qu'on les ait découverts, ce mot, ce verbe, cet adjectif, et ne jamais se contenter de l'à-peu-près.' His manner of telling a story is detached and objective, but there are traces of irony and a fundamentally pessimistic outlook. He was at his best when describing ordinary folk: shopkeepers and tradesmen, private soldiers and peasants and prostitutes. For R. Ritchie, he was 'in many respects the greatest and most successful of the Naturalists'.

Further reading

Selected Short Stories – Maupassant, ed. J. Matthews (1959); J. Dugan, *Illusion and Reality* (1973); M. MacNamara, *Style and Vision in Maupassant's Nouvelles* (1986).

Workpoints

1 *His subject*
   'Maupassant is at his best when writing of the middle-class and of the peasants of his native Normandy' (*G. Brereton*).
   'If he is misanthropic in general, his particular hatred is for women' (*B. Nicholas*).
   'A cynical, amusing observer of human folly' (*D. Charlton*).

2 *Style and the use of visual details*
   Find examples of what Martin Turnell has called Maupassant's 'unerring eye for graphic detail'.
   Henry James saw in Maupassant's work 'a sort of bird's-eye view contempt'.
   'We never have the impression of "literature"; it is the direct narrative of the eye-witness or actor' (*R. Ritchie*).

3 *His importance*
   'A very great and original artist' (*F. Green*) or 'a minor author' (*B. Nicholas*)?

'A splendid entertainer and a superb technician, but he did not possess the moral or the intellectual qualities which are essential to the great writer' (*M. Turnell*).

'A beaucoup d'égards le vrai et l'unique successeur de Flaubert' (*H. Taine*).

Prosper MERIMEE (1803–70)

The *nouvelle* is the genre in which Mérimée excelled. The most famous works are *Colomba* (1841), describing a Corsican vendetta, and *Carmen* (1847), the story of a young Basque soldier's fatal love for a wild gypsy-girl which forms the basis of Bizet's opera.

Mérimée's life and career reveal a man of surprising contrasts. He was probably the most scholarly and erudite of all the nineteenth-century writers, but his passion for history and archaeology never prevented him from being a first-rate story-teller; as Inspector of Historical Monuments, he was a high-ranking and influential member of the Civil Service, a rare profession in which to earn a reputation as a celebrated practical joker; he was a member of the French Senate and close friend of Napoleon III and the Empress Eugénie, but beneath the social polish and urbanity there was, as his choice of fictional subjects reveals, a fondness for the wild and untamed, the violent and savage.

At a time when the historical novels of Walter Scott were attracting the attention of Romantic writers, it is hardly surprising that one of Mérimée's first ventures was a reconstruction of the Massacre of Saint-Bartholomew under the title of *Chronique du règne de Charles X* (1829). (In fact, his very first work was an elaborate and convincing hoax: *Le Théâtre de Clara Gazul* (1825), which Mérimée claimed to have discovered and translated, sent earnest scholars in search of the neglected Spanish dramatist only to find that the plays, like the playwright herself, were a complete fabrication.) To his historical fiction and to the *nouvelles*, Mérimée brought the precision and accuracy of the professional historian and scholar, a treatment very different from the flamboyant, sometimes fantastical, manner of the Romantic novelist. The activities of his outlaws and of his vital and dynamic heroines are presented with an objectivity and concision which increase the narrative force; the vivid yet precise use of local colour is all the more effective for being subdued. The result is an unusually effective combination of controlled Romanticism and compelling realism.

Further reading

Carmen, ed. M. Tilby (1981); *Colomba*, ed. J. Fontaine (1973).

Workpoints

'One of the most exquisite masters of French prose the nineteenth
century has seen' (*G. Saintsbury*).
'Mérimée may fairly be classed as a repressed Romantic' (*G.
Brereton*).
'Mérimée est purement artiste: son œuvre relève de la théorie de
l'art pour l'art. Il tient dans le roman la place que tient Gautier
dans la poésie' (*G. Lanson*).

Alfred de MUSSET (1810–57)

'Enfant prodige', 'enfant gâté'; these labels point to Musset's
youth, his virtuosity and his self-indulgence, but fail to do justice
to his complex presentation of human nature and to his humour.
He joined enthusiastically in the first forays of Romanticism with
picturesque, stylish and light-hearted plays and poems, *Contes
d'Espagne et d'Italie* (1830), rivalling Hugo in his use of everyday
language and supple rhythms. The best known is probably
'Ballade à la lune' with its flippant opening:

> C'était, dans la nuit brune,
> Sur le clocher jauni,
>   La lune,
> Comme un point sur un i.

In the same year the failure of his first staged play led him to write
plays for reading rather than performance: *Un Spectacle dans un
fauteuil*.

After 1830 Musset parted company with the other Romantics,
liking neither the concept of poet as social reformer and leader of
the people nor the impersonality of Art for Art's sake. When
Hugo, Lamartine and Gautier were moving in one or other of
these directions, Musset developed more deeply the idea of poetry
as the expression of personal experience. His dramatic love affair
with George Sand, from 1833 to 1835, led to an outburst of lyric
poetry, notably the four poems of 'Les Nuits'. Now he is no
longer playing with verse, but pouring out his deep suffering in the
context of a dialogue between himself and his muse, or himself and
his mysterious double. In 'La Nuit de mai' he rejects all the many
kinds of poetry available, paradoxically asserting the impossibility
of communicating even his grief:

> Je ne chante ni l'espérance,
> Ni la gloire, ni le bonheur,
> Hélas! pas même la souffrance.
> La bouche garde le silence
> Pour écouter parler le cœur.

'Les Nuits' are his most prestigious poems, but there is something more immediately appealing in the unrhetorical simplicity of a poem like 'Tristesse':

> J'ai perdu ma force et ma vie
> Et mes amis et ma gaîté;
> . J'ai perdu jusqu'à la fierté
> Qui faisait croire à mon génie.

In the prose work *La Confession d'un enfant du siècle* (1836), Musset analyses this sadness in terms of the whole generation to which he belongs.

This melancholy Musset is the familiar stereotype, yet there was another, equally important, side to Musset, one which many people prefer and which appears in his amusing account of two men's futile attempts to find out what Romanticism really is (*Lettres de Dupuis et Cotonet* (1836–7), and in his varied dramatic output. Here we find delicate plays, hovering between comedy and tragedy – *Les Caprices de Marianne* (1833), *On ne badine pas avec l'amour* (1834), *Fantasio* (1834) – and charming, elegant and witty one-act *proverbes* including *Un Caprice* (1837) and *Il faut qu'une porte soit ouverte ou fermée* (1845). These plays, light of touch, reminiscent of Marivaux in their sparkling, subtle dialogue and of Shakespeare in their fantasy, are performed more frequently than many serious Romantic dramas, and could even be considered the most lasting theatre produced in this period.

However, Musset's most ambitious theatrical work was the historical drama *Lorenzaccio*, published in 1834 but not performed until long after his death, in 1896. With thirty-eight scenes and a cast of more than forty, it was clearly not written with performance in mind, but is far from shapeless despite its multiplicity of settings and characters. In this dramatization of the assassination of the corrupt duc de Médicis, the assassin Lorenzaccio is a complex, tormented, ironic soul, more interesting than the relatively simple, symbolic Hugolian heroes. He involves himself in a life of corruption in order to win the trust of the debauched duke and, on the point of committing the murder, knows that he has ended by corrupting himself: 'Le vice a été pour moi un vêtement, maintenant il est collé à ma peau.' He knows too that his action will be futile, which indeed it proves to be; one corrupt ruler is simply replaced by another, and Lorenzaccio is murdered by one of the common people for a reward. The poetic, flowery language of this play, full of highly developed images, is Romantic, but the ambiguity of motives and the pessimism make it seem strangely modern.

Further reading

Contes d'Espagne et d'Italie, ed. M. Rees (1973); H. Gochberg, *Stage of Dreams. The Dramatic Art of Alfred de Musset (1828– 1834)* (1967); C. Affron, *A Stage for Poets. Studies in the Theatre of Hugo and Musset* (1971); D. Sices, *Theater of Solitude. The Drama of Alfred de Musset* (1974); C. Crossley, *Musset: 'Lorenzaccio'* (1983).

Workpoints

1   Ceri Crossley writes of 'the profound bleakness of Musset's moral vision' in *Lorenzaccio*. Do you agree with this and, if so, what contributes to this bleakness?

2   Marjorie Shaw writes of *Lorenzaccio* and *Un Caprice* that they 'are so different from one another, that they might have been written by different authors'. Comment on these differences. Are there any similarities?

3   'On ne saurait être trop sévère pour Alfred de Musset. Il est, avec Lamartine, qui s'en est repenti, responsable d'un faux sentimentalisme qui a empoisonné plusieurs générations' (*B. Lalande*). How just do you find this criticism? Is Musset falsely sentimental?

4   'Se sentir coupé de soi, se regarder parler ou agir du dehors, comme on le ferait pour un étranger; c'est l'une des originalités de la vie de la conscience chez Musset' (*J.-P. Richard*). Find examples of this split consciousness in Musset's poems and plays, and attempt to assess its importance.

Arthur RIMBAUD (1854–91)

Rimbaud had a violent and meteoric career. The whole of his startling and revolutionary poetry was concentrated into six years, from 1869 to 1875, ending when he was 21. An explosively rebellious childhood in the provinces was followed by a stay in Paris, where he sympathized with the revolutionaries of the Commune and alienated the literary establishment. A stormy relationship with Verlaine came to an end with a shooting incident in Brussels in 1872 for which Verlaine was imprisoned. In 1875 Rimbaud totally abandoned poetry, first travelling in Europe, then involving himself in gun-running in Africa.

Rimbaud's early poetry is characterized by a vehement rejection of middle-class values and religion, expressed in forceful, scornful, physical language. He describes the tense relationship with his authoritarian mother in 'Les Poètes de sept ans', and celebrates a joyful escape from restrictions in 'Ma Bohème':

> Je m'en allais, les poings dans mes poches crevées;
> Mon paletot aussi devenait idéal;
> J'allais sous le ciel, Muse! et j'étais ton féal;
> Oh! là là! que d'amours splendides j'ai rêvées!

'Les Chercheuses de poux' weaves a magical web of Baudelairean *correspondances* around the repellent theme of delousing:

> Elles asseoient l'enfant devant une croisée
> Grande ouverte où l'air bleu baigne un fouillis de fleurs,
> Et dans ses lourds cheveux où tombe la rosée
> Promènent leurs doigts fins, terribles et charmeurs.

In these poems Rimbaud shows a complete mastery of all current styles and, by 1871, was looking for a new kind of poetry. He wrote in the 'Lettre du voyant' that he wanted to become a seer, someone who would go beyond normal human experience and arrive at 'l'inconnu'. To do this he was prepared to inflict upon himself 'amour, souffrance, folie' and drugs, in order to achieve 'un long, immense et raisonné *dérèglement* de tous les sens'. His new kind of poetry appears in the sonnet 'Voyelles', in 'L'étoile a pleuré rose' and above all in 'Le Bateau ivre', which Rimbaud took with him as his entrée to Parisian literary circles. Here language is used in a powerful, uncompromising, immediate way, exploding with images:

> J'ai rêvé la nuit verte aux neiges éblouies,
> Baiser montant aux yeux des mers avec lenteurs,
> La circulation des sèves inouïes,
> Et l'éveil jaune et bleu des phosphores chanteurs!

Some of the poems that followed, collected under the title 'Vers nouveaux' or 'Derniers vers', show a calmer, more reflective mood in, for example, the song-like simplicity of 'L'Eternité':

> Elle est retrouvée
> Quoi? – L'Eternité.
> C'est la mer allée
> Avec le soleil.

But the main development now was towards the prose poem. Rimbaud's last two works – and no-one has yet established with any certainty which was written first – were the fragmented series of prose poems, the *Illuminations*, and the dramatized confession, *Une Saison en enfer*.

'Illuminations' can mean both coloured plates (Rimbaud's subtitle) and spiritual enlightenment, and this collection of poetry, which he also referred to as 'parade sauvage' and 'opéra fabuleux', can be understood in both these ways. Vivid images of amazing freshness, dream-like sequences of magical delight or disturbing hallucination follow one another in this new attempt to become the 'voyant'. The first poem, 'Après le déluge', has been seen as containing the essential theme of the whole collection: the contrast between a destructive, bourgeois civilization and the vision of a new, pure, dream-world. 'Aube' captures the freshness of a child's (and a poet's) vision in an attempt to fuse with nature itself: 'J'ai embrassé l'aube d'été.' 'Phrases' leaves the real world altogether for an idyllic expression of lyrical joy: 'J'ai tendu des cordes de clocher à clocher; des guirlandes de fenêtre à fenêtre; des chaînes d'or d'étoile à étoile, et je danse.' With *Une Saison en enfer* Rimbaud dramatically expresses all his conflicts, aspirations and failures, until he reaches the point at which his poetry must be abandoned and another reality sought: 'Moi! moi qui me suis dit mage ou ange, dispensé de toute morale, je suis rendu au sol, avec un devoir à chercher, et la réalité rugueuse à étreindre! Paysan!'

Rimbaud has had a great influence on other poets, especially on the Surrealists with their wish to tap the hidden dream-worlds of the subconscious and of childhood. With his development of the prose poem, with his continual pushing back of the frontiers of language, and with his aggressive, restless approach, he can be seen as opening a new era in French poetry.

Further reading

E. Starkie, *Arthur Rimbaud* (1938, 1972); J. Houston, *The Design of Rimbaud's Poetry* (1963); W. Frohock, *Rimbaud's Poetic Practice* (1963); C. Hackett, *Rimbaud: a Critical Introduction* (1980); *Illuminations: Coloured Plates*, ed. N. Osmond (1976); R. Little, *Rimbaud: 'Illuminations'* (1983).

Workpoints

1 'It is possible to see Rimbaud as the last and most audacious of the Romantic poets, in that he pushed to an extreme conclusion a belief in the poet as prophet, seer, magus or *voyant* – a privileged person endowed with special, if not divine powers' (*C. Hackett*).

2 ' "*Le Bateau ivre*" represents a journey of liberation, beyond all restrictions, into fabulous oceans of vision, synæsthesia, colour and sound which seem to convey some supernatural meaning and cannot be reduced to the language of reason' (*Broome and Chesters*).

3   'If at one level *Une Saison en enfer* expresses the crisis in the
    life of an adolescent struggling for self-fulfilment in the year
    1873, at another level it represents a crisis in our own
    materialistic civilization' (*C. Hackett*). Look at the poems
    from this point of view.

4   'Rimbaud's is the kind of poetry in which expression remains
    exploration, pushing back, through its defiance of the accepted
    relationship between words and objects, events, actions or
    concepts, the frontiers of logic and language' (*R. Little*).

STENDHAL (pseudonym for Henri Beyle) (1783–1842)

Stendhal came late to the novel, making his first attempt with
Armance (1827) at the age of 44. Before that, preoccupied with
literature although ostensibly pursuing a career in the Napoleonic
army, he had exercised his talents in various writings of a critical
and analytical nature. In love with Italy, which he had discovered
during the Napoleonic campaigns, he spent the last years of his life
alternating between vacations in Paris and his post as consul in
Civita Vecchia.

He can be seen as a writer who bestrides two centuries – one
foot in the eighteenth with his cool, rational, analytical approach,
and the other in the nineteenth with his passionate Romantic
sensibility and cult of energy. The tension between the two creates
a recognizably Stendhalian brand of irony as the head looks
ironically at the follies of the heart and the heart always goes
beyond the dictates of reason.

Other paradoxes abound: a mathematician who wanted logic
and clarity above all, yet admired the violent, irrational passions of
tales of Renaissance Italy; a Frenchman more at home in Italy.
Hating the crassness of post-Napoleonic France yet averse to the
vague socialism and lyrical pomposity of other Romantics, he
writes for the future: ('J'aurai peut-être quelque succès vers 1860
ou 1880') and for a small group who would share his individualistic
values: the 'Happy Few' mentioned at the end of *La Chartreuse de
Parme*. Stendhal adopted the philosophy of the *Idéologues*,
inheritors of the *Encyclopédie* tradition at the turn of the century,
a materialist philosophy stressing man's ability to analyse himself
and act upon the results of his analysis in the pursuit of happiness.
Yet Stendhal himself, and his heroes and heroines, although highly
intelligent, always go beyond this rational approach and act out of
passion and enthusiasm.

Stendhal's field of interest was 'le cœur humain' and, to portray
it, he needed facts – many, many little details – for this was where

he felt the truth lay, not in vague generalizations, and he wanted these 'petits faits' to be recorded in a clear style: 'Je cherche à raconter: 1° avec vérité; 2° avec clarté ce qui se passe dans un cœur.' He wanted to show characters in action, not describe them in static passages of analysis; to do this he needed a good basic story, obtained from a newspaper report of a trial (*Le Rouge et le Noir*) or an old Italian chronicle (*La Chartreuse de Parme*), so that, without having to worry about what E. M. Forster called 'this constant "and then . . . and then"' he could take his characters through infinitely complicated twists and turns of emotion and behaviour.

By this interest in the human heart he continues the tradition of the psychological novel, begun by Madame de Lafayette with *La Princesse de Clèves*, and, by his insistence on 'petits faits', he is, in his own way, a realist in the sense of a realistic observer of human psychology. He can also be called a realist because he sets his novels in the present, or the very recent past, and links his characters very closely with society and with political events. In an image which seems to be perfect for a realist, but which needs to be treated carefully, he defined the novel many times as a mirror carried along a road, reflecting the blue of the sky or the mud on the ground. This seems to imply that the novel will deal with all classes of people and all kinds of society, but this is not the case with Stendhal; his heroes and heroines are highly sensitive and intelligent *âmes généreuses*. Nor does this image imply impersonality in a work of art; Stendhal intervenes constantly (although he also makes use of the impersonal technique used later so effectively by Flaubert and Zola, whereby incidents and places are viewed through the eyes of the character). In fact he usually refers to the novel as a mirror in order to defend himself against a censorious readership. 'Don't blame me', he is saying, 'if my characters are anti-government or immoral; I am only describing what is there.'

Another definition of the novel – the violin bow drawn across the responsive violin, with its emphasis on the reader's response and the way the writer will play upon him, provoking, cajoling, enlisting his sympathy – brings us much closer than the mirror image to the characteristic flavour of Stendhal.

His first novel *Armance* is a perplexing work. It has been variously seen as a *roman à clef* (incomprehensible without information, not provided within the text, about the hero's dreadful secret – his impotence), as a tragic novel of misunderstanding, and as a comic satire on the *mal du siècle*, that melancholy frame of mind that makes happiness impossible. Less accomplished than the later novels, it nevertheless shows Stendhal well on the way to mastering a narrative technique and structure of his own. The background of Restoration society is there, the intermittent ironic references to the hero, the pattern of happiness found but jeopardized by the characters themselves.

The concern with the individual in contemporary society can be seen clearly in *Le Rouge et le Noir*, published in 1830 and subtitled *Chronique de 1830*. A fascinating picture of society in the last six years of the reign of Charles X emerges, as the hero, Julien Sorel, moves from the provinces to Paris, and from small town to seminary to aristocratic household, in pursuit of ambition and what he takes to be happiness. Only at the end, in prison and about to be executed for attempted murder, does he realize that true happiness lay in the love between himself and Madame de Rênal. Here Stendhal has perfected an ironic, elusive style, but one which he considered too abrupt, too *sec*. His next novels would be much more expansive.

Lucien Leuwen, begun in 1834, has the same linear structure as the preceding novels, in which a young man learns about life. This time the events are set in the July Monarchy, and the political satire is much more scathing. The love between Lucien and Madame de Chasteller is also developed at much greater length, with scenes of great delicacy in which fine nuances of feeling are exposed. This approximates more than any of the other novels to the analysis of the various stages of love outlined in Stendhal's idiosyncratic *De l'amour* (1822), supposedly a treatise on love but actually a collection of fascinating jottings and personal experiences. *Lucien Leuwen* was obviously going to grow to an inordinate length and Stendhal abandoned it.

His next novel, *La Chartreuse de Parme* (1839), drawn from a Renaissance tale similar to those of *Chroniques italiennes* (also 1839), is set in Italy and has all the charm of Stendhal's memories of a place where he had been happy. The biting satire is diminished, the dry style balanced by harmonious passages evoking a mood of happiness and tranquillity. This is a more free-wheeling novel than *Le Rouge et le Noir*; its hero, Fabrice, is not tormented by ambition like Julien, and entangles himself in an endearingly naive way in many adventures, including the battle of Waterloo, until he arrives at *le bonheur* in his love for Clélia. In this novel we have a band of passionate souls gathered around the hero, embodying the values of courage, gaiety and generosity in the face of a petty world.

Stendhal's heroes have been seen as various projections of Stendhal himself, but Stendhal also wrote autobiographical works, notably *Souvenirs d'égotisme* and *Vie de Henri Brulard*, both published after his death. The latter is a fascinating discourse on the difficulties inherent in writing an autobiography: what is truth? how will the reader know if he is reading the retrospective reflections of a 50-year-old or the impressions of a child? how can the author avoid the eternal repetition of *je* and *moi*? Informal, jumping from one thing to another, talking to the reader, this is a book which some prefer even to the novels.

Stendhal was one of the few nineteenth-century writers to have taken part in the Napoleonic campaigns, and Napoleon is an inspiration to most of his heroes: Julien reading the *Mémorial de Saint-Hélène*, Fabrice playing his muddled part in the battle of Waterloo. Yet this heroic past remains firmly in the past, and attempts to apply it to the present fail dismally and are treated ironically. Fulfilment for Stendhal's fictional heroes lies not in traditionally heroic exploits, but in love and in preserving an individual integrity in a corrupt and materialistic society. However, Stendhal's ever-present irony is such that one can never quite pin him down, and his novels, for this reason, are constantly stimulating. The reader has to be awake to every elusive reference, to every unexpected twist of phrase, as the sentences shoot off in different directions, each clause undermining the previous one. Undoubtedly a 'good read' and full of articulate, charming and intelligent characters, Stendhal's novels require a great deal of attention from the reader aspiring to join 'The Happy Few'.

Further reading

V. Brombert (ed.), *Stendhal. A Collection of Critical Essays* (1962); F. Hemmings, *Stendhal. A Study of his Novels* (1964); J. Atherton, *Stendhal* (1965); V. Brombert, *Stendhal: Fiction and the Themes of Freedom* (1968); M. Tillet, *Stendhal. The Background to the Novels* (1971); M. Wood, *Stendhal* (1971); G. Strickland, *Stendhal. The Education of a Novelist* (1974); J. Mitchell, *Stendhal: 'Le Rouge et le Noir'* (1973); A. Finch, *Stendhal: 'La Chartreuse de Parme'* (1984).

Workpoints

1 Stendhal wrote: 'Or, la première qualité d'un roman doit être raconter, amuser par des récits, et, pour pouvoir amuser les gens sensés, peindre des caractères qui soient dans la nature.' Look at the many implications in this quotation and apply them to Stendhal's novels.

2 'Ce mélange intime de lyrisme et de critique dont est faite l'originalité de son génie' (*J. Prevost*). See how these two elements combine in Stendhal's novels.

3 'Like all Stendhal's heroes, Lucien Leuwen is disorientated and unattached, a stranger in the fictional world in which he moves' (*R. Giraud*). Look at Stendhal's heroes in the light of this quotation.

4 'Stendhal's novels are never cynical or sarcastic (*M. Wood*). Do you agree?

5 Flaubert considered *Le Rouge et le Noir* to be 'mal écrit et incompréhensible, comme caractères et intentions'. Can you explain Flaubert's disapproval?

6 'To the extent that they deal with politics, Stendhal's novels ask one question over and over again: how can we – Europeans of cultivated tastes – survive in this era of cant and reaction?' (*I. Howe*). Look at the treatment of politics in Stendhal's novels, bearing this quotation in mind.

7 'Etre vrai et simplement vrai' (*Stendhal*). Is this possible in an autobiographical work? To what extent does Stendhal achieve this ambition?

Paul VERLAINE (1844–96)

Verlaine's life, with its ups and downs of depression and debauchery, cheerful bohemianism and maudlin self-pity, and including a period of imprisonment for shooting his friend and fellow poet Rimbaud in the wrist, has always attracted a good deal of attention. It may indeed be helpful to link collections of poems with his turbulent life: *La Bonne Chanson* (1870) reflecting his momentary calm in marriage with Mathilde Mauté; *Romances sans paroles* (1874) his distress and perplexity as the marriage disintegrates and a complex, tempestuous relationship develops with Rimbaud; *Sagesse* (1881) his religious awakening during his term of imprisonment.

Verlaine's poetry is extremely varied but he is best known for a kind of dreamy, sad musicality in which the outside world reflects the melancholy of the poet. Examples showing different ways of expressing this relationship can be found throughout his work. The early 'Chanson d'automne' of *Poèmes saturniens* (1866) inextricably links the sobbing sound of violins with the melancholy of autumn and its debilitating effect on the poet:

> Les sanglots longs
> Des violons
>   De l'automne
> Blessent mon cœur
> D'une langueur
>   Monotone.

Here there is none of the profuse rhetoric of Lamartine, even though the sentiments are often similar, but a concise construction and an evocative, economical use of words. The six-syllable lines of 'Il pleure dans mon cœur' of *Romances sans paroles* make a similar connection, this time using an apparently straightforward simile to compare the sadness in the poet's heart with the rain falling on the town:

Il pleure dans mon cœur
Comme il pleut sur la ville;
Quelle est cette langueur
Qui pénètre mon cœur?

There is, however, great artistry and great subtlety in this apparent simplicity, as Verlaine modifies the expected *Je pleure* to the impersonal *Il pleure*, forming an echo with *il pleut*, and builds up a mood of lyrical melancholy with the rhymes of *pleure*, *cœur*, *langueur*. The melancholy of the poet is again connected with the outside world in 'Je ne sais pourquoi', the seagull poem of *Sagesse*, but this time in a more complicated structure. Instead of directly comparing his heart to a seagull, he refers to his spirit flying in distress above the sea. Only in the second verse is the direct identification made: 'Mouette à l'essor mélancolique, / Elle suit la vague, ma pensée.' The metre of this poem is also more complicated. Verlaine uses an unusual combination of five and thirteen syllable lines to convey a sense – in the first verse, with its proliferation of mute 'e's – of the frantic search of the seagull: 'D'une aile inquiète et folle vole sur la mer' and, in the third verse, with this measured line, of serene, instinctive flight: 'Un instinct la guide à travers cette immensité.' In each of these poems Verlaine uses a haunting repetition of sounds, words and phrases to create a song-like, lingering quality in the verse. Questions give an underlying note of uncertainty: 'Pourquoi? Pourquoi?' becomes the mournful note of the seagull; '— Qu'as-tu fait, ô toi que voilà / Pleurant sans cesse, / Dis, qu'as-tu fait, toi que voilà, / De ta jeunesse?' is the final verse of the apparently calm 'Le ciel est par-dessus le toit' of *Sagesse*. These poems seem to exemplify the kind of poetry advocated by Verlaine in his 'Art poétique', with its emphasis on musicality above all else, on suggestion rather than direct statement and on shades of emotion and colour: 'De la musique avant toute chose. . . .'

Although musicality is the most characteristic feature of Verlaine's poetry, he can also create a vivid picture in words. In 'Effet de nuit' for example, from *Poèmes saturniens*, a stark, black and white picture, like an etching, is built up in blocks and lines:

La nuit. La pluie. Un ciel blafard que déchiquette
De flèches et de tours à jour la silhouette
D'une ville gothique éteinte au lointain gris.

In *Fêtes galantes* (1869) the inspiration is again painting, though the verse is still often enchantingly musical – the frivolous, languid, eighteenth-century paintings of Watteau providing the starting point for a series of scenes in which charming, flirtatious yet sad figures flit through a landscape of formal gardens, fading at the end into an image of neglect and desolation with the 'vieux parc solitaire et glacé' of 'Colloque sentimental'. Yet these apparently objective scenes reflect, as do the more obviously personal poems, the melancholy soul of the poet:

> Votre âme est un paysage choisi
> Que vont charmant masques et bergamasques
> Jouant du luth et dansant et quasi
> Tristes sous leur déguisements fantasques.

Even in the collection *Romances sans paroles*, whose title would seem to indicate an exclusive preoccupation with musicality, there is a section called *Paysages belges* in which a bright and cheerful picture of Walcourt is built up through a series of nouns, dotted like splashes of colour on canvas and reminiscent of an Impressionist painting:

> Briques et tuiles,
> O les charmants
> Petits asiles
> Pour les amants!

The same collection contains a poem in which stark colours are used to create a landscape of vivid permanence to contrast with the poet's emotional insecurity:

> Les roses étaient toutes rouges
> Et les lierres étaient tout noirs.
>
> Chère, pour peu que tu te bouges,
> Renaissent tous mes désespoirs.

Other poems, especially in the collection *Sagesse*, exchange vague suggestion for more formal allegory, in which a moral quality or emotion is personified in a clear one-to-one relationship: 'Bon chevalier masqué qui chevauche en silence, / Le Malheur a percé mon vieux cœur de sa lance.' Or the sonnet form gives a framework for complex debate in 'Les faux beaux jours ont lui tout le jour, ma pauvre âme', and 'Sagesse d'un Louis Racine, je t'envie!' Nor is humour absent from Verlaine's work, from the satirical 'Monsieur Prudhomme' of *Poèmes saturniens* to the light-hearted 'Colombine' of *Fêtes galantes* and the self-parody of 'A la manière de Paul Verlaine' of *Parallèlement* (1889), with its exaggerated internal rhymes and ironic reference to moonlight:

C'est à cause du clair de lune
Que j'assume ce masque nocturne
Et de Saturne penchant son urne
Et de ces lunes l'une après l'une.

However, for all this variety of subject and tone and constant experimenting with verse form, Verlaine's popularity rests on his intensely personal poems of sadness, reflected in features of the natural world, and expressed with subtlety and haunting lyricism in delicately musical verse.

Further reading

Editions: *Selected Poems*, ed. R. Perman (1965); '*Sagesse*', ed. C. Chadwick (1973); '*Romances sans paroles*', ed. D. Hillery (1976).

Biography: J. Richardson, *Verlaine* (1971).

Criticism: A.Carter, *Paul Verlaine* (1971); C. Chadwick, *Verlaine* (1973); S. Taylor-Horrex, *Verlaine: 'Fêtes galantes' and 'Romances sans paroles'* (1988).

Workpoints

1 'Verlaine's tenuous, impressionistic effects are obtained by the intelligent exploitation of his own stock of poetic devices' (*N. Osmond*). What are the poetic devices he uses for these effects?

2 'De la musique avant toute chose,' wrote Verlaine. Analyse the means (rhyme, alliteration, assonance, rhythm) by which he achieves this musicality.

3 'Verlaine's output is far more varied than one might at first imagine' (*R. Perman*). Find examples of this variety.

4 Analyse Verlaine's techniques as a painter of landscapes.

Alfred de VIGNY (1797–1863)

Vigny stands out in a very distinctive way from the rest of the Romantics. Sombre and pessimistically atheistic, averse to the vague Lamartinian idea that nature is a consoling force, he pins his hope on the stoic suffering of the transient human being: 'Plus que tout votre règne et que ses splendeurs vaines, / J'aime la majesté des souffrances humaines.' These are the lines addressed to nature in 'La Maison du berger', which he said could be taken as 'le sens de tous mes poèmes philosophiques'.

This attitude can partly be explained by his life. From a minor aristocratic family ruined by the Revolution, he prepared for a career in the army but was disappointed by routine garrison life during the uneventful Restoration; turning to drama and poetry, he was eclipsed as leader of the young Romantics by Hugo, in spite of adaptations of Shakespeare (*Le More de Venise*, 1829), a historical novel (*Cinq-Mars*, 1826), and *Poèmes antiques et modernes* (1826–37). 1835 saw the successful performance of his thoughtful prose drama *Chatterton*, with its theme, now something of a cliché, of the poverty-stricken poet, ignored by society, escaping from his torment through suicide. In the same year a collection of three short stories (*Servitude et grandeur militaires*) describes the loneliness of the soldier, condemned, like the poet, to misunderstanding from society, but finding refuge in a personal sense of honour. A religious crisis in 1837, the death of his mother and the collapse of his love affair with the actress Marie Dorval led to a complete pessimism, expressed in a series of poems: 'La Mort du loup', 'Le Mont des Oliviers', 'La Colère de Samson', though a more hopeful philosophy appears in the 1840s with 'La Maison du berger' and 'La Bouteille à la mer', published after his death in *Les Destinées. Poèmes philosophiques*.

The isolation of the man of genius is expressed in poems and on stage. Already 'Moïse' (written 1822) showed, not the biblical Moses, but 'l'homme de génie, las de son éternel veuvage et désespéré de voir sa solitude plus vaste et plus aride à mesure qu'il grandit'. Here we see a Romantic figure different from the sad, lamenting figures of Chateaubriand or Lamartine. This is the exceptional hero and leader, adored by the multitude but isolated by his very grandeur and genius.

If society is hostile, nature does not provide the maternal refuge hymned by Lamartine ('Mais la nature est là qui t'invite et qui t'aime'). In 'La Maison du berger', nature expresses her indifference to humanity in magnificent, stately verse:

> On me dit une mère, et je suis une tombe.
> Mon hiver prend vos morts comme son hécatombe,
> Mon printemps ne sent pas vos adorations.

In the face of inevitable human suffering Vigny sees a lesson for man in the silent and dignified death of the wolf ('La Mort du loup'):

> Gémir, pleurer, prier est également lâche.
> Fais énergiquement ta longue et lourde tâche
> Dans la voie où le sort a voulu t'appeler,
> Puis, après, comme moi, souffre et meurs sans parler.

'Les Destinées' and 'Le Mont des Oliviers' offer a still more pessimistic vision: since even God refuses to answer the call for help, man's dignified reaction should be silence. 'La Bouteille à la mer' and 'L'Esprit pur' lighten this sombre picture with a confidence in man. The 'trésor de la pensée', like the bottle cast on the waves, will endure.

Not only are the ideas behind Vigny's poetry different from those of other Romantics, but also his mode of expression. Poetry for him was concentrated thought, 'perle de la pensée', and his poems usually take the form of little epics, with a strong dramatic quality, illustrating a central idea. The forcefulness of his vision expresses itself in great blocks of alexandrines and memorable, lapidary messages. The dominant tonality is violent: dramatic reds and blacks, storms and tempests, whether in the biblical desert or the French Landes. His poetry gives the impression of objectivity but is clearly personal, fuelled by his own experience. Powerfully expressed, it transcends the limits of purely didactic poetry and, in the more complex 'La Maison du berger', is both moving and beautiful.

Bibliography

R. Buss, *Vigny: 'Chatterton'* (1984); K. Wren, *Vigny: 'Les Destinées'* (1985).

Workpoints

1 'Vigny, if not entirely "modern", nonetheless communicates an intellectual toughness, a grim perception of what life is like, that render him more acceptable to our disillusioned generation than his contemporaries' (*K. Wren*). Do you agree?

2 'The first shots in the war that was now beginning between the artist or man of letters and bourgeois society'; this is how Alfred Cobban describes *Chatterton*. How is this theme presented by Vigny?

3 'A number of critics have seen in Vigny an ancestor of the symbolists. . . . More recent critics have often refused to use the term symbol in connection with Vigny' (*M. Gilman*). Look at Vigny's use of the symbol in the light of this quotation.

Emile ZOLA (1840–1902)

Zola rose from humble origins in southern France to great fame in the capital as one of the most commercially successful men of letters of his century. Having endured poverty in Aix-en-Provence and then as a clerk in Paris, in 1863 he began his long career in journalism, among other things championing the emergent Impressionists, whose approach and subject-matter would find echoes in his own mature work. His early fiction was by turns naïve and dream-like, but with *Thérèse Raquin* (1867) he found his characteristic manner, and by 1868 he was planning the determinedly realistic novel-cycle which was to dominate the next two decades of his life. By the time the twenty-volume *Rougon-Macquart* series was completed, however, some of Zola's supporters were looking for a different sort of literature, and he changed course himself in *Trois Villes* (1894–8) and *Les Quatre Evangiles* (1899–1902) – now largely unread – which tackled religious and moral issues. In 1898, unusually for a nineteenth-century novelist, he found himself at the centre of political controversy following 'J'accuse!', his famous open letter to the President of France, in which he demanded justice for Dreyfus, the army officer wrongly imprisoned for espionage four years earlier.

Thérèse Raquin is a lurid story of two adulterous lovers who murder the woman's husband but are destroyed by nightmarish remorse and terror. The novel was denounced as immoral, yet sold in its thousands. As an example of Zola's attitudes, however, it is significant above all for the claims Zola makes in the preface: 'J'ai voulu étudier des tempéraments et non des caractères. . . . J'ai simplement fait sur deux corps vivants le travail analytique que les chirurgiens font sur des cadavres.' The propagandist's confident invocation of science – an increasingly plausible discipline at this stage of the nineteenth century – and the apparent reduction of human beings to the level of animals are both dominant themes in the *Rougon-Macquart* period. Imbued with Darwin's ideas on evolution, Taine's determinism, and the *Traité de l'hérédité* of Prosper Lucas, among other influences, he aimed to write the 'histoire naturelle et sociale d'une famille sous le Second Empire' – his subtitle for the series. The novels trace five generations of the descendants of a peasant woman from Plassans (a fictionalized Aix), who had a legitimate son – a Rougon – and after her husband's death gave birth to the son and daughter of her lover, called Macquart. The family tree, revealing the inherited traits of each character, appears in *Une Page d'amour* (1878) and *Le Docteur Pascal* (1893).

Zola distinguished his work from Balzac's as being 'moins social que scientifique'. In practice, heredity receives less emphasis than the other key determining factor, environment, as the various members of the family are dispersed geographically (in Plassans, Brittany, Paris, the north-east and elsewhere) and in different milieux (the financial world, the Church, politics, the coal-mines, for instance). The historical setting, from Louis-Napoleon's *coup d'état* in 1851 via Haussmann's transformation of Paris to the collapse of the Second Empire in 1870, is carefully described. Zola makes much of his Naturalism, particularly in the theoretical work *Le Roman expérimental* (1880), inspired by Claude Bernard's *Introduction à l'étude de la médecine expérimentale*. Here Zola assimilates the novelist to the impassive scientific experimenter documenting his observations. And indeed the working-class Paris of *L'Assommoir* (1877), and the mining community of *Germinal* (1885) reflect just such a method. But the documentation is not always so scrupulous – as in *Pot-Bouille* (1882), where the observation of upper-class society is far less acute. In any case, the analogy of the experimenter breaks down when Zola's methods are closely examined. His novels centre on an initial idea, as is clear from his *ébauches* or preparatory sketches, rather than emerging from a mass of accumulated evidence; in this way *Germinal*, for example, is intended to portray 'la lutte du capital contre le travail' and to predict twentieth-century conditions. Further, the novels are informed by a vision of the world which is creative and imaginative, rather than merely passive. Characters may be to some extent dehumanized: the very title of the railway novel, *La Bête humaine*, is an obvious illustration; but people can also coalesce into groups (the 'troupeau' of workers trudging into Paris at the beginning of *L'Assommoir*, or the mass of striking miners in *Germinal*), which develop a collective identity, revealing Zola's unique talent for animating crowds. As the individual is reduced, so elements of the environment take on a menacing life of their own: in *Germinal*, as Etienne Lantier observes the coal-mine known as Le Voreux, 'cette fosse . . . lui semblait avoir un air mauvais de bête goulue, accroupie là pour manger le monde'; in *L'Assommoir* Paris itself 'devours' the workers as they come down from the northern *faubourgs*, and the still in Père Colombe's drinking establishment casts sinister shadows: 'des figures avec des queues, des monstres ouvrant leurs mâchoires comme pour avaler le monde'. Talking of his novels, Zola repeatedly used the term 'poème': *La Terre* (1887), set among the peasantry of the Beauce, was to be 'le poème vivant de la terre'; *Au Bonheur des dames* (1883), devoted to the new department stores, he saw as the 'poem' of modern commerce. Flaubert, a mentor to the younger writer, wrote of the enigmatic prostitute, 'Nana tourne au mythe, sans cesser d'être réelle.' The novels cannot be taken as mere clinical analysis, and a wide range of critical approaches has revealed many other qualities in them. Marxists have studied the presentation of the class struggle in *Germinal*, and psychoanalysts have probed the sexual obsessions in *La Bête humaine*; Zola's visual style has not only been linked with the Impressionists, but also seen as an anticipation of the art of cinema. And while none of these interpretations tells the whole story, together they bring home the novelist's real depth and diversity.

His narrative skill is at its peak in *L'Assommoir*, with the symmetrical curve of Gervaise's fortunes poised on parallel scenes: the initial situation, when she looks out on the boulevard de la Chapelle as a newcomer with her life in front of her, and her 'errance' nearly twenty years later, as she covers the same ground on foot, a broken woman near to death. The upward and downward movements are set against the dramatic moments of her career, most notably her birthday feast in the central chapter, when her standing is at its highest. The use of an unobtrusive narrator, who can move into Gervaise's thoughts and words by means of *style indirect libre*, is another vital factor in the novel's success. Other impressive features occur in a number of texts, notably the powerful, panoramic openings (Etienne striding across the darkened plan in *Germinal*, or the coaches returning from the bois de Boulogne in *La Curée* (1879)). Similarly, Zola's gift for evoking the sights, sounds and smells of the physical world – the steamy, noisy wash-house visited by Gervaise, or the engines' smoke and din at the Gare Saint-Lazare – enriches every text.

Zola's scientific propaganda is a clear indication of how far he was caught up in the mentality of his age; but his best novels, for all the stress on the urbanization and industrialization transforming the France of the 1850s and 1860s, still speak vigorously and vividly to their readers more than a century later.

Further reading

A. Wilson, *Emile Zola: An Introductory Study of his Novels* (1952, 1964); F. Hemmings, *Emile Zola* (1966); E. Grant, *Zola's 'Germinal'* (1962); C. Smethurst, *Zola: 'Germinal'* (1974); F. Hemmings, *The Life and Times of Emile Zola* (1977); B. Nelson, *Emile Zola: a Selective Analytical Bibliography* (1982); R. Butler, *Zola: 'La Terre'* (1984); P. Walker, *Zola* (1985); *Thérèse Raquin*, ed. B. Nelson (1987).

Workpoints

1 *The significance of Naturalism.* Zola admitted to Flaubert: 'Je me moque comme vous de ce mot *naturalisme*, et cependant, je le répéterai, parce qu'il faut un baptême aux choses, pour que le public les croie neuves.' Does Zola use the word purely for publicity reasons? or are there real indications of a naturalist technique in his novels?

2 *The world of Rougon-Macquart.* Jules Lemaître called the cycle 'une épopée pessimiste de l'animalité humaine'. What are

its epic qualities? Is it, ultimately, pessimistic? Is 'l'animalité humaine' its main theme?

3   *Zola as a novelist.* 'L'art de Zola, dans ses meilleures réussites, tenait à une heureuse conciliation du roman et de l'épopée, de la documentation et de la poésie, du réel et du mythe' (*M. Raimond*). What evidence is there of these different qualities, and how are they reconciled and balanced?

5

The twentieth century

As the Dreyfus Affair receded into history (Dreyfus was finally declared innocent in 1906), there was in France a stronger sense of stability and continuity. The population had not increased nearly as rapidly as that of Britain or Germany (it was 36 million in 1870 and still under 40 million in 1914), and industrialization had not developed to the same extent as it had in these neighbouring countries. France was still, in the early years of the twentieth century, a country of small towns and small-scale enterprises, and by the time war broke out, half of its people were still working in agriculture. During the 1880s and 1890s there had, though, been a considerable expansion of France's colonial empire, to include Madagascar and parts of black Africa, as well as protectorates over Morocco and Tunisia. If this process was not universally popular in France, its results came to be accepted as an indication of the nation's renewed prestige after the humiliations of 1870–1. And even allowing for internal conflict, as in the religious dispute which led to the separation of church and state in 1905, the Third Republic succeeded in establishing itself so firmly that no internal force could overthrow it. The general standard of living and foreign trade improved greatly; education helped to convey the idea of national unity; and there was widespread sense of well-being among the people. It would become customary to look back nostalgically on the period before 1914 as 'la Belle Epoque'.

Everything was soon to be transformed. Friction between the major European powers was apparent in various incidents, as in 1911, when Germany sent a gunboat to the Moroccan port of Agadir to protest against French policy in Africa. War broke out because France, Britain and Germany were all sucked into the affairs of eastern Europe, but the main theatre of hostilities was the north-eastern corner of France. Many initially greeted the war with patriotic enthusiasm: President Poincaré called for 'L'union sacrée' of his people, and the crowds shouted 'A Berlin!'. Yet rapidly it became clear that the nation was involved in butchery on an unprecedented scale. Over a quarter of a million Frenchmen had died by the end of 1914; battles such as Verdun in 1916 caused massive loss of life, and by the armistice 16 per cent of all those mobilized had been killed.

For the next ten years, France, like the rest of Europe, struggled to recover from the traumas of war. Much reconstruction was achieved, although it was obvious that the pre-war world could never return. By the mid-1920s, for instance, the growth of new industries meant that production rates easily outstripped those of fifteen years earlier. The political situation, with power moving between centre-right and centre-left, was also relatively stable. At the same time, long-term changes were in prospect. At the Congress of the Socialist Party held at Tours in 1920, a majority vote set up the French Communist Party, and although it would be some time before the Communists would become a major force, the political spectrum was already being significantly widened. The mood of prosperity was to continue until the end of the decade, and France seemed once more secure in her foreign affairs. In order to protect the eastern frontiers, and following the lesson of fortified defence lines learned at Verdun, the government decided in 1928 to build the Maginot Line between Belgium and the Swiss frontier.

Once again, however, outside pressures were to transform the situation within France, and set off further conflicts. When the New York stock exchange crashed at the end of 1929, the immediate impact was obviously felt in the United States, but within a year or two declining trade, failure of business and growing unemployment spread across the western world – and France was not immune. It is argued that unemployment was lower in France than in some other countries – but no less dramatic because France was not nearly as familiar with the problem. Soon Hitler was to become Chancellor of Germany (in 1933) and create another Fascist state on France's borders, Italy having acquired an all-Fascist parliament in 1929. In 1929, too, Poincaré retired as Prime Minister, and with him went the fragile consensus France had briefly known. The field of extreme attitudes was opening up: on the left, many looked to Communism as a radical way out of crisis; on the right, others, including ex-servicemen's groups, sought to emulate the discipline and strong government that Fascism seemed to offer. As with its earlier revolutions, as with the Dreyfus affair, splits were appearing in the fabric of French society, and threatened to tear the whole country apart. The crisis intensified in 1934, when the Right took to the streets (perhaps with a view to marching on the Chambre des Députés) in protest against government corruption. And this galvanized the Left into a rare unity, whereby Communists co-operated with Socialists and Radicals, coming to power as the reforming Popular Front government under Léon Blum in 1936, but lasting less than a year before running out of energy and support.

With hindsight it seems clear that war with Hitler's Germany was quite inevitable, yet France, like Britain, does not appear to have been particularly well-prepared. And even after war was declared, during the inertia of the 'drôle de guerre', there was none of the conviction of 1914, and much complacency persisted about the strength of France's position. The German invasion of May–June 1940 was therefore an immense shock, as was the subsequent division of the country into an Occupied Zone and – south of the Loire – the so-called 'Zone Libre' under the Vichy government of Marshal Pétain, an authoritarian regime well-suited to coexisting with Nazism. Opposition remained alive – immediately, in the form of De Gaulle's Free French in London, and increasingly via Resistance groups on French territory. The liberation of France in 1944 removed the occupying forces, but the antagonisms between 'Résistants' and 'Collabos' were much slower to disappear.

De Gaulle led France for over a year, from August 1944, as the country set about re-establishing its shattered economy and creating a new constitution, the Third Republic having been ended by referendum. Unable to achieve the 'strong' constitution he believed in, De Gaulle resigned, no doubt hoping he would be invited back to power. During the twelve years of the Fourth Republic, France moved into a closer relationship with her European neighbours, through the coal and steel agreements of 1951 and then the Rome treaties for the Common Market in 1957. At the same time, she found herself disengaging from her colonies, pulling out of Indo-China in 1954, and granting independence to Morocco in 1956. Algeria, first colonized in 1830, was to be a more intractable problem, with the independence movement, the FLN, fighting to expel the French, and the sizeable European population, backed by the clandestine OAS, demanding to stay. With no-one else able to offer firm direction, De Gaulle returned to power in 1958, created a new constitution strengthening the powers of the president *vis-à-vis* parliament, and, in 1962, after much manœuvring, gave Algeria its independence. Once free of this immediate problem, De Gaulle was able to pursue his overriding aim of making France once again a great nation. He achieved a strong position in world affairs, for instance by committing himself to an independent nuclear deterrent and withdrawing from NATO. The French economy grew at an unprecedented rate, individual prosperity increased, and, under De Gaulle's Minister for Culture, André Malraux, the country took a new pride in its artistic achievements. In May 1968 there was a violent swing of the pendulum, when student disturbances –

initially an expression of frustration with the university system – set off a general wave of unrest. The police, the state-controlled broadcasting service, and the government itself were further targets; indeed it seemed as if the whole of the Establishment was being rejected. When industrial workers went on strike, the state itself seemed to be threatened. Although De Gaulle rode out the storm, trading on the public's deep-seated fear of disorder, he was to fall from power after narrowly losing in a referendum on political reform, in 1969. He died in the following year, but the state he had created remained, to be run first by his conservative successors Pompidou and Giscard d'Estaing, and then by the first Socialist President of the Fifth Republic, François Mitterand.

*   *   *

The cultural climate is always as volatile as the historical situation: ideas, moods and fashions overlap and replace one another from decade to decade, sometimes from year to year. At the beginning of the twentieth century, with the Positivism of Comte and Taine out of favour, the influence of Henri Bergson remains strong. His emphasis on human beings as intuitive and creative, rather than reducible to a set of predictable, mechanical categories, parallels Proust's approach in the novel, and represents a prevailing attitude. The rejection of the rationalist view takes on a fresh impetus following the translation into French of the work of Sigmund Freud, during the 1920s. The word 'psychanalyse' had entered the language (1914), and soon a whole new perspective opens up, revealing perhaps more fully than ever before the irrational side of man – his neuroses and obsessions, his sexuality, his dreams and fantasies.

Within the arts, too, there is a similar sense of rapid progress and renewal. The Impressionists and their successors had already pictured the world in a new way from the 1860s, by stressing the artist's immediate perceptions rather than attempting any objective portrayal of their subjects. Soon after the turn of the century the Cubist movement was moving a stage further, by shifting the emphasis from the way objects appeared to the eye, and concentrating instead on the *idea* of them – faces, musical instruments, kitchen utensils – choosing whatever aspects or angles seemed most apt, regardless of their actual physical relationship with one another. As Georges Braque put it: 'Les sens déforment, l'esprit forme.' From about the time of Picasso's *Demoiselles d'Avignon* (1907) Cubism was to flourish for a decade. The radical originality of the movement is matched in the other arts; and it is a characteristic of the twentieth century that artists working in different media frequently interact, so that, say, the Cubist paintings of Picasso and Braque have their counterparts in the poems of Apollinaire and Max Jacob. At much the same time, composers such as Debussy and Ravel were creating new languages and harmonies in music, drawing inspiration from Symbolist writers and Impressionist painting.

A more drastic artistic revolution was under way before the end of the First World War, and – another feature typical of modernist movements – its origins are truly international. Dada, born in Zurich of the chaos war had brought, stood for wildness, instinctive behaviour, and the destruction of all conventional values and standards – mostly through the shock tactics of its poetry and painting. Its leading light, the Rumanian Tristan Tzara, brought his ideas to Paris in 1920, but before long the initial impetus of Dada was exhausted. However, the anarchic spirit lived on in a number of writers, especially André Breton, who emerged as the leader of a new group including Aragon and Eluard; it spread also to painters such as Picasso and Dali. While Dada had apparently existed above all to disturb, Surrealism (the name was first used by Apollinaire) mobilized freshly liberated energies for more constructive purposes. Breton, an early disciple of Freud, whom he met in 1921, saw the freeing of the subconscious as a vital means of artistic creation. In his first *Manifeste du surréalisme* (1924), Breton defines the term as: 'Automatisme psychique pur par lequel on se propose d'exprimer, soit verbalement, soit par écrit, soit de toute autre manière, le fonctionnement réel de la pensée. Dictée de la pensée, en l'absence de tout contrôle exercé par la raison en dehors de toute préoccupation esthétique ou morale.' As this suggests, the movement embraced various forms, including cinema (with Luis Buñuel) and the novel (through Aragon's *Le Paysan de Paris* of 1926, and Breton's *Nadja* of 1928). Important Surrealist works range from the 'écriture automatique' and the 'récits de rêves' which allowed the free play of the poet's mind, to the haunting landscapes by painters such as Dali or Max Ernst. The movement was anything but unified: it could, by turns, be earnest and whimsical, profound and superficial, and it was marked by endless personality clashes involving the domineering Breton. By the end of the 1920s, as political realities impinged even on this rarefied environment, serious ideological divisions opened up. Breton tried, unsuccessfully, to reconcile Surrealism with Communism, while Aragon became a committed party member. By the early 1930s many had left the movement altogether, and its importance was in sharp decline.

Around 1930 occurred a critical turning point in world affairs, and sooner or later the fact became apparent to all. As Sartre was to put it: 'A partir de 1930, la crise mondiale, l'avènement du nazisme, les événements de Chine, la guerre d'Espagne, nous ouvrirent les yeux. . . . Du coup nous nous sentîmes brusquement *situés*.' As the new decade progressed, writers of all kinds felt obliged to take up a clear political stance. Some, like Aragon or Malraux, adopted positions on the left – and even the ageing Gide travelled to Russia, the better to understand Communism in practice; others saw salvation in Fascism (if not necessarily the varieties current among France's neighbours): among these were Pierre Drieu la Rochelle and Robert Brasillach, disgusted by what they saw as the laxity and disorder of modern life and keen for a return to discipline and authority. This sort of polarization continued through the period of the Popular Front government and then during the Second World War, with writers supporting the Resistance, often forced to publish their poems and essays clandestinely, set against those who approved of the German occupying forces, or at least were prepared to coexist with them.

While various vigorous defences of orthodox Christianity continue to be made by thinkers such as Teilhard de Chardin, the dominant strand in French thinking immediately after the Second World War is Existentialism. Its roots go back at least as far as the nineteenth-century Danish theologian Kierkegaard, and can be traced through more recent German philosophers such as Heidegger. In Sartre's version it is a denial of the idea that man has any 'essence' or pre-ordained, ideal being; it asserts instead that each individual must confront the realities of his actual existence, in a universe without a god or any other source of meaning. The positive side of this, for Sartre, is that it leaves us free to define our responsibilities, make our own choices and thereby justify ourselves. While his strictly academic accounts of Existentialism – most notably *L'Etre et le néant* (1943) – remain the preserve of specialist philosophers, his ideas have reached a much wider audience through his plays, in which the problem of choosing appropriate action is thoroughly explored. In his own life Sartre increasingly saw himself as committed ('engagé'): duty-bound to play an active role in contemporary events, as he did in the Vietnam protests of the 1960s. In this way he clearly differentiated himself from the partisans of a new intellectual trend, Structuralism, which did not in itself presuppose a political dimension.

The theories of Structuralism derive principally from the Swiss linguist Ferdinand de Saussure (1857–1913), who saw language as a system of relations between components such as words or sounds, rather than the expression of some pre-existing meaning. Thus the critic Roland Barthes, in his Structuralist phase, would approach works of literature as independent patterns or codes which do not necessarily reflect some prior idea or reality. It is also a sign of the times that, during the 1960s and 1970s, literary criticism claims more and more attention as an activity in its own right. But the influence of Structuralism makes itself felt still more widely, as with its application to anthropology, where Claude Lévi-Strauss analyses kinship-systems and primitive beliefs in similar terms.

Roland Barthes, however, is a significant figure far beyond his involvement with Structuralism. His writings draw on most of the major strands of thought of the century – psychoanalysis, Marxism, Existentialism and others. Just as important, particularly in his later work, is the fact that he breaks down the traditional barriers between criticism and imaginative literature, offering instead a creative 'écriture', as in *Roland Barthes par Roland Barthes* (1975) or *Fragments d'un discours amoureux* (1977). In so doing he crystallizes one of the most striking features of twentieth-century writing: the constant challenge to time-worn categories.

This tendency becomes increasingly apparent as time goes on, but even in the 1940s a critic could write: 'La "République des Lettres", si bien organisée aux époques classiques – ou du moins on nous l'a fait croire – fait place à l'anarchie littéraire. . . . Toutes les manières se mêlent; toutes les définitions demandent à être révisées.' The evidence accumulates: Gide warning against a facile use of the term 'roman' by denying it to most of his fiction; the division between 'serious' and 'light' literature meaning less and less when, say, the *romans policiers* of Georges Simenon command so much respect; the distinction between comedy and tragedy becoming irrelevant with the plays of Beckett or Ionesco. And it is not simply that the interior walls within the house of literature are being radically altered. Literature is to be found remarkably often on the boundaries with other art-forms: Prévert's poems can readily turn into popular songs (and, one might add, the songs of Georges Brassens can just as easily go in the opposite direction); Robbe-Grillet blurs the differences separating novel and film-scenario; Nathalie Sarraute can write for radio as well as for the printed page. It is, indeed, perhaps in this perspective that traditional notions of genre can best be placed.

*   *   *

Poetry in the twentieth century is a network of individual talents, in which trends present in the nineteenth century are developed and new, revolutionary modes created. Baudelaire as poet of the modern city finds his successor in Apollinaire; the mysterious quest of the poet, delving into an unknown world, represented by Nerval and Rimbaud as well as by Baudelaire and Hugo, flourishes in the Surrealist school with Breton, Aragon and Eluard; religious poetry revives with Jammes, Péguy and Claudel.

The century divides naturally into four periods: pre-war and the First World War (1900–18); the inter-war years (1918–39); the Second World War (1939–45); and post-war up to the present.

At the beginning of the century Symbolist poetry continued and the influence of Mallarmé's salons was still felt. Paul Valéry, with *La Jeune Parque* (1917) and *Charmes* (1922), containing his best-known poem, 'Le Cimetière marin', followed the Mallarméan tradition of intelligent, impersonal poetry. However, where Mallarmé had tried to evoke the ideal world behind reality, Valéry – in a classically restrained and musically complex verse – investigated the workings of the mind and the nature of poetry.

In contrast, there was a resurgence of religious poetry with the later collections of Francis Jammes (from *Clairières dans le ciel*, 1906, to *Ma France poétique*, 1926); the long litanies of Charles Péguy, inspired by the association of his strongly patriotic Catholic faith with the countryside of La Beauce (*La Tapisserie de sainte Geneviève et de Jeanne d'Arc*, 1912); and the cosmic *Cinq grandes odes* (1900) of Paul Claudel, a widely travelled diplomat, influenced by Rimbaud and by the rhythms of the Bible and Greek tragedy. Saint-John Perse, also a diplomat, writing from outside France, developed, later in the century, a similar vein of grand, universal, epic poetry in a kind of fluid, musical prose, with symbolic titles such as *Pluies* (1943) and *Amers* (1957).

A third, almost aggressively modern development appears with Apollinaire, who, like Picasso and the Cubists in painting, put together disparate objects and moods, broke up a coherent whole into fragmented and surprising juxtapositions and mingled traditional lyrical themes with strident modern images in *Alcools* (1913).

Surrealism dominated the inter-war years. It was both a social and a poetic revolution, attacking the norms of bourgeois society and aspiring to a poetry that would give a totally new perception of the world. The ideas behind it can be seen clearly in André Breton's Surrealist manifestos of 1924 and 1930, where he criticizes both society and the rationalist tendency to organize, explain and classify. He asserts even more firmly than writers of the nineteenth century the poet's role as investigator of the world behind reality and as searcher after truth. Stressing the value of the dream-world and the immediacy of childhood experience, acknowledging a great debt to Freud in the liberation of the subconscious, experimenting with automatic writing, fascinated by mental disorders, Breton wanted to tap the sources of poetic imagination and bring them to the surface in the power of the startling image, which he compared to a short circuit, fusing dream and reality into a kind of *surréalité*, and opening up vistas onto *le merveilleux*. Surrealist poetry therefore, like the paintings of Salvador Dali, is full of extraordinary images, often impossible to explain in rational terms and, indeed, intended to be virtually inexplicable. The best images, said Breton, are those which take the longest to 'traduire en langage pratique'.

Many modern poets began with the Surrealist movement and its negative predecessor Dadaism, although they moved eventually in different directions. Paul Eluard is perhaps the best-known, moving from Surrealist poetry in *La Vie immédiate* (1932), to a simpler lyricism in the committed poems of Resistance in occupied France (*Au Rendez-vous allemand*, 1944), and combining both kinds of inspiration in the collections of the post-war years. Like Breton he stresses the total power of poetry to break down barriers and renew life for everyone, not just for an élite. His work is often more immediately moving than that of other Surrealists because, writing above all about love, he draws on natural images of earth, fire, water, trees and flowers, and intersperses dense clutches of images with simple, though at times enigmatic statements. His poems frequently address his beloved (through whom the diversity of the world can be understood) and make her one with the natural elements in images of total intermingling. René Char, considered by some critics to be particularly representative of contemporary French poetry, followed a similar pattern, progressing from Surrealism to an active poetry of Resistance and, after the war, to the elaboration of a new, though fragile, faith in man.

The Second World War produced a great upsurge in poetry, accessible to a wide readership. Poems, with their allusive style, could pass the censor where prose could not. Themes of love, friendship, brotherhood and patriotism raised people's spirits and the very act of writing or reading poetry gave them a sense of dignity. Many well-known poets, some with their roots in Surrealism, produced 'popular' poems at this time – Desnos, Tardieu, Emmanuel, Char – but the best-known are probably Eluard and Aragon. Aragon drew on legends of old France to revive a spirit of patriotism and attained a simple directness of style in *Le Crève-cœur* (1941), *Les Yeux d'Elsa* (1942) and *La Diane française* (1945). Eluard's 'Liberté' became almost the hymn of the Resistance when it was adopted by the Gaullists in London and copies were parachuted into France.

During and after the war, poetry was also developing in many different ways with highly individual poets. Jules Supervielle, writing from South America, worked outside the mainstream with a fresh poetry of nature. Jacques Prévert, drawing on both the rhythms and language of the popular cabaret song and on the violent juxtaposed images of Surrealism, writes poems which typically attack bourgeois conventions and hypocrisy or evoke modern life and love in a wry, mocking yet sentimental vein (*Paroles*, 1946; *La Pluie et le beau temps*, 1955). Francis Ponge, whose best-known works are *Le Parti pris des choses* (1942) and *Proêmes* (1948), in poems very close to prose, full of wit and fantasy, writes a kind of 'scientific' poetry of objects, 'objeux', a mixture of 'objet' and 'jeu de mots'. Henri Michaux, from *Au Pays de la magie* (1941) to *Moments: traversées du temps* (1973), in a poetic prose of great vigour, explores the conflict between the self and the world, describing both real and imaginary countries and renewing the theme of the journey so important in the poetry of Baudelaire and Rimbaud. André Frénaud, after the Resistance poems of *Les Rois-Mages* (1943), with *Depuis toujours déjà* (1970) and *La Sorcière de Rome* (1973), evokes the paradoxes of time and death in what has been called 'un style sans repos d'une beauté mouvementée et contradictoire'.

After Michaux and Frénaud other poets have become established: Yves Bonnefoy, André du Bouchet, Philippe Jaccottet, Jacques Dupin, Michel Deguy, to name but a few, and a new generation is emerging, associated with the reviews *Action Poétique* (Jacques Roubaud) and *Tel Quel*.

One of the most important developments in French poetry has been the movement away from traditional verse forms to a free verse which is difficult to distinguish from poetic prose. In the nineteenth century Baudelaire had dreamt of 'le miracle d'une prose poétique, musicale sans rythme ni rime, assez souple et assez heurtée pour s'adapter aux mouvements lyriques de l'âme, aux ondulations de la rêverie, aux soubresauts de la conscience'. In the twentieth century the formal structures of French verse are finally abandoned. 'L'ancien jeu des vers' (Apollinaire) is replaced by a concern for poetic vision, for the suggestive power of imagery and by a love of rhythm which can function without any formal framework.

*　　　*　　　*

For theatre in France, the twentieth century has been a time of evolution and revolution. Although any attempt to contain within a few pages the heterogeneity of themes, styles, playwrights and plays must cut corners, it is hoped that by adopting two (of many possible) viewpoints, the dangers of arbitrary classifications and oversimplifications can be reduced.

The evolutionary processes are visible in the persistence or renewal of theatrical traditions which link modern drama to Greek and Roman antiquity, to the tragedy and comedy of classical French literature, to medieval religious drama and nineteenth-century Romanticism, at a time when playwrights and producers were adapting to such external forces as the arrival of cinema and television, and to changes in the political, philosophical and social climate caused by two world wars, the advent of Freudian psychoanalysis, Existentialism and the emancipation of women.

The revolutionary processes are particularly apparent on two occasions, both inspired as much by theatre's own internal dissatisfactions as by external pressures: the first occurs in the inter-war years when, through the collaboration of a talented group of producers like Jacques Copeau and gifted writers such as Cocteau, Giraudoux, Salacrou and Anouilh, there was a decisive reaction against 'slice of life' realism and facile, undemanding boulevard theatre; the second occurs in the 1950s with the eruption onto the Parisian stage of plays by Ionesco and Beckett who, with others, provide the latter half of the century with the Theatre of the Absurd or, as it is sometimes called, 'anti-théâtre'.

One particularly notable feature of the evolutionary process can be described as the *courant antique*, with plays like those of seventeenth-century tragedy, based on the myths and legends of classical antiquity. Gide's *Œdipe* (1931) and Giraudoux's *Electre* (1937) were followed by Sartre's treatment of the Orestes story in *Les Mouches* (1943) and by Anouilh's *Antigone* (1944). Comedy, too, has retained links with classical theatre: Giraudoux's *Amphi-tryon 38* (1929) is set in antiquity, whereas Anouilh's *Ornifle* (1955) is visibly and explicitly a modernization of the Don Juan theme treated by Molière, the dramatist to whom he refers as 'notre saint patron'. Traditional comedy based upon the exploitation of human weakness and the careful study of human psychology continues in plays like *Knock* (1923) by Jules Romains.

Another important thread can be called the *courant religieux*, providing a counterpoint to the humanism of Giraudoux and the atheism of Sartre. Within the period stretching from the miracle plays of Ghéon at the start of the century to the post-war drama of François Mauriac, the outstanding religious playwright is Paul Claudel. Whatever their spiritual effects, plays like *L'Annonce faite à Marie* (1916), set in the days when medieval cathedrals were under construction, and *Le Soulier de satin* (1943), a panorama of seventeenth-century Spanish colonialism and catholicism, have exerted an incalculable influence on modern theatre.

If this thematic approach is now translated into chronological terms, these and other elements of theatrical evolution, such as the recent emergence of the new or absurdist theatre, can be traced in three broad stages: first, drama in the post-Romantic and Naturalistic modes of the late nineteenth and early twentieth centuries, sometimes called the 'Belle Epoque'; then the inter-war years; and finally, the period since 1950 in which a new style of drama provides the theatrical equivalent of Surrealist poetry, post-Impressionist painting and the *nouveau roman*.

During the period up to the First World War and the early 1920s, theatre was active but somewhat repetitive and uninspiring. There were exceptions: the neo-Romantic plays of Rostand, such as *Cyrano de Bergerac* (1899) and *L'Aiglon* (1900), brought to the stage colour, energy and a swashbuckling splendour in a style that was particularly appealing when enlivened by the acting of Sarah Bernhardt or another of the *vedettes* of popular theatre; and there were the earnest examinations of contemporary problems by Eugène Brieux, whose treatment of motherhood in *Les Remplaçantes* (1900), of venereal disease in *Les Avariés* (1905), and of legal integrity in *L'Avocat* (1922) tend nowadays to be dismissed, perhaps a little too readily, as mere *pièces à thèse*. This period is best remembered for its frivolous and light-hearted dramatists. The plays of Courteline and Feydeau, of Flers and Caillavet, continued the mood of the 'naughty nineties' and attracted large audiences to what was skilful entertainment in the form of bedroom farces and trivial domestic upheavals. Inevitably, most of the plays in this first period have disappeared without trace, and the theatre of the day is considered drab and dull (hardly surprising, of course, in view of the lingering Naturalist mood). The tendency is to denigrate what remains by applying terms such as 'boulevard' or 'commercial'. However, 'boulevard theatre' has endured. In any case, theatre is both an artistic and a commercial endeavour, and this stock drama provided theatres, actors and audiences, essential ingredients without which revolutions later in the century could not prosper.

It was in the inter-war years that the first major revitalization of theatre occurred. Whether this phenomenon is called a 'flight from Naturalism' or given a label like 'studio theatre' or 'experimental drama', it is possible to isolate two particular factors which contributed to the creation of a new theatrical climate. The first was a changing attitude to the nature of drama, precipitated by the theories of Copeau and a group of influential directors known as the 'Cartel des Quatre', which consisted of Jouvet, Dullin, Pitoëff and Baty; the second was the simultaneous emergence of talented dramatists, like Cocteau and Giraudoux, Salacrou and Anouilh, to mention only a few, whose work shows a decisive reaction against 'slice of life' realism. Close collaboration between, for example, Dullin and Salacrou, and between Giraudoux and Jouvet brought with it a freshness and enthusiasm which stimulated the interest of practitioners and public in the act of theatrical creation, quite as much as in the 'tale to be told', and far more than in the photographic realism or the lavish splendour of earlier documentary and boulevard drama.

In the 1920s and 1930s, Cocteau and Salacrou presented unusual plays which disturbed the public by the novelty of their technique and their unfamiliar poetry. Whereas Cocteau, to the end of his career, retained his fondness for the eccentric and spectacular to the point of introducing motorcycles in his Orpheus films, and contriving statues in which the circulation of blood was visible, Salacrou adopted a more accessible manner, but without sacrificing inventiveness. His sureness of theatrical touch is apparent in plays like *L'Inconnue d'Arras* (1935), which deals with an incident in the First World War, and *Les Nuits de la colère* (1946), whose subject is the Resistance movement in the Second World War. One of his most powerful plays is *Boulevard Durand* (1961), the chronicle of a trade union leader wrongfully punished for strike action in 1910, when Salacrou was a boy living in Le Havre. Giraudoux, coming to theatre as an established novelist, provided a successful series of more literary plays. Anouilh has been dubbed the poor man's Giraudoux, and, even though the majority of his plays have been produced since 1945, his work as playwright is essentially in the spirit of pre-war theatre.

The second theatrical revolution took place soon after the Second World War. In the 1950s, a tremor was felt in small Parisian theatres on the Left Bank, the effects of which have been quite as influential and enduring as the upheaval in French poetry in the 1920s or as the advent of the *nouveau roman*.

In fact, the first stirrings of this new drama can be traced as far back as Alfred Jarry, whose grotesque character, King Ubu, began to bludgeon Parisian audiences from his very first word ('Merdre') in 1896; or Apollinaire's *Les Mamelles de Tirésias* (1917), whose heroine decided to divest herself of her femininity, become a soldier (at which moment two balloons erupt from her corsage, dangling overhead for the remainder of the play), and leave to her husband the task of raising a family (of 49,212 children). Hardly surprisingly, such totally non-realist plays, as they became more popular in the 1950s, were grouped together under the title of the Theatre of the Absurd.

Of the many writers, such as Genet, Audiberti, Vian and Schehadé whose plays belong to this new theatrical style, probably the best-known are Eugène Ionesco and Samuel Beckett; but there are, between them and between the other dramatists, so many differences that this *nouveau théâtre* or avant-garde theatre should not be seen as a unified phenomenon. However, even if these playwrights do not form as coherent a school as the nineteenth-century Romantics, there are common qualities and characteristics, the most obvious of which is that they struggle consciously, often self-consciously, to avoid resembling traditional theatre. Even the subtitles of Ionesco's early plays advertise the mood of this 'anti-théâtre': *La Cantatrice chauve* is called an *anti-pièce*; *La Leçon* is a *drame comique*; and *Les Chaises* is a *farce tragique*.

In spite of its varied manifestations, the Theatre of the Absurd differs significantly from earlier theatre in its attitude or mood and in its methods. Behind the wild, frenetic humour, the point of view of this new theatrical activity is one of despair and anguish with an insistence on the absurdity of the human condition.

Anguish, of course, recalls Jean-Paul Sartre, just as the notion of absurdity recalls both Sartre and Albert Camus, two more conventional dramatists whose plays belong chronologically to the third period of twentieth-century theatre. In addition to re-explorations of antiquity (Sartre's *Les Mouches*), both wrote plays on political and historical subjects; and in at least one play each of them attempted to convey the absurdity of the human condition by choosing a central character who was mad (Franz in Sartre's *Les Séquestrés d'Altona*, 1959, and Camus's hero in *Caligula*, 1945). Their methods differ markedly, however, from those of the new dramatists.

The genuinely post-war theatre does not argue about the absurdity of the world; it demonstrates it. Indeed, it abuses, misuses and denigrates language so that, instead of rational argument and discursive thought, the audience is presented with theatrical images designed to portray the absurd. The aim is not to make the spectator intellectually conscious, but to provoke an emotional response by a violent onslaught of absurdity presented physically.

La Cantatrice chauve is a good example. At the superficial level of 'What happens?', the answer must be 'Not much!' In their middle-class, suburban English home, Mr and Mrs Smith are waiting for their maid to return from the cinema and for their guests, Monsieur and Madame Martin, to arrive. They do – together with another unexpected guest – and that is the sum total of the plot. It may strike us as odd that, at the end of the play, the Smiths leave and the Martins occupy their chairs by the fireside – but if that is the first thing to strike the audience, something has gone wrong with the production. Much is striking, starting with the English chimes of the English clock which punctuate the dialogue – and the choice of the word dialogue is important, for the exchanges never form a conversation if that term indicates any degree of communication. The characters do not listen to each other; Monsieur and Madame Martin do not even recognize each other; the only person quite sure of her identity is the maid who proclaims: 'My name is Sherlock Holmes.' The idiocy of the comments spills over into the stage directions: we are, for

example, told at one point that 'M. Martin embrasse ou n'embrasse
pas Madame Smith'. There is, as Ionesco describes it in his *Notes et
contre-notes*, 'a collapse of reality'.

The other major figure whose plays continue to shock and
disturb and entertain is Samuel Beckett. It is hard to describe
today the sensation created by the appearance of *En attendant
Godot* (1953). The acting profession and theatre-goers have grown
accustomed to the new style which this play introduced, and
which Beckett has sustained at regular intervals with such other
plays as *Fin de partie* (1957) and *La Dernière Bande* (1958). His
later plays became so lean and taut, to the point of dispensing not
only with plot but also dialogue, that Beckett seemed to be veering
towards a 'theatre of nothingness'.

The course of twentieth-century drama, from the documentary
dramas of Brieux to the absurdist theatre, might be called a flight,
not only from Naturalism, but also from the natural and normal; a
flight not only from Realism but even from reality itself, as the
public is transported more and more frequently into worlds of
fantasy and illusion, insanity and derangement, dream and
nightmare, to make the acquaintance there of characters who are
progressively deprived of such normal attributes as a recognizably
standard mind, a recognizable body and even of life itself. In one
sense, there might even seem to be a flight from theatre itself: there
are fewer theatres, dwindling audiences and a reduced number of
dramatists in France – as in other European countries. Contemporary drama, reflecting a loss of confidence in traditional values
and producing a laughter which is often sour and bitter, has caused
some critics to despair. Tynan looked unhopefully for a new
generation of writers who would leave 'the blind alley into which
Messrs Beckett and Ionesco have beguiled them'. The future will
show whether theatre returns to the distortions produced by the
camera or whether today's imaginative representations continue to
be accepted as the truer reality.

*   *   *

The novel, like any other genre, reflects the radical upheavals in
the wider world during the twentieth century. Initially it
undergoes numerous technical changes – in structure, narrative
point of view and style. It also performs a wide variety of different
tasks: some writers see it as an instrument of self-discovery, others
as a way of bearing witness to historical realities, yet others as a
forum for examining religious or political beliefs – and the list is
nowhere near complete. Before the middle of the century the pre-
eminence it has enjoyed since Balzac and Stendhal is increasingly

being questioned, as newer art-forms come to rival its popularity, and its traditional territories of social analysis and psychological exploration have to be shared with rising academic disciplines.

By the beginning of the century Naturalism was in serious decline. Zola's own last novels with their spiritual dimension were far removed from the atmosphere of *Thérèse Raquin* and *L'Assommoir*, and his followers had moved off in other directions – Huysmans, for instance, writing a series tracing the progress of a largely autobiographical hero towards Catholicism. More and more it was felt that fiction based on determinist principles was a dead end – hence, in the resolutely undeterminist *Les Caves du Vatican* (1913), Gide giving his central character an address in the '*impasse* Claude Bernard', a clear hint that Zola's mentor was no longer leading anywhere. The novelists most solidly established in the pre-war years were Maurice Barrès, a pillar of French nationalism (and thus, thirty years on, the object of Sartre's displeasure in *La Nausée*), and Anatole France, one of the models for Proust's Bergotte and author of *Les Dieux ont soif* (1912), an outstanding novel of the 1789 Revolution.

It is, however, Proust and Gide themselves who dominate the first two decades. In *A la recherche du temps perdu* (1913–27) Proust certainly plays the traditional role of social chronicler, but he combines this with tracing his narrator's path to self-discovery; as Ramon Fernandez puts it, the work is 'à la fois l'histoire d'une époque et l'histoire d'une conscience'. And the second element is the one which stands out. For all the brilliant observation (high society, bourgeois family life, homosexual behaviour, Paris in wartime) the introspective first-person narrative gives the main emphasis to the quest which ends with the discovery of an artistic vocation. Introspection and the values of art are also keynotes of Gide's work, in spite of the considerable differences between the two writers. *Récits* such as *L'Immoraliste* (1902) and *La Porte étroite* (1909), again using first-person narrators, chart the extremes of self-absorption; *Les Faux-Monnayeurs* (1926) – the only work of Gide's which he consistently thought worthy of the label *roman* – turns the form in on itself by following the development of a novel in progress (itself to be called *Les Faux-Monnayeurs*).

Gide's subsequent fiction had relatively little impact; Proust died in 1922, and the final volume of his novel appeared five years later; and Alain-Fournier, author of the poetic evocation of lost youth, *Le Grand Meaulnes* (1913), had been killed at the beginning of the Great War. By the end of the 1920s the recently-dominant elements have effectively receded. The First World War had produced convincing testimonies of the fighting, such as Barbusse's *Le Feu* (1916) and Dorgelès's *Les Croix de bois* (1919), but during the 1920s a reaction set in, and the novel often served as a form of escapism, an antidote to contemporary disasters. Alain-Fournier's 'domaine merveilleux' was sought, in different ways, by both Cocteau in *Les Enfants terribles* (1929) and by Colette in *La Fin de Chéri* (1926). Jean Giraudoux's stories, while revealing an awareness of recent history, are best characterized by their vein of poetic fantasy, as in *Siegfried et le Limousin* (1922). But this mood of 'grandes vacances' could not last indefinitely; in the telling image of one critic, the literary Maginot Line was circumvented – just as the physical one would be. Serious issues once more forced their way into the realm of fiction: towards the end of the decade a number of important writers were, for instance, exploring moral and religious dilemmas. Although Julien Green, François Mauriac and Georges Bernanos were all Catholics, it is perhaps wise to respect their individuality by avoiding the term 'the Catholic novel'. Nevertheless, in Green's *Léviathan* (1929), Bernanos's *Sous le soleil de Satan* (1926), or any of Mauriac's works, metaphysical evil is a powerful and destructive force.

It is in this period, too, that contemporary events again demand a prominent place. The economic crisis following the Wall Street crash of 1929 was severely affecting the life of France by the early 1930s, and a new generation of novelists could not turn their backs on history in the making. It was soon apparent that a crucial change was taking place. In the words of Michel Raimond, 'aux romanciers tournés vers eux-mêmes succèdent, en 1930, les romanciers tournés vers le monde'. Céline, in *Voyage au bout de la nuit* (1932), goes back to the beginning of the Great War, but then exposes in devastating detail the horrors of the crazy modern world – the exploitation of the colonies, the dehumanization of the production line in America, the squalor and disease of the working-class suburbs of Paris. Others, too, would recall the war, but Céline's style, annexing the rhythms and vocabulary of popular speech, gives his work a unique flavour. An equally noteworthy novel is André Malraux's *La Condition humaine* (1933). True to its ambitious title, it rises above the minutiae of history, using the communist uprising in Shanghai in 1927 to present a whole universe of conflict – between tradition and change, left and right, oriental and western values, action and passivity. Characters are significant less as individuals than as representative figures – Tchen the terrorist, Gisors the intellectual, Katow the Communist Party faithful, Ferral the capitalist. But no simple solution is offered for the problems of mankind: this would be quite out of keeping for a writer who saw the modern novel as 'un moyen d'expression privilégié du tragique de l'homme'. Malraux's work is also distinguished by its innovative technique, which draws on, for instance, cinematic montage and journalistic presentation; it is no coincidence that Malraux was at different times involved in films and in the production of newspapers. Others promoted specific political viewpoints in their fiction – whether of the Right (Drieu la Rochelle, Brasillach) or the Left (Aragon, Nizan). Less tendentiously, novel-cycles (*romans-fleuve*), such as Martin du Gard's *Les Thibault* and Duhamel's *Chronique des Pasquier*, embraced recent or contemporary history while focusing on one character, or family or other social group.

Various writers shared Malraux's practice of making fiction an access to the world of action. Most typical of these, Saint-Exupéry introduces his reader to the experience of flying, and contrasts the sharpened awareness of the pilot with the inert, banal existence of the modern man in the street. But Saint-Exupéry came closer to the bulk of his contemporaries when he found himself inextricably involved in historical events after the outbreak of the Second World War. His *Pilote de guerre* (published in New York in 1942) was the work of a Frenchman prepared to express his hostility to the German invasion. The conditions of the Occupation obviously had a great effect on literary production; poetry was better suited to clandestine distribution than the novel, and was perhaps more likely to escape censorship. Even so, notable works of fiction did appear, such as *Le Silence de la mer* (1942) by the Resistance writer known as 'Vercors', who with this volume launched the publishing house Les Editions de Minuit.

Once the war was over, a different atmosphere was perceptible. Jean-Paul Sartre had started writing fiction somewhat earlier, but his novel *La Nausée* (1938) pointed forward rather than back. One perceptive critic has suggested 'the invasion of the novel by metaphysics' as the outstanding development between the 1930s and the 1960s; this fictionalized diary – a form which enables Sartre to present the absurdity of society and the material world as lived experience, not abstract philosophy – is a key example of the process. Sartre also published the short stories of *Le Mur* (1939), and three volumes of the uncompleted cycle *Les Chemins de la liberté* (1945–9), before abandoning this form of literature altogether. Simone de Beauvoir, perhaps best known for her feminist study *Le Deuxième Sexe* (1949) and her later autobiographical writings, tackled ethical issues in novels such as *Le Sang des autres* (1945), which covered the period of the Occupation and the Resistance. But the greatest achievement within this philosophically-based group (given his personal opposition to it, 'Existentialist' may seem a questionable label) is no doubt that of Albert Camus. *L'Etranger* (1942) is a classic study of nonconformism and alienation, the more compelling for being presented from Meursault's own, uncompromising point of view. With *La Peste* (1947), Camus adds a stoical brand of resistance to his statement of the absurdity of life: the efforts of Dr Rieux and his colleagues in their fight against the symbolic plague have a positive value, and their exemplary solidarity supports Rieux's contention that 'il y a dans les hommes plus de choses à admirer que de choses à mépriser'. On the other hand, in *La Chute* (1956), a series of monologues (or, more accurately, one side of a set of dialogues) offers a much darker, more cynical view, as the renegade lawyer Clamence displays his own reprehensible characteristics and then subtly insinuates that they apply equally to his interlocutor – or, perhaps, to the reader.

The prominence of Sartre and Camus in the 1940s and 1950s should not obscure the variety of forms and directions the novel takes before, during and after their heyday. Raymond Queneau, whose best novel, *Le Chiendent*, dates from 1933, explores the vast potential of the genre, experimenting – often playfully – with language and narrative technique, while at the same time treating serious traditional novelistic themes. His younger contemporary, Boris Vian, creates a world of fantasy and verbal invention in texts such as *L'Ecume des jours* (1947). Jean Giono, whose career began with idyllic nature novels in the vein of *Colline* (1928), goes on to write a well-received account of the Great War in *Le Grand Troupeau* (1931), and, later, *Le Hussard sur le toit* (1951), a Stendhalian evocation of the 1830s. Henry de Montherlant, most readily associated with a cult of heroism and masculinity (*Les Bestiaires*, 1926; *Pitié pour les femmes*, 1936), remains a significant figure into the 1970s.

By the early 1950s a number of major writers can be seen to break radically with widely held traditional novelistic attitudes, including the ambition of attracting a large readership – and with more recent notions such as that of 'committed' literature. Beckett's trilogy of *Molloy*, *Malone meurt* and *L'Innommable* (1951–3), for example, tends to abandon the recognizable world of physical objects for an unstable territory of verbal confusion. Nathalie Sarraute, in the essays of *L'Ere du soupçon*, challenges the technique of characterization established in the nineteenth century and so often uncritically accepted thereafter. In her own creative works, such as the early *Tropismes* (1939) or *Martereau* (1953), she aims at a less stereotyped presentation of personality and behaviour. Alain Robbe-Grillet, from his first novel *Les Gommes* (1953), turns away from most of the conventions on which the novel has hitherto been built – plot, chronology, and what, in one of his essays, he calls 'les "significations" (psychologiques, sociales, fonctionnelles)'. Michel Butor, who explicitly considers the novel to be a 'recherche', reworks notions of time and space in *Degrés* (1960), and disturbs the normal relationship between narrator and reader by beginning *La Modification* (1957) with a disconcerting

'Vous'. Claude Simon exploits the uncertainties of language and chronological development in early novels such as *La Route des Flandres* (1960), and conceives some of his later works as systems of collages. The term 'nouveau roman' becomes an increasingly unsatisfactory one. For one thing, the common ground between the authors in question is slight: little beyond a general hostility to ossified tradition and, in most cases, the fact of being published by Les Editions de Minuit. For another, with the passing of time, newness is less and less the preserve of Robbe-Grillet or Butor.

Subsequent developments are by no means easy to chart. It would be impossible, for instance, to locate precisely a writer such as Marguerite Duras, whose use of dialogue and silence brilliantly communicates the dilemmas of her none-too-articulate characters. Elsewhere Georges Pérec has continued Queneau's explorations in his own idiosyncratic style; Michel Tournier has found new ways to reactivate ancient myths; and, meanwhile, other writers have been making their mark in more accessible and even traditional idioms – Françoise Sagan, with her pessimistic but plausible pictures of modern love; Christiane Rochefort, capturing with humour and realism the experiences of a young girl reaching maturity in the Parisian suburbs; Patrick Modiano, recalling the mood of the 1940s.

Further reading

J. Ardagh, *France in the 1980s* (1982); J. Flower (ed.), *France Today* (5th edn 1983); J. McMillan, *Dreyfus to De Gaulle* (1984); P. Ouston, *France in the Twentieth Century* (1972).

J. Bersani *et al.*, *La Littérature en France de 1945 à 1968* (1970); M. Bradbury and J. McFarlane (eds.), *Modernism (1890–1930)*, (1976); J. Flower, *Writers and Politics in Modern France (1909–1961)*, (1977); W. Fowlie, *A Guide to Contemporary French Literature from Valéry to Sartre* (1957); H. Moore, *Twentieth-Century French Literature to World War II* (1966); C. Robinson, *French Literature in the Twentieth Century* (1980); B. Vercier *et al.*, *La Littérature en France depuis 1968* (1982).

T. Hawkes, *Structuralism and Semiotics* (1977); J. Macquarrie, *Existentialism* (1973); M. Nadeau, *History of Surrealism* (1965); R. Shattuck, *The Banquet Years: the Arts in France 1885–1915* (1958); C. Smith, *Contemporary French Philosophy* (1964); J. Sturrock (ed.), *Structuralism and Since: from Levi-Strauss to Derrida* (1979); K. Reader, *Intellectuals and the French Left in France since 1968* (1987).

M. Bishop, *The Contemporary Poetry of France* (1985); M. Bishop (ed.), *The Language of Poetry: Crisis and Solution* (1980);

M. Caws, *The Poetry of Dada and Surrealism* (1970); M. Caws (ed.), *About French Poetry from Dada to 'Tel Quel'; Text and Theory* (1974); C. Hackett, *New French Poetry. An Anthology* (1973); I. Higgins (ed.), *Anthology of Second World War French Poetry* (1982); J. Matthews, *Surrealist Poetry in France* (1969); J. Rousselot (ed.), *Dictionnaire de la poésie française contemporaine* (1968); J.-P. Richard, *Onze études sur la poésie moderne* (1974).

D. Bradby, *Modern French Drama, 1940–80* (1984); J. Chiari, *The Contemporary French Theatre* (1958); M. Esslin, *The Theatre of the Absurd* (1962); D. Grossvogel, *Twentieth-Century French Drama* (1958); J. Guicharnaud, *Modern French Theatre from Giraudoux to Beckett* (1961); H. Hobson, *French Theatre of Today* (1953); D. Knowles, *French Drama of the Inter-War Years 1918–39* (1967); R. Lalou, *Le Théâtre en France depuis 1900* (1961); L. Pronko, *Avant-Garde – the Experimental Theatre in France* (1964); P.-H. Simon, *Théâtre et destin* (1959).

G. Brée and M. Guiton, *An Age of Fiction: the French Novel from Gide to Camus* (1957); J. Cruickshank (ed.), *The Novelist as Philosopher: Studies in French Fiction, 1935–1960* (1962); A. Jefferson, *The Nouveau Roman and the Poetics of Fiction* (1980); V. Mercier, *The French New Novel: from Queneau to Pinget* (1971); H. Peyre, *French Novelists of Today* (1967); M. Raimond, *La Crise du roman: des lendemains du naturalisme aux années vingt* (1966); J. Sturrock, *The French New Novel* (1969).

ALAIN-FOURNIER (Henri-Alban Fournier) (1886–1914)

Alain-Fournier was a schoolmaster's son from the Sologne, south of the Loire, and both of these biographical circumstances feature prominently in his writing. In a short, unspectacular career he studied in Paris and worked as a literary journalist before dying in action at the beginning of the First World War. He left unfinished a novel and a play, while much of his completed work was published in *Miracles* (1924). However, his reputation rests almost entirely on one immensely successful novel, *Le Grand Meaulnes*, which has been widely read and discussed ever since its appearance in 1913.

As a young writer Alain-Fournier was firmly opposed to the excesses of the nineteenth-century realistic novel, preferring instead the poetry of Laforgue and Rimbaud; and even when, by 1910, he was drawn to narrative fiction, the same instincts remained. The prose of the finished novel is rhythmic and musical, and makes effective use of devices such as alliteration, which are more usually a feature of verse. There is a powerful visual appeal, too; a whole country scene can be captured in a sentence such as: 'Sur la route blanchie de givre, les petits oiseaux tourbillonnaient autour des pieds de l'âne trottinant.' The text also owes much of its strength to the pervasive patterns of imagery, such as that relating to the sea: the houses at La Ferté-d'Angillon resemble moored boats; Meaulnes and Yvonne, alone after their wedding, are like 'deux passagers dans un bateau à la dérive'. The story – from Meaulnes's dramatic arrival in Sainte-Agathe, his stumbling on the seemingly enchanted world of the 'domaine mystérieux', his quest to find Frantz's lost fiancée, and the death of Yvonne, on to the hero's final return – is told by Meaulnes's friend François Seurel. His narrative, dating from fifteen years or more after the events described, maintains a strong sense of mystery by reproducing events as Seurel learned of them, rather than using the benefits of hindsight. It is, moreover, extremely effective in conveying the perceptions and outlook of the young Seurel – his attitude to school routine, his delight in the beauties of nature, his personal diffidence – and, more generally, in putting forward a youthful view of things. Adults count for relatively little in this world, and the main characters – especially Seurel – are often shown as being reluctant to grow up. This ethos admirably serves the theme of the friendship of the young, linking Meaulnes with Frantz, and Seurel with Yvonne, as well as binding together the two major figures; equally, it is an apt setting for the exploration of love, both the idealized desire Meaulnes feels for Yvonne and his more earth-bound relationship with Valentine. Meaulnes's burden of guilt (after he unwittingly becomes engaged to Frantz's fiancée), and the grim dénouement (with Yvonne dying in childbirth, and then Meaulnes returning to take the baby from Seurel) might suggest that the work is a tragedy. However, this is but one reading among many, for interpretations vary widely. *Le Grand Meaulnes* has been praised as a romance like *Wuthering Heights* or even a successor to the stories of the Round Table knights, criticized as an exercise in irresponsible wish-fulfilment, and proclaimed to have a Christian message. On a formal level, some have hailed it as a classically balanced novel, while others have seen nothing more than an overblown short story. All of which, at the very least, proves its rich diversity. But given both the central theme of irretrievable purity and the fact of Alain-Fournier's premature death, most readers will be left with a double sense of loss.

Further reading

Le Grand Meaulnes, ed. R. Gibson (1968); R. Gibson, *The Land Without a Name* (1975); D. Arkell, *Alain-Fournier: A Brief Life (1886–1914)* (1986); R. Gibson, *Alain-Fournier: 'Le Grand Meaulnes'* (1986).

Workpoints

1   'Poetry' or 'Realism'? What is the balance between observed reality and creative imagination in *Le Grand Meaulnes*? Consider the claim that: 'Ce n'était pas seulement le domaine merveilleux qui laissait paraître une réalité transfigurée; mais la réalité la plus quotidienne était pénétrée de poésie' (*M. Raimond*).

2   *The Narrator*. How important is his contribution to the story? How does it compare with that of the other main characters? How far would you agree that 'his imprint on the book is . . . so indelible that it could, perfectly appropriately, have borne the title *Le Petit Seurel*' (*R. Gibson*)?

3   *Interpretation*. Discuss Alain-Fournier's own claim: 'Je n'ai pas pensé à faire un livre de moral. J'ai voulu faire un livre vivant. . . . Je n'ai pas voulu faire des personnages moraux ni sympathiques. J'ai d'abord pensé à les faire vivants.'

Jean ANOUILH (1910–87)

In a declaration made to Hubert Gignoux when the first critical study of his drama was being prepared, Anouilh said: 'Je n'ai pas de biographie et j'en suis très content.' He maintained this modest attitude throughout his entire, entirely successful career as playwright and latterly as director, preferring to be remembered as a craftsman of theatre: 'un homme de métier', 'un fabricant de pièces' rather than as a celebrity.

Little by little, various biographical details have emerged: he was born in Bordeaux where his father was a tailor (like Messerschmann in *L'Invitation au château*, 1946); his mother was a musician (which suggests some private joke in his frequent references to the Conservatoire d'Arcachon); like Molière, for whom he had an immense admiration, he studied law, but Anouilh then settled for work as a copywriter in an advertising agency until he had the opportunity to move into the theatre as secretary to Louis Jouvet, one of the outstanding actors and directors of the inter-war years. For personal reasons, this two-year collaboration (1930–2) was far from successful; but it was during this time that Anouilh's first play was performed (not by Jouvet) and he took the decision to devote himself to theatre.

His first major success was *Le Voyageur sans bagage* (1936), and thereafter the story of his life for thirty or forty years was really a list of his plays, a regular succession of Parisian triumphs, many of which were rapidly translated and performed abroad. They have been grouped into collections with very distinctive titles such as

Pièces roses, *Pièces noires*, *Pièces brillantes* and *Pièces grinçantes*, but there is no really valid distinction between the pink and the black. Anouilh contrives a highly individual and skilful fusion of the comic and the tragic, not merely within any particular play or scene but even within an isolated speech. Colette was clearly captivated by Anouilh's extraordinary skill in changing key, when she wrote: 'Il m'est doux, dans *Le Voyageur sans bagage*, qu'un sanglot crève en éclat de rire et qu'un échange comique de reparties amasse des larmes.' The technical brilliance of his theatre is universally acknowledged, even by those critics for whom Anouilh's plays lack depth and substance.

In addition to the contribution made by Molière to his apprenticeship, the 'bon artisan' readily acknowledges the influence of Marivaux and Giraudoux whose charm, graceful language, wit and ingenuity have appreciably influenced his own style. And yet, from the earliest of his *pièces roses* and *pièces noires*, Anouilh presented an unmistakably personal flavour and a distinctive outlook. *Le Bal des voleurs* (1932) and *Léocadia* (1939) are delightful, light-hearted comedies remarkable for their freshness and humour, and above all for an atmosphere of enchantment and unreality. Even so, beneath the pink, sugar-coated surface, there is already a trace of the sadness and despair of the black plays in his repertory; for the conventional happy ending which unites the young lovers in both plays is so improbable that, by its artificiality, it raises doubts about the durability of the relationship; it hints at an eventual outcome diametrically opposed to the mood and tone of the preceding play.

The impossibility of attaining any lasting happiness without sacrificing personal integrity is the central problem which emerges more clearly in the *pièces noires*, of which *La Sauvage* (1934) is an early example. When she rejects the man with whom she is sincerely in love, Thérèse Tarde establishes herself as the first of a long line of heroines in Anouilh's theatre who say 'No' to a life of unworthy compromise. In *Antigone* (1944), and in *L'Alouette* (1952), the imaginatively dramatized history of Joan of Arc, the two heroines prefer to die rather than allow themselves to be tainted by the corrupting influences and mediocre satisfactions of life.

There is undeniably a sameness in Anouilh's theatre. As W. D. Howarth puts it: 'No reader can penetrate far into Anouilh's theatre without being struck by "family likenesses" between the individual plays; the recurrence of similar themes, characters and human relationships, the echoing of sentiments from one play to another . . . soon become familiar characteristics.' Indeed, it is this similarity which gives cohesion to the entire work. Its appeal comes in part from the sparkling inventiveness of dialogue and in part from the altered shading, the slight, almost imperceptible variations which Anouilh brings to a persistent theme: the dramatist's attempt to explore, perhaps to define, and certainly to come to terms with an elusive ideal.

For numerous critics, if not for the theatre-going public, the new wave of absurdist theatre has swept Anouilh away, with the result that his evolution in recent years has been neglected. The dramatist is, like the ideal itself, elusive, not simply because of his modesty, but because of his reluctance to espouse some philosophical, social or political creed, and because of his determination to remain a dramatist rather than become a theoretician. There has been recognition of what Gabriel Marcel calls 'ce sens proprement infaillible de l'efficacité théâtrale'; there has been little analysis of his deceptively commonplace yet poetic dialogue, and little investigation of his tenacious concern for the processes of theatrical creativity, which can be traced not in manifestos but in the occasional programme note, not in pronouncements but in a series of later plays starting with *La Grotte* (1960).

Further reading

E. Marsh, *Jean Anouilh, Poet of Pierrot and Pantaloon* (1953); J. Harvey, *Anouilh, a Study in Theatrics* (1964); M. Archer, *Jean Anouilh* (1971); H. McIntyre, *The Theatre of Jean Anouilh* (1981). Critical editions with useful introductions: *Antigone*, ed. W. Landers (1960); *Le Bal des Voleurs*, ed. W. Howarth (1960); *L'Alouette*, ed. M. Thomas and S. Lee (1964); *Le Voyageur sans bagage*, ed. W. Hodson (1986).

Workpoints

1 *Anouilh's technical skill*: 'As a craftsman, Anouilh is second to none in the contemporary French theatre' (*D. Knowles*). 'The striking but frequently shallow theatricalism of Anouilh' (*K. Tynan*).

2 *Characterization*: 'Le théâtre, c'est d'abord et avant tout des personnages' (*J. Anouilh*). 'The character (usually a young girl) who refuses to compromise with life and prefers death or certain unhappiness is in most of his plays' (*G. Brereton*). 'Human beings are replaced by brilliant talking marionettes' (*M. McGowan*).

3 *Ideas*: 'It is hardly an exaggeration to say that there is only one central theme running through the whole of Anouilh's work – the eternal and universal conflict between idealism and reality' (*H. McIntyre*).

'Je n'ai pas de pensées politiques. . . . La critique sociale ne m'intéresse pas. Il faut moquer l'homme, cela suffit' (*J. Anouilh*).

4 *Outlook*: 'En dépit d'une fantasie et d'un génie comique souvent irrésistibles, Anouilh est franchement pessimiste' (*Lagarde et Michard*).
'Anouilh has marked out for himself an idiosyncratic no-man's land between comedy and tragedy' (*W. Howarth*).

Guillaume APOLLINAIRE (Wilhelm Apollinaris de Kostrowitsky) (1880–1918)

Apollinaire is a poet of contrasts, bestriding two centuries, combining the old and the new in both content and form, marked by a restlessness and desire for permanence which in part is explained by his rootless life.

His biography is one which lends itself to myth-making, and Apollinaire himself was not averse to making it seem more bizarre than it already was. Born of a Polish adventuress and an unidentified father (actually an Italian officer, although Apollinaire liked to give a more scandalous parentage in the Vatican), he settled with his mother in Paris and made France his adopted country. Two other regions left their mark on his literary output: the Belgian Ardennes where he spent a brief holiday in 1899 and began to write stories and poems, and the German Rhineland where, he was inspired by the forests and legends of Germany. While employed as a tutor, he fell unhappily in love with an English governess, Annie Pleyden. Many of the poems in his best-known collection of poetry, *Alcools* (published 1913), found their source here.

Back in Paris he moved in a circle of poets and painters, notably Picasso and the Cubists, with whose work his poetry has often been compared. In their different ways they were all restructuring reality into new into new and startling forms. Apollinaire's precarious hold on a stable existence in France was threatened at this point by an extraordinary episode, typical of his irreverent and exuberant life, in which he was arrested in 1911 and held briefly on suspicion of having stolen the *Mona Lisa*. On the outbreak of war he enlisted and was severely wounded. Returning to Paris he had his Surrealist play, *Les Mamelles de Tirésias*, performed, and his second collection of poetry, *Calligrammes*, was published a few months before his death in 1918.

In one sense Apollinaire was a traditional lyric poet, drawing inspiration from personal experience: 'Chacun de mes poèmes est la commémoration d'un événement de ma vie et le plus souvent il s'agit de tristesse, mais j'ai des joies aussi que je chante.' Lost love, the passing of time, autumn, death: one could almost be enumerating the themes of a Romantic poet like Lamartine rather than a twentieth-century poet lauded by the Surrealists. An anthology piece like 'Le Pont Mirabeau' with its haunting refrain and song-like development of a single central image – the flowing river as symbol of the passing of time and love – reinforces this view of Apollinaire, as do some of the simpler Rhineland poems of *Alcools*.

However this simple, lyrical tone is not Apollinaire's characteristic style. A poem of *Calligrammes*, 'La Jolie Rousse', expresses his position between the old and the new: 'Je juge cette longue querelle de la tradition et de l'invention / De l'Ordre et de l'Aventure,' and his poems typically combine, in new and surprising juxtapositions, traditional lyricism with jarring, modern subject-matter and language, and a broken verse-form. The spell of a unified, musical verse is shattered by ironic or humorous asides; incongruous details stray across the scene; strange and often violent images surface. The discordant jangle of the modern city makes its most strident entry into French poetry. The opening poem of *Alcools* gives the characteristic note with its assimilation of the shepherdess watching her flocks and the Eiffel tower watching over the bridges of Paris: 'Bergère ô tour Eiffel le troupeau des ponts bêle ce soir.'

Apollinaire's search for identity in this fragmented world permeates many of his poems, several of them containing wandering, restless figures: gypsies, strolling players. It is expressed particularly clearly in 'Cortège':

> Un jour je m'attendais moi-même
> Je me disais Guillaume il est temps que tu viennes
> Et d'un lyrique pas s'avançaient ceux que j'aime
> Parmi lesquels je n'étais pas.

Apollinaire experimented with many verse-forms, both traditional and free verse, but above all he wanted the freedom to use whatever form and whatever language seemed appropriate. After Hugo's injection of life into a dying classical vocabulary, we now have a second revolution in which all kinds of language, from slang to high-flown classical allusion, can be mixed and mingled in the same poem. The most obvious experimentation with form is in the poems of *Calligrammes*, which use typographical layout to reinforce the meaning of the poems, but *Alcools* also has great variety and is immediately striking in its total lack of punctuation. This flexibility of form, total mixing of varied subject-matter and different registers of language, of deep seriousness and flippant levity, make Apollinaire one of the first truly twentieth-century poets.

Further reading

M. Davies, *Apollinaire* (1964); S. Bates, *Guillaume Apollinaire* (1967); L. Breunig, *Guillaume Apollinaire* (1969); R. Little, *Apollinaire* (1976); '*Alcools*', ed. G. Rees (1975).

Workpoints

1 'Apollinaire is indeed much less a love poet than a poet of lost love' (*R. Little*).

2 'Apollinaire was rarely solemn and played a major part in putting the fun back into poetry' (*R. Little*).

3 Georges Duhamel wrote a devastating review of *Alcools* when it appeared, comparing it to a junk shop full of miscellaneous bric-à-brac, none of it original. Do you think there is any justification for this opinion? How would you refute it?

4 'He is at the same time a poet belonging to a bygone age and the most dynamic symbol of his own era' (*Broome and Chesters*). Identify these two sides of Apollinaire's poetry and see how they are combined.

5 '*Alcools* apparaît comme un manuel pour duper le temps par le souvenir de l'amour, pour confondre passé et présent. C'est le poème du Temps' (*J. Roudaut*). Look at the different ways the theme of time is treated in *Alcools*.

Samuel BECKETT (b. 1906)

Beckett is one of the major figures of modern European drama, a remarkable achievement for one who has said: 'I am not interested in the theatre.' The production of his first play, *En attendant Godot* (1953), created a sensation. The public was bewildered by its novelty and fascinated or appalled by its disturbing blend of tragedy and farce. At first, many were inclined to dismiss it, but the play ran far longer than Beckett or his critics expected. Notoriety based on shock gradually changed into success based on respect for the bleak but skilful portrayal of suffering in an absurd world, and for the play's daringly original technique. *En attendant Godot* is now established as a classic in the Theatre of the Absurd. It has been translated and performed in over twenty countries. Beckett continued to write for the theatre (usually in French because, he claims, it is easier to write without style in a foreign language) and in 1969 he was awarded the Nobel Prize for Literature. For an Irishman to achieve a worldwide reputation with a first play written in French at the age of 47 is only slightly less surprising when one considers the dramatist's background.

Samuel Beckett was born in County Dublin and seemed, as a young man, to be destined for a distinguished academic career. After school, he went to Trinity College, Dublin, and read for a modern languages degree in French and Italian. For two years he worked as *lecteur* in Paris and prepared a thesis on Proust; but a post as assistant lecturer back in Dublin held only a brief attraction (he considered it presumptuous to teach what he did not know), and he preferred to travel throughout Europe and write fiction. He was a close friend of another Dubliner, James Joyce, and the two writers worked together for a while in Paris where, since 1937, Beckett has settled. By the time of his emergence as a dramatist, he had written several novels, starting in English with *Murphy* (1938) and continuing in French with others such as *Molloy* (1951), but it is above all for a number of highly unconventional plays that he has acquired a truly international reputation.

For audiences in the 1950s, everything about *En attendant Godot* was unusual. Whereas the traditional play has incident and climax, exposition and dénouement, Beckett's play presents a situation. Two men – Vladimir (Didi) and Estragon (Gogo) – wait throughout Act I for Godot to arrive. Apart from the interruption of a bullying oaf called Pozzo and Lucky, his slave, nothing happens; their time is spent in apparently inconsequential talk and unproductive gestures until, at the very end, a boy comes to tell them that Godot will arrive tomorrow. Even though, by the next evening (whenever that is!), a bare and forlorn tree has sprouted some leaves, Lucky is dumb and Pozzo has lost his sight, the pattern of Act II is virtually identical: Vladimir and Estragon wait, nothing happens, and Godot again fails to appear.

The initial reaction of theatre-goers and critics was to look for some rational explanation or to evaluate the play in terms of traditional criteria. The invisible, perhaps non-existent, Godot was interpreted in various ways ranging from God (which led to religious and metaphysical interpretations of this play by an atheist) to Godeau, a former cycling champion (which tended to confirm the view that the play was a hoax). Looking for a foothold in more normal drama, Kenneth Tynan said of the London production: 'The bleak, denuded vision of man as a forlorn biped condemned to die alone has a tragic honesty that Aeschylus would have recognized if not comprehended.' Others dismissed the entire enterprise, or neglected the serious element to concentrate upon its triviality or comedy. Such confusion of opinions is hardly surprising for much in modern theatre is not susceptible of a rational explanation. Where logic provided no key, alarm set in. As Colin Duckworth has put it, *Godot* is 'a play which entertained and disturbed in a completely new and revolutionary way'. Time and familiarity with Beckett's later plays have reduced the confusion, as critics and public have become accustomed to the idiosyncratic fusion of farce and pathos. 'Although by the skilful use of music-hall techniques, Beckett presents his tramps in the guise of amusing clowns, they are at the same time pathetically human,' according to L. M. Barker, 'as they waver between suicide and irrational hope.' On the whole, there is now broad agreement about the mood and tone of *En attendant Godot*, and about the dramatist's serious intentions, even if there is disagreement over interpretation: 'Godot is a spiritual signpost' (*K. Tynan*). 'Godot's function seems to be to keep his dependents unconscious' (*E. Metman*). 'The play as a whole is a most complex dramatic symbol expressing man's anxiety and suffering as to his origin and destination' (*L. Barker*). 'Underlying *Waiting for Godot* there is a deep sense of evil, of fear and apprehension' (*C. Duckworth*). 'So Vladimir – East European name – and Estragon – French tarragon which flavours vinegar, soured wine – share circus clown's garb of big boots, capacious pockets, everlasting hand-me-down clothing, and the diminished respectability and gentility of bowler hats in a no-man's-land of despair and emptiness' (*F. Doherty*). Beckett's 'sometimes barely human characters, subject to extremes of physical humiliation, drag out a meaningless existence in a physical waste dominated by the fact of suffering and the eroding action of time' (*D. G. Charlton*). *En attendant Godot* will continue to intrigue, to baffle and perplex, and no-one can expect to find the final solution: like *Hamlet* and *Phèdre*, it is a play, not a riddle.

Even so, in his later plays from *Fin de partie* (1957) to *Souffle* (1969), Beckett continues the process of pruning his images and paring his ideas until, by a process of distillation and condensation, he eventually reaches a point where, by their brevity, his plays may seem to present the audience with a form of dramatic conundrum.

Fin de partie also depicts a static and wretched situation. Hamm is blind, paralysed, confined to a chair and dependent on his servant, Clov. The other two inhabitants of the claustrophobic room are Nag and Nell, legless and confined to dustbins. In *Happy Days* (1961), there is only one character, an elderly woman called Winnie who, at the start of the play, is buried in a mound of sand up to her waist and, by the end of the play, has so far submerged that only her head is visible. Subsequently, Beckett's plays became even barer and shorter. Some of his more recent sketches or 'dramaticules' are mime dramas, as titles like *Acte sans paroles* indicate. Beckett has said: 'At the end of my work there is nothing but dust,' and he seemed almost to have reached that ultimate point with *Breath* where there is a stage littered with rubbish and no actor. In the space of thirty seconds, the audience hears the cry of a new-born child, an inhalation of breath during which the lighting is raised, followed by an exhalation during which the lights dim to total darkness.

However denuded Beckett's theatre may become, *Breath* carries a clear though barely perceptible echo of the comment in *Godot*: 'They give birth astride a grave,' and so, in a few seconds, confirms the existence in Beckett's theatre of constants of theme and technique: immobility and extinction, surprise and an ambiguous, ambivalent humour.

Further reading

R. Coe, *Samuel Beckett* (1964); M. Esslin (ed.), *Samuel Beckett* (1965); C. Duckworth, *Angels of Darkness* (1972); V. Cook (ed.), *Beckett on File* (1985).

Workpoints

1 'Beckett's plays are acted out in a kind of purgatory of eternal waiting' (*C. Duckworth*).

2 'Whatever medium of drama Beckett has worked in, the resulting creation has that characteristic density, sparseness and desolation which one comes to associate with all his work' (*F. Doherty*).

3 'All the theatre of Samuel Beckett is a sustained meditation on death' (*S. John*).

4 'Beckett wanted his private fantasy to be accepted as objective truth' (*K. Tynan*).

5 'Beckett's chief weakness as a dramatist is that the action and visual imagery are frequently too static (*L. Barker*).

Albert CAMUS (1913–60)

Camus was born in Algeria and, although by the time of his death in a car crash in 1960 he had lived in metropolitan France for many years, taken an active part in the Resistance movement and acquired a reputation as one of France's leading post-war writers, much of the drama and fiction for which he is particularly remembered is set in a North African context. His fondness for the sun-drenched Mediterranean is recorded in an early collection of essays, *Noces* (1938); and, in an even earlier collection called *L'Envers et l'endroit* (1937), it is significant that the third piece, a description of Camus's first visit to Europe, is called 'La Mort dans l'âme', whereas the fourth, an account of his joy and relief on returning to a warm climate, is entitled 'Amour de vivre'. Algeria is also the background of the two major novels which established his international reputation, *L'Etranger* (1942) and *La Peste* (1947); and because both works portray different forms of isolation and imprisonment, the occasions when characters contrive to escape and enjoy or recall the sensual pleasures of Mediterranean life are particularly powerful and memorable.

The true significance of Camus's work – his fiction, theatre and a number of important essays – depends, however, not so much upon his evocation of the natural delights of earth, sun and sea as upon his fervent and unrelenting struggle to find a humane and humanitarian solution to the 'absurdity' of the modern world, its poverty, injustice, violence and tyranny. The tension between two cultures and climates, between the country of his birth and (from the late 1930s) his adopted country, reappears in his later fiction: *La Chute* (1956) plunged the reader into the gloomy atmosphere of an Amsterdam bar where the guilt-ridden Clamence confesses his cowardice and injustice; *L'Exil et le royaume* (1957) is a collection of *nouvelles* in a number of which the setting is again North Africa; there is, within all Camus's creative and critical work, a deeper tension as the author strives to establish an appropriate moral and political attitude towards the dilemmas which confront mankind in the twentieth century.

Camus's own life, itself marked by struggle and exile, can in some senses be considered highly successful: he freed himself from the sad and restricted circumstances into which he was born, from the limitations of his upbringing in the poor quarter of Algiers; his zest for life enabled him to overcome a serious illness; by his fiction and his theatrical work he achieved an international reputation; and a few years after the publication of his major philosophical essay, *L'Homme révolté* (1951), he was awarded the Nobel Prize for Literature. Measured in other ways, however, Camus's struggle may seem less productive. He was acutely saddened by his inability to mediate effectively at the time of the Algerian war, even though he was ideally qualified to understand the outlook of both countries. In his later works there is more than a hint of this distress, more than a trace of his growing despair.

The Second World War exerted a profound influence on Camus, as on many other French writers. A comparison of his two major novels reveals, as Camus himself pointed out, that between *L'Etranger* and *La Peste* there was an important re-orientation of the author's attitude, which can broadly be described as a move from the negative to the positive. This analysis is confirmed by comparing plays and essays written before 1945 with those written after.

L'Etranger is the story of Meursault, an outsider in the sense that he never conforms to the values of a false and hypocritical society. As Camus has said: 'Meursault ne joue pas le jeu.' He fails to demonstrate conventional grief at his mother's funeral; he refuses to feign any regret at having killed an Arab. The events are related by Meursault himself in two parts, the first extending from his mother's death to the death of the Arab, the second describing his imprisonment and trial. During Meursault's time in jail, he discovers a curious snippet from a newspaper which describes a traveller returning after many years to his home where, because he is not recognized, he is murdered by his own family. Having read the story countless times, Meursault's verdict was that the traveller was himself responsible for his death because 'il ne faut jamais jouer'. Camus was obviously intrigued by this incident, and he expanded what in *L'Etranger* occupies no more than twenty lines into a full-length play, *Le Malentendu* (1944).

As well as being the narrative of a man who, in Camus's terms, 'accepte de mourir pour la vérité', *L'Etranger* has been interpreted as an indictment of modern society, an attack upon its empty values, its inadequacies and flaws. An alternative interpretation argues that Meursault is not totally honest and that 'his attitude has dangerously inhuman or sub-human implications'. To convey the attitude and outlook of his anti-hero, or hero of restricted sensibility, Camus adopts an economical style, placing the emphasis upon the immediate and physical rather than on the abstract and philosophical. Meursault acts and reacts, but the author does not provide explanatory or causal links.

It is appropriate to associate with *L'Etranger* and *Le Malentendu* a long and important essay, *Le Mythe de Sisyphe* (1943), in which Camus compares the life of modern man to the endeavours of Sisyphus, condemned in Greek mythology to the arduous and fruitless task of repeatedly pushing a rock to the top of a hill. The essay's opening sentence makes the dramatic assertion that the major philosophical dilemma is whether man should or should not commit suicide, Camus's essential point being to question the value of man's endeavours in an absurd world where, like the gravitational pull on Sisyphus's rock, there are forces which doom all human activity to inevitable failure. 'Je ne suis pas un philosophe,' said Camus in an interview in 1945, 'je ne crois pas assez à la raison pour avoir un système. Ce qui m'intéresse, c'est de savoir comment il faut se conduire. Et plus précisément comment on peut se conduire quand on ne croit ni en Dieu ni en la raison.'

Together, these three wartime works can be considered as Camus's examination of 'l'absurde'. His response, a positive one, was already perceptible in Meursault's experiences: as his execution drew nearer, the outsider's attitude was modified not by a fear of death or by any form of religious conversion, but by the discovery of life's intrinsic worth. This positive element is expressed more fully in three corresponding works written in the immediate post-war period. The novel *La Peste* which demonstrates that although traditional values are futile in the plague-infested town of Oran, men can collaborate even when confronted with the certainty of death and, by their collaboration, create positive values and reasons for optimism. The play, *L'Etat de siège* (1948), as the title suggests, deals with problems of isolation and extinction similar to those endured by the inhabitants of Oran. A lengthy essay, *L'Homme révolté* (1951), re-asserts the need for men of good will to rebel collectively against the 'absurd' whether it be of human or natural origin.

Camus's reputation depends upon the combination of his very considerable skill as a writer in portraying the human predicament and his earnest and honest attempts to create a just form of society. These two elements of his work are inseparable. Together they constitute a persuasive plea for moderation and understanding, rather than an advocacy of violence and bloodshed: 'Le monde où je vis me répugne', wrote Camus, 'mais je me sens solidaire des hommes qui y souffrent.' Revolt cannot be interpreted in narrow political terms; the broader philosophical implications for those who share his belief in human liberty and respect for human life are contained in Camus's rewording of the Cartesian *cogito*: 'Je me révolte, donc nous sommes.'

Further reading

P. Thody, *Albert Camus 1913–60* (1957); J. Cruickshank, *Albert Camus and the Literature of Revolt* (1959); D. Haggis, *Camus: 'La Peste'* (1962); C. O'Brien, *Camus* (1970); G. Banks, *Camus: 'L'Etranger'* (1976); R. Jones, *Camus: 'L'Etranger' and 'La Chute'* (1980).

Critical editions with useful introductions: *L'Etranger*, ed. G. Brée and C. Lynes (1958); *Les Justes*, ed. E. Marsh (1960); *L'Exil et le royaume*, ed. D. Walker (1981); *Selected Political Writings*, ed. J. King (1981).

Workpoints

1 '*L'Etranger* is a work of creative fiction, not a moral tract or a philosophical essay; it does not contain a coherent system of thought or offer practical solutions to the problems it raises' (*G. Brée and C. Lynes*).

2   *La Peste* has been interpreted on three levels: the narrative
plane dealing with an imaginary epidemic in Oran in the 1940s;
the political plane in which the plague represents 'la peste
brune' as the invading Nazi army was described in occupied
France; and the philosophical plane in which 'la peste'
symbolizes the absurdity of the human condition. How valid
are the following two criticisms of Camus's symbolism?
'Assimiler l'occupation à un fléau naturel, c'était encore un
moyen de fuir l'Histoire et les vrais problèmes' (*S. de
Beauvoir*).
'Camus is tending towards the humanist folly by disregarding
the evil resultant from human origins' (*J. Cruickshank*).

Jean COCTEAU (1889–1963)

Cocteau was a creative artist of immense talent and a quite
amazing versatility. A public reading of his poetry when Cocteau
was only 19 led to contact with influential figures in the artistic
world. Characteristically he was attracted by the unconventional
(Apollinaire, Picasso and, in the realm of ballet, Diaghilev and
Nijinsky). This association of precocious amateurism with pro-
fessionals who, however unconventional, were highly disciplined
artists, provides a clue to two important threads discernible in all
Cocteau's subsequent work: the first, an emphasis upon poetry in
many guises; the second, a desire to shock and astound. It was
Diaghilev who one day said: 'Jean, étonne-moi!'; and from the
time of his adolescent poetry to the summit of his career as a
French Academician, a member of the Royal Belgian Academy
and a doctor *honoris causa* of Oxford University, Cocteau never
ceased to astonish the public.

Poetry was the label that Cocteau applied not merely to his
thirty collections of verse but also to his forty-five critical works
(*poésie critique*), to his celebrated pen and ink drawings (*poésie
graphique*), and to his six novels (*poésie de roman*). His *poésie de
théâtre* consists of twelve full-length plays, numerous sketches and
one-acters, not to mention seven films. Such considerable output
is all the more remarkable when it is realized that he was not
merely the playwright: he was often producer, director, actor and
even costume designer. He has been called a supreme showman,
and throughout his flamboyant and exhibitionist career (for it is
hard to talk, in his case, of a private life), Cocteau contrived to be
involved in many unusual or sensational events: he was nearly
awarded the Croix de Guerre for bravery during the First World
War; he recovered from an addiction to opium; he successfully
organized the professional rehabilitation of Al Brown, a former
boxing champion; and he won a wager with a national newspaper

that he could equal the record of Jules Verne's hero by travelling round the world in eighty days. His personal behaviour was similarly unconventional and, with Gide, he came to be classified by the title of one of his own novels, *Les Enfants terribles* (1929).

In fact, by its considerable variety, Cocteau's theatre – like the dramatist himself – defies any simple classification. He started with short plays and sketches or playlets in the 1920s. An early example of his unusual style is *Les Mariés de la Tour Eiffel* (1924) in which a wedding breakfast is invaded by an ostrich and various unexpected arrivals. Unfortunately the photographer's equipment is faulty and, when he says 'Watch the birdie', his camera proceeds to disgorge a bathing beauty, a cyclist and even a tiger which ends up by devouring the guests. In more controlled ways, Cocteau's later plays reveal his continuing interest in the fantastical, in dreams and the subconscious, with the result that he was associated in the public mind with his contemporaries, the Surrealists, although he was never a member of any literary movement or school.

It was more a perverse sense of humour or a desire to shock that persuaded Cocteau to include in his version of the Orpheus legend (*Orphée*, 1927) a pantomime horse with unmistakably human legs, and a talking flower in his medieval play about the court of King Arthur, *Les Chevaliers de la Table Ronde* (1937). His was a consciously experimental theatre, designed to question basic assumptions and standard attitudes: Cocteau's intention was invariably to refurbish or rehabilitate the humdrum and common-place, in other words to renew the spectator's vision. He aimed to revitalize theatre which, in his view, was 'pourri de littérature'. His *poésie de théâtre* must not be confused with *la poésie au théâtre* even if, in a play like *Renaud et Armide* (1943), he abandoned a prose dialogue for the rhyming couplets of classical French tragedy. Theatre was not to be the exclusive realm of poetry; in a *spectacle complet* there is a need for all nine muses to be incorporated, and so he engaged artists like Dufy and Picasso to design the sets, composers like Milhaud and Honegger to prepare the musical score, and clowns or ballet dancers to animate the performance.

A perfect example of his skill in revitalizing the commonplace is *La Voix humaine* (1930), written for and performed by the celebrated singer and cabaret artiste, Edith Piaf. Cocteau takes from popular boulevard theatre the most banal of its themes, the eternal triangle: an affair ends when a woman is abandoned by her lover. The treatment is brilliantly original in that the audience sees and hears only one-third of the triangle, and the entire play consists of one actress, alone on stage, talking on the telephone for the last time to the man with whom, clearly, she is still very much in love. It is a daring treatment and, for the solitary performer, an exceptionally demanding role, particularly as the pauses while the man replies must be of credible length, which means that, for about half of this one-hour solo, the audience is sitting in complete silence. The play's immediate acceptance by the Comédie Française is proof of Cocteau's achievement, his technical skill and his infallible sense of theatre.

However unanimous the view of his stagecraft, opinion has always been divided about the substance of his work. Nor were criticisms of emptiness or flimsiness helped by his irreverent treatment of the classics, for example with the introduction of jazz music on the battlements of Thebes in the opening scene of his version of the Oedipus legend, *La Machine infernale* (1934). To counter such criticisms, attempts to demonstrate a positive element have referred mainly to charm, grace and scenic originality, thereby reinforcing rather than refuting accusations of what Eric Bentley has called the 'awful vacuity' at the centre of Cocteau's work. There is, it is claimed, too much magic and too little moral substance. Certainly Cocteau made no claim, in public or in private, to conventional moral attitudes; and at a time when writers like Camus and Sartre felt the need to be *engagés*, Cocteau resolutely refused all forms of social, philosophical and political commitment. The opposite and entirely reasonable view is that such critics have missed the essential point of Cocteau's work and attitude. Liberty is the central feature of all his work and, instead of conformity, Cocteau is advocating individual freedom, which he describes as the hardest discipline of all.

Further reading

La Machine infernale, ed. W. Landers (1957); N. Oxenhandler, *Scandal and Parade* (1958).

Workpoints

'A versatile writer whose acute intelligence and sensitivity made him the spearhead of literary and artistic movements between the 1914–18 and the 1939–45 wars' (*J. Reid*).

'Cocteau has been too consistently inventive to be dismissed lightly' (*G. Brereton*).

'He is the supreme showman among French dramatists, and it has been suggested that his plays are really a succession of confidence tricks, all technique and no substance' (*S. Taylor*).

'An important and gifted *animateur* who finally lacked that intense concentration of talent which characterized most of the greatest artists' (*D. Charlton*).

'The general impression is that Cocteau has always something to do if not always something to say' (*J. Guicharnaud*).

Sidonie-Gabrielle COLETTE (1873–1954)

Few writers, and particularly few women writers, have been President of the Académie Goncourt, the committee responsible for the annual award of one of France's prestigious literary prizes. Fewer still have earned their living for almost ten years as a music hall entertainer. Colette did both. It is a mark of her energy and of her varied and highly individual talent that, from the Burgundy countryside of her childhood, she should acquire national and international fame (or, for the more puritanical, notoriety) as an important literary figure.

Colette's experiences in vaudeville, recorded in, for example, *La Vagabonde* (1910), constitute an important period of her life, as she recovered from her first, unsuccessful marriage to the charming but unreliable Willy; but they form only a relatively minor element in her largely autobiographical writings. She is remembered above all for the affectionate portrayal of her home, her native village, the surrounding countryside and its inhabitants, both human and animal, in a series of novels which began with *Claudine à l'école* (1900). Just as Claudine leaves the village of Montigny for the capital (*Claudine à Paris*, 1901), Colette left her native Saint-Sauveur-en-Puisaye and bounded into the Parisian salons of the 'Belle Epoque'. Her frank and ingenuous manner, her enthusiasm for sensual pleasures, her exuberance and candour created a sensation which Willy, a professional opportunist, persuaded her to exploit. In those early novels and more confidently – when she had shaken free from his influence – in later works such as *La Maison de Claudine* (1923), she displays a particular talent for capturing and crystallizing the episodic. It is a work based on incidents and fleeting sensations, memorable for the clanking of a blacksmith's forge or the barely perceptible breathing of a cat, for the scent of honeysuckle and acacia, the savour of apricots and peaches, the cool shade of a walnut tree. There is a persistent echo of her own vigour and vitality in the novels she wrote about young people, notably *Le Blé en herbe* (1923) and *Gigi* (1943).

The fictional world she chose to describe may be limited, but her prose has its own idiosyncratic flavour and harmony. Even with dissonant elements which range from the rattling of a shutter against a farmhouse wall to the rhythmical clatter of dancing feet on a tawdry stage, Colette created a personal music which enchanted a wide public. She was the first French woman to be honoured by a state funeral.

Further reading

La Maison de Claudine, ed. H. Shelley (1964); N. Ward Jouve, *Colette* (1987).

Workpoints

'The deliberately limited universe of Colette is a universe of the senses, whose perceptions she expresses with astonishing skill' (*G. Brereton*).

'Her talent, if minor, was perfect of its kind, and she possessed astonishing gifts as a stylist' (*D.Charlton*).

'Les bêtes et les fleurs sont des personnages innombrables et toujours présents dans l'œuvre de Colette' (*L. Perche*).

André GIDE (1869–1951)

Gide was born in Paris of a southern father and a Norman mother, and considered his origins as symbolic of the tensions and paradoxes which he saw as marking both his life and his work. He received an austere Protestant upbringing and a fragmented education during a childhood disrupted by illness; and much of his early adulthood was devoted to throwing off his moral inhibitions. A notable stage in this process took place during a lengthy stay in North Africa, where he became fully receptive to the life of the senses and the appeal of homosexuality. His inherited wealth gave him the leisure to write and travel, and from about 1910, as his work became known to the public, he enjoyed increasing prominence and influence.

The earliest writings – lyrical poetry and prose, including *Les Cahiers d'André Walter* (1891) – bore the influence of Symbolism, but Gide's individual literary identity is clear in *Les Nourritures terrestres* (1897), a manifesto for *disponibilité* – an openness to the maximum range of sensations and experiences leading to a more authentic personal existence. The book concludes with a characteristic piece of advice to the disciple to whom it is addressed: 'Jette mon livre; dis-toi bien que ce n'est là qu'*une* des mille postures possibles en face de la vie'; in this way *disponibilité* is to be maintained to the end. Gide's moral preoccupations are combined with a scrupulous concern for appropriate literary form in his narrative fiction, which he divided into the broad categories of *récit*, *sotie* and *roman*. The major *récits* are generally concise and intense accounts of personal crisis, related either by a protagonist (Michel in *L'Immoraliste* (1902), the pastor–diarist in *La Symphonie pastorale* of 1919) or by a privileged observer (Gérard in *Isabelle*, 1911), though in *La Porte étroite* (1909) the technique involves a more complex interplay of narrative monologue, letters and diary. The *soties* – a term originally applied to satirical, anti-clerical farces of the medieval period – tend away from both the seriousness and the intensity of the *récits*, adopting a comic view of human affairs (*Paludes*, 1896; *Le Prométhée mal enchaîné*, 1899), borrowing from other genres such as the adventure novel, and favouring an intrusive narrator and an involved plot (*Les Caves du Vatican*, 1914). The main connecting thread between these disparate texts is that of a theory or principle serving as an ironic yardstick against which to measure the actual conduct and attitudes of the major characters. Michel's aim of absolute moral freedom is shown to be a fantasy ('Savoir se libérer n'est rien; l'ardu, c'est savoir être libre'), and Alissa's aspiration to an unattainable perfect spirituality, in *La Porte étroite*, merely negates all reasonable values, whether worldly or religious; similarly the pastor, having represented his attraction to the blind foundling Gertrude as disinterested Christian charity, and Gérard, after his idealization of the vulgar Isabelle, eventually come to understand their self-delusion. In the same way, too, in *Les Caves du Vatican*, the *acte gratuit* – an act devoid of all motivation – is demonstrably a pure abstraction: the stuff of much theorizing on the part of the novelist Julius de Baraglioul, but unachievable even by the *disponible* Lafcadio, who pushes Amédée Fleurissoire from a railway carriage not, in fact, gratuitously, but in order to satisfy his curiosity about his own reactions. With its greater density and range, *Les Caves* points ahead to *Les Faux-Monnayeurs* (1926), the only one of his works Gide considered diverse enough to merit the label *roman*. Here the unrealizable concept is the ambition of a central figure, Edouard, to write a *roman pur* – a novel purged of all accessory features such as realistic representation. Given Edouard's inevitable failure, the *roman pur* exists merely as a bench-mark against which to measure Gide's own novel – or indeed any other. The moral dilemmas of individual liberty and authenticity reappear here, notably via the career of the young Bernard Profitendieu, who discovers himself to be an illegitimate child (like Lafcadio before him) and thereafter struggles with the problems of a new-found independence. But there is a marked shift to a greater emphasis on aesthetic concerns, already present to some extent in *Les Caves*. A good example is the device of *mise en abyme* (a technique borrowed from the visual arts whereby the work as a whole is reflected, in miniature, in some element within it) when, at the very centre of *Les Faux-Monnayeurs*, Edouard discusses the nature of the book he wishes to write. Many of Edouard's reflections are recorded in a diary, and these are paralleled in the *Journal des Faux-Monnayeurs* (1926), which Gide himself kept while writing his novel. A diary covering most of his creative life (*Journal 1885–1939*) offers illuminating insights into his major intellectual and literary interests, and the latter also generate a substantial body of critical work, incuding books on Dostoyevsky and Montaigne. Gide's fiction after *Les Faux-Monnayeurs* is of less note, but his highly developed introspection found many outlets, not only in the journals, but also in *Corydon* (first published in 1911), with its apologia for homosexuality, and *Si le grain ne meurt* (1926), a candid autobiography running from his first childhood memories to his North African experiences and the death of his mother. The self-absorption of texts such as these is ultimately a more essential part of Gide than the socio-political themes of *Voyage au Congo* (1927), or of *Retour de l'U.R.S.S.* (1936), an account of his disenchantment with Stalin's Russia.

A relatively obscure figure in his Symbolist period, a champion of freedom and unorthodoxy by the 1920s, a Nobel prizewinner in 1947 and an acknowledged precursor of the Existentialists, Gide saw his reputation fluctuate dramatically within his own lifetime, and opinions still vary greatly as to his final standing. But if some of the values he proclaimed seem uncontroversial or even shallow now, the commitment and the formal skill with which he articulated them continue to command respect.

Further reading

G. Brée, *Gide* (1963); G. Ireland, *Gide* (1963) and *André Gide – A Study of his Creative Writings* (1970); D. Littlewood (ed.), *Gide: A Collection of Critical Essays* (1970); C. Bettinson, *Gide: A Study* (1977); J. Davies, *Gide: 'L'Immoraliste' and 'La Porte étroite'* (1972); C. Bettinson, *Gide: 'Les Caves du Vatican'* (1972); C. Tolton, *André Gide and the Art of Autobiography: A Study of 'Si le grain ne meurt'* (1975); M. Tilby, *Gide: 'Les Faux-Monnayeurs'* (1981).

Workpoints

1   *Gide*: 'L'œuvre d'art, c'est une idée qu'on exagère.'
    'Toute théorie n'est bonne qu'à condition de s'en servir pour passer outre.'
    'Le point de vue esthétique est le seul où il faille se placer pour juger sainement de mon œuvre.'
    'Je ne crois pas du tout à un acte gratuit, même je tiens ceci pour tout à fait impossible à concevoir.'
    'J'appelle un livre manqué celui qui laisse intact son lecteur.'

2   *Gide's critics*: 'Considering his work as a whole, Gide emerges as an artist forever seeking after new modes of thought and new forms of expression, but lacking the intellectual rigour and artistic power fully to achieve either' (*I. Walker*).
    'Profondément traditionnelle et radicalement révolutionnaire,

[l'œuvre d'André Gide] témoigne d'une conscience probe et courageuse de la grandeur de l'homme' (*C. Martin*).

'The "liberator of youth" appears irrelevant to those who have long since lost their chains' (*J. Cruickshank*).

'Gide's art aims to establish a compromise between risk and rule, in him are balanced Protestant law and the nonconformity of the homosexual, the arrogant individualism of the rich bourgeois, and the puritan taste for social restraint. . . . This play of counter-balances is at the roots of the inestimable service which Gide has rendered contemporary literature' (*J.-P. Sartre*).

'The work of Gide is the expression of neither a system of thought nor a fixed personality: it is first and foremost the search for, and the elaboration of, a style' (*G. Picon*).

Jean GIRAUDOUX (1882–1944)

Nationally and internationally, Giraudoux made a resounding success of two simultaneous careers, the one as a diplomat and the other as a writer. His first literary work was in fiction; but, in 1928, a chance meeting with Louis Jouvet, one of the most influential personalities of French theatre in the inter-war years, led to a happy coincidence of talents. Thereafter Giraudoux delighted Paris with a theatrical 'hit' every other year until the outbreak of the Second World War. His plays are remembered above all for their wit and charm and for the distinctive eloquence of their dialogue.

From Giraudoux's choice of subjects, his theatre would appear to be varied and diverse: *Siegfried* (1928) and *Intermezzo* (1933) are set in twentieth-century Germany and France; *Amphitryon 38* (1929) and *La Guerre de Troie n'aura pas lieu* (1935) are taken from classical antiquity; *Ondine* (1939) is a delightful fairy story in which a water sprite leaves the enchanted realm of the undines to live as a human in medieval Germany, where she falls in love with a blundering knight in armour. Such diversity of subject would seem to entail a variety of characters ranging, in *Electre* (1937), from the rulers of Argos to the palace gardener, and in *La Folle de Chaillot* (produced in 1945 after Giraudoux's death), from a Parisian rag-and-bone man to oil magnates and captains of industry. In reality, Giraudoux's theatre is less remarkable for its breadth than for its depth, which is derived from two persistent features: whatever the setting, whatever the century, there is in every one of his plays a similarity of thematic preoccupations and of style.

Giraudoux was born and brought up in Bellac, not far from Limoges. He was a countryman through and through until, after a brilliant school career at the Lycée de Châteauroux, he moved to

Paris and studied at the Lycée Lakanal and the Ecole Normale Supérieure. His subject was German, and he once described *Ondine* as the *explication de texte* which he never quite managed to submit to his professor when he was a student. More seriously, throughout the remainder of his life, Giraudoux's interests and activities were constantly drawn towards the problem of Franco-German relationships: militarily, because he served in the French army in the First World War and was twice wounded; theatrically, because the traditional hostility between the two countries and the conflict between two cultures were uppermost in his mind as he considered the problem of war in the modern context of *Siegfried* and in the ancient context of the Trojan War; and professionally, in that his work as a senior civil servant in the Ministry of Foreign Affairs focused upon this precise facet of French policy, vividly and acutely alive in the national consciousness since the Franco-Prussian war in the late nineteenth century. Through the summit conference of Hector and Ulysses in *La Guerre de Troie*, Giraudoux makes a searing denunciation of modern war, its futility and its savagery. This theme recurs even in the delightful light comedy called *Amphitryon 38*, so named, it is said, because before Giraudoux thirty-seven other dramatists had already portrayed the myth in which Jupiter seduces the hero's wife, Alcmène, by taking on her husband's form. Giraudoux died in 1944, that is, before the end of the war which, in his official and dramatic work, he had foreseen and dreaded, the war in which he had been appointed Minister of Information. It is an unkind irony that he should have been selected for the task of exhorting France to fight in a war whose approach and menace he had so often denounced.

To counterbalance the inevitability of human conflict, Giraudoux's work concentrates upon love, friendship and the simple pleasures of life, both natural and human or social. In almost every one of his plays there is an example of a devoted couple and an examination of love and friendship; there is often an amazingly sensitive and radiantly attractive heroine. Siegfried, who lost his memory in the First World War and has since become the national hero of Germany, is lured back to his native France by the devotion of Geneviève, his fiancée; Alcmène, although duped by Jupiter into infidelity, so impresses the god by her constancy, grace and – above all – her love of Amphitryon, that he erases all memory of the night in which Hercules was conceived; indeed the Trojan War might have been averted if only Paris and Helen of Troy had been truly in love.

More noticeable even than the recurrence of themes in Giraudoux's theatre is the similarity of style in which are discernible echoes of seventeenth-century *préciosité* and of the graceful exchanges found in plays by Marivaux and Musset. Whether in Argos or Germany, in Paris or the provinces, the distinctive feature of Giraudoux's dialogue is its charm, in the two senses of elegance and enchantment. It is an idiosyncratic style whose sparkle comes from the deft combination of paradox and pun, anachronism and poetry, gentle irony and good-natured mockery. This language is, for some, excessively intellectual, too removed from everyday life, too dependent on literary allusions. In one sense, the accusation is justified, for Giraudoux makes no concession to threadbare realism, and a witty aphorism or a whimsically bantering rejoinder may just as soon spring from the mouth of a vulgar matelot as from the mind of a distinguished general. Every play is a dazzling debate which provides the audience with an opportunity to hear Giraudoux arguing with Giraudoux.

Préciosité in its pejorative sense is the label with which many critics tried to qualify the whirling constellations of Giraudoux's wit, allusions and insight, and to impose a tidy framework on the enchanting arabesques of his intricately contrived style. Giraudoux himself justifies the highly artificial and consciously adopted flavour of his plays by pointing out that: 'Le théâtre n'est pas un théorème, mais un spectacle, pas une leçon, mais un filtre.' Giraudoux makes no attempt to photograph reality. Art is a transposition, not a slavish imitation. As a scholar and a linguist, he is aware of the real power of language. Mankind needs to be wary of the faulty, warped and tendentious use of words. It was, after all, the propagandists who provided the catalyst for the Trojan War. Giraudoux's concern for the accurate and attractive use of language is visible in all his characters, who are not everyday, ordinary mortals but rather creations of his own vivid imagination, projections of his own lively mind. However light-hearted and frivolous or even flippant the dialogue may be, there is within it a serious idea which Giraudoux often conveys more effectively because of his unemphatic mode.

This is particularly true of *Intermezzo*, the story of a primary school mistress in the provinces, which by its title implies an interlude in a line of productions on more serious topics. From one angle it is a delightful fantasy, a none-too-chilling ghost story, for Isabelle has been enticed from the world of humans towards a supernatural force in the form of a spectre who roams the woods around the village. For all the frivolity and fun, it can be argued that *Intermezzo* is more a central pivot of Giraudoux's theatre than an unimportant intermission. Giraudoux was a countryman before he was ever a politician, a Parisian playwright or an apparently dandified diplomat. This subject allows him to reveal the real potential and the simple pleasures of rural life at the

expense of man's socialized and civilized follies. Just as the
gardener in *Electre* represented the 'natural' by his unsophisticated
delight in trees, shrubs, plants, vines and even their irrigation, so
the modest joys and familiar sounds of village life are powerful
enough for Isabelle to overcome the lure of the supernatural; and
the rural education which she provides in the meadows outside the
classroom enables her pupils to retain a little longer the language
which every baby knows at birth, but which official education
systematically crushes and destroys. *Intermezzo* is therefore an
opportunity for Giraudoux to mock the shortsightedness of
human endeavour. There is, for instance, an amusing dig at male
vanity when the spectre describes man as an animal who has
learned to stand on his back legs in order to 'recevoir moins de
pluie et accrocher des médailles sur sa poitrine'. Behind this
mockery, there lurks a serious preoccupation with man's tragic
condition. It is significant that Giraudoux, on another occasion,
should define tragedy in a way reminiscent of the spectre's
definition of man. 'Qu'est-ce que la tragédie?' asks Giraudoux, in
a collection of essays and speeches entitled *Littérature* (1942).
'C'est l'affirmation d'un lien horrible entre l'humanité et un destin
plus grand que le destin humain; c'est l'homme arraché à sa
position horizontale de quadrupède par une laisse qui le retient
debout, mais dont il sait toute la tyrannie et dont il ignore la
volonté.' The tension at the heart of *Intermezzo* was to develop
into a more perceptible distress in later plays. Even at its most
light-hearted moments, Giraudoux's frivolity is always closer to
the tragic than to the trivial.

Further reading

D. Inskip, *Jean Giraudoux, the Making of a Dramatist* (1958); *La
Guerre de Troie n'aura pas lieu*, ed. H. Godin (1958); *Amphitryon
38*, ed. R. Totton (1969).

Workpoints

1   Is Giraudoux frivolous and superficial?
    'His ideas and thought cannot be abstracted from the deft and
    poetic expression of them, and when he treats serious themes
    he does it with a light touch' (*R. Totton*).

2   Does Giraudoux, a novelist-turned-dramatist, allow literary
    longueurs to spoil his theatre?
    'A playwright is a man who can forget himself long enough to
    be other people; and a poet is a man who can forget other
    people long enough to be himself. In Giraudoux, as in few
    others, the two vocations are fused like Siamese twins. The
    playwright sets the scene, and in the *tirades* the poet takes

over; and by a miracle of collaboration the poet's eloquence
nearly always crowns an arch which the playwright has built'
(*K. Tynan*)

3 Is Giraudoux's theatrical world merely fanciful and fantastic?
'Giraudoux est un magicien du théâtre' (*L. Jouvet*).
'Looked at closely, Giraudoux's characters are most unnatural'
(*M. McGowan*).

4 Is there a lasting value in Giraudoux's theatre?
'The shallowness of his plays, and their intellectual coolness,
will finally prove them ephemeral' (*J. Taylor*).

Eugène IONESCO (b. 1912)

The totally unconventional theatrical work of this Rumanian
dramatist erupted onto the Paris stage in the 1950s and led to
international acclaim and to his election to the Académie Française
in 1971. Ionesco, a graduate in French literature, seems to have had
little early taste for the theatre, with the possible exception of
Punch and Judy. It was an attempt to learn English in 1948 which
led to the first of his plays: the string of platitudes in an elementary
language primer were so incongruous that they provided the
flavour for the dialogue of *La Cantatrice chauve* (1950). Other
early one-acters and sketches were performed in *théâtres de poche*
on the Left Bank, and their shock tactics and irrational substance
were slowly accepted by small if sometimes bewildered audiences.
An excellent example of his work is *Les Chaises* (1951) which
almost totally inverts traditional, accepted theatrical conventions:
if the standard 'boulevard' play consists of a young or middle-aged
couple who 'live through' an 'event', here we have two octogen-
arians who die through a 'non-event'. In the semi-circular set, Le
Vieux and La Vieille anxiously await the arrival of an Orator who
will deliver the Old Man's message, the truth of a lifetime's
experience. What the audience experiences is a room progressively
filled with chairs, which are real, and characters which are unreal,
since everyone in the vast throng of guests is invisible. This
proliferation of material things is characteristic of later, sometimes
longer plays: in *Amédée* (1954), the huge feet and legs of a corpse
in the next room gradually invade the stage; in *Le Nouveau
Locataire* (1955), the new tenant is overwhelmed by his furniture
and possessions.

Much of Ionesco's drama is based upon a sort of linguistic
explosion: a blend of exuberance, incoherence, distortions and
contradictions places a question mark over the value of language as
a valid means of communication. By raising doubts about
linguistic meaning, Ionesco queries all basic assumptions and all

rational or traditional beliefs. The very nature of human existence is called into question by characters who behave like puppets or animals (in *Jacques*, 1955, and *Rhinocéros*, 1960, they wear masks) and who lack any individuality, even a distinctive name. A frequent target for his iconoclasm is traditional theatre: he parodies its realistic conversations, its preoccupation with the affairs of couples and eternal triangles, its dependence upon plot and psychology. The total vacuity of these enactments creates the impression of a meaningless, gratuitous humanity, increasingly mechanized, steadily overwhelmed by material objects. The outcome seems inevitably to involve violence, suffering and death, for a crescendo of humour or nonsense is resolved by some form of catastrophe or extinction.

Further reading

R. Coe, *Ionesco* (1961); R. Hayman, *Eugène Ionesco* (1972); A. Lewis, *Ionesco* (1972); *Tueur sans gages*, ed. J. McCormick (1982).

Workpoints

'He turns classic comedy on its head' (*R. Schechner*).
'Ionesco [is] preoccupied with death' (*A. Lewis*).
'A drama of dissent' (*R. Coe*).
'*The Bald Soprano* is a powerful indictment of the sterility of bourgeois life' (*A. Lewis*).
'Une œuvre d'art n'a rien à voir avec les doctrines' (*Ionesco*).
'The theme of senseless brutality substituted for order and justice is found everywhere in Ionesco' (*R. Coe*).
'We need humour and fantasy. . . . Humour brings us a free and lucid realization of the tragic or derisory condition of man' (*Ionesco*).
'As a thinker he is banal; as a word-trickster he is no more than ingenious; but as a comic inventor he is superb and classical' (*K. Tynan*).

François MAURIAC (1885–1970)

Mauriac enjoyed a notably successful career as a man of letters, earning early popular acclaim, being elected to the Académie Française (in 1933), and winning the Nobel Prize for Literature (in 1952). His prolific output embraced literary criticism, memoirs and plays, as well as polemical journalism defending the Republican cause in Spain and the French Resistance. But it is, of course, the fiction he wrote, mostly in the 1920s and 1930s, which claims the

closest attention. *Le Baiser au lépreux* (1922), a brief, poignant
domestic drama of self-sacrifice, and *Génitrix* (1923), a portrait of
possessive motherhood set in a vast, gloomy house, are two major
works from his early years.

By the middle of the 1920s, Mauriac's mature manner is
established. A strong sense of place is a constant feature: the
majority of his novels are located in his native Bordeaux, in the
nearby wine-growing areas or in the Landes, the sandy coastal
region covered in pine-forests. The other recurrent setting, Paris,
features far less, except in, say, *La Fin de la nuit* (1935); it
functions essentially as a remote and superficial respite (usually
only temporary) from the claustrophobic, isolated *bordelais*
country, whose oppressive atmosphere envelops and smothers its
inhabitants. The effect of this ambiance is enhanced by the skilful
use of local motifs and imagery – the torrid heat in *Le Baiser au
lépreux*, the cold and decaying house in *Génitrix*, the barren
countryside which indelibly marks *Thérèse Desqueyroux* ('J'ai été
créée à l'image de ce pays aride où rien n'est vivant'). Mauriac's
landscape is social as well as physical: his novels are solidly based
on the prosperous middle-class community he knew from
childhood, which grows rich on the vineyards and the pines.
Individual lives are geared to the acquisition and preservation of
property and wealth; even the outsider Thérèse 'avait toujours eu
la propriété dans le sang'. Similarly, marriages are arranged to
assure the continuity of private fortunes, and family life is
accordingly stultified. To emphasize the close-knit nature of this
society, Mauriac has characters appearing in more than one novel,
and actually writes sequels for *Thérèse Desqueyroux* (1927) and *La
Pharisienne* (1941).

Beyond the physical and the social, Mauriac's fictional world
has another dimension, and this, too, derives from his origins. As a
lifelong Catholic, he was forever engaged in religious debate, and
particularly concerned with the problem of how to integrate his
Catholic beliefs into his novels (see his essays *Le Roman*, 1928, and
Le Romancier et ses personnages, 1933). This did not, however,
lead him to preach. He constantly resisted the label 'romancier
catholique', asking instead to be thought of as a Catholic who
wrote novels. In practice, his major works, with their stress on
destructive passion, tend to depict the darker, unhappier side of
human nature. The need for divine salvation may be implied here,
but it is hardly explicit. The comparison with Pascal's 'misère de
l'homme sans Dieu' has often been made; Mauriac saw himself
creating an 'indirect apology for Christianity'. *Le Désert de
l'amour* (1925) examines the frustrated loves of father and son for
the same woman, and their common tragedy of non-communi-
cation; as Maria Cross puts it: 'Nos proches sont ceux que nous

ignorons le plus.' *Thérèse Desqueyroux* traces its heroine's troubled life from childhood to her attempt to poison her crass, uncomprehending husband. Thérèse is oppressed by her guilt, and may have the capacity for spiritual renewal – at the end of the novel she envisages a return to Argelouse: 'toute une vie de méditation . . . l'aventure intérieure, la recherche de Dieu'. Yet there is no certainty that, with her new-found independence in Paris, she will achieve any such thing; for all his sympathy, Mauriac presents Thérèse as an insoluble enigma.

There has often been praise for the skill of Mauriac's narratives, where devices such as flashback (as in *Thérèse*, *Le Désert de l'amour* and *Génitrix*) allow sharp, economical highlighting of personal crises. The main critical objection to his technique, voiced most forcefully about *La Fin de la nuit* by Sartre, concerns his apparent weakness for authorial 'omniscience' and intervention. However, at his best, Mauriac shows consummate skill in reconciling personal convictions and artistic needs.

Further reading

C. Jenkins, *Mauriac* (1965); J. Flower, *Intention and Achievement* (1969); C. O'Brien, *Maria Cross* (1954).

Workpoints

1 *Character*: Discuss Mauriac's fiction in the light of his claim that 'l'ambition du romancier moderne est . . . d'appréhender l'homme tout entier avec ses contradictions et avec ses remous. Il n'existe pas dans la réalité de belles âmes à l'état pur'.

2 *Society*: Consider and illustrate J. Flower's description of Mauriac's south-western France: 'Insulated from the outside world, hemmed in and controlled by certain standards and requirements which ensure its continuing prosperity.'

3 *The outer and the inner world*: 'Il opère avec toutes les ressources d'une prose savante une sorte de fusion du monde extérieur et du monde intérieur' (*M. Raimond*). In what ways (imagery? choice of detail? use of setting?) does Mauriac blend the physical and the non-physical?

4 *Thérèse Desqueyroux*: Mauriac is quoted as claiming that *Thérèse* is not a Christian novel, but that only a Christian could have written it. Explain and discuss.

5 *Le Désert de l'amour*: Benjamin Crémieux saw in the novel 'un nouveau romantisme de l'isolement'. Consider its main themes in the light of this remark.

Marcel PAGNOL (1895–1974)

Pagnol was born near Marseilles, and of all his works as playwright and film-maker, the most successful and the most enduring are those whose characters are drawn from the South of France, either from the port of Marseilles itself or from the surrounding Provençal countryside.

His career started with some years as a teacher of English, and he worked in the south before moving to the Lycée Condorcet in Paris, an experience which provided the setting for his first real success, *Topaze* (1928), which ran for three years. The hero, a simple school master in a private boarding school, is dismissed for honesty: his candid comments about his pupils have offended the wealthy parents and may therefore endanger the headmaster's income. A ruthless local councillor sees Topaze as an ideally naive and respectable partner for some unscrupulous business dealings; but makes a serious miscalculation. Topaze turns out to be an even more unscrupulous operator, and the lamb devours the lion. The play is popular less as a moral commentary on political and financial dishonesty than as an example of Pagnol's uncomplicated style and lively humour.

These are the striking qualities of three plays he set in an unpretentious dockside café in le vieux Port of his native Marseilles. *Marius* (1930), *Fanny* (1931) and *César* (filmed in 1933 and subsequently staged), are delightfully entertaining tales involving the bartender, the ferry boat skipper, the proprietor and his regular customers, and characters from the fishmarket whose conversations form a characteristically lively and humorous dialogue.

In the 1930s, Pagnol decided to concentrate upon cinema. Many of his best films were adaptations of fiction which, like Daudet's *Lettres de mon moulin* and Giono's *Regain*, are rooted in the Provençal countryside of his childhood. Pagnol became a member of the Académie Française in 1946.

Further reading

La Gloire de mon père, ed. J. Meuks (1962); *Topaze*, ed. D. Coward (1981).

Workpoints

'*Topaze* is worthy of the best traditions of French satirical comedy' (*A. Bovee*).

'Unlike most comedies of manners, bound as they are to the times they depict, the Marius trilogy is evergreen' (*D. Knowles*).

Marcel PROUST (1871–1922)

A la recherche du temps perdu (1913–27) is in many ways the culmination of the hundred years, beginning with Balzac and Stendhal, in which the novel dominates literary output. The ambitious scope and level of achievement of the *Recherche* set it among the very greatest works of fiction. Its creator was the son of a wealthy family whose comfortable finances left him free to indulge his interests. Proust's intense relationship with his mother, his homosexuality and his delicate health are among the crucial features of his youth on which he draws for his novel; but all are deftly transposed to meet artistic needs: there is no question of autobiography for its own sake. As a young man he enjoyed the fashionable Parisian social life of the 1890s, but also – as is less well remembered – campaigned vigorously for Dreyfus towards the end of the decade. By this stage his artistic and literary inclinations had led him to translate Ruskin, and to publish some sketches and short stories (*Les Plaisirs et les jours*, 1896). He wrote some important literary criticism, now collected in *Contre Sainte-Beuve* (1954), the main issue of which is his attack on the biographical approach to literature typified by the nineteenth-century writer. The novel, *Jean Santeuil* (published 1952) was abandoned by 1902. But, as has repeatedly been pointed out, Proust was a 'one-book man': the first part of his life was an apprenticeship for the *Recherche*; and by 1910 he was devoting himself entirely to his novel, living as a recluse in his famous cork-lined room, which insulated him from the rest of the world. Although the first volume, *Du côté de chez Swann* (1913) attracted little interest initially, the second, *A l'ombre des jeunes filles en fleurs* (1919) won the prix Goncourt, and by the time of his death, although he had not added the finishing touches, the importance of the work was clearly recognized.

The essence of the *Recherche* – a quest which, after much disappointment and difficulty, ends in fulfilment – is simple enough. The Narrator, after a series of failures in love and in his social life, finally recognizes his vocation as an artist: 'la vocation invisible dont cet ouvrage est l'histoire'. But the text is infinitely more complex and subtle than any brief summary could suggest. From the beginning – when the middle-aged Narrator describes his painful search for identity as he lies in bed sleeping, waking, dreaming – and even from the first, endlessly quoted sentence ('Longtemps je me suis couché de bonne heure'), the reader is caught up in a disconcerting shuttling movement between the unspecified present of the narration and various points in the near and more remote past. One thing that rapidly becomes apparent is that the novel is the record, not of events, but of a consciousness: a mind feeding on and processing the data of the outside world. As the text progresses, time becomes somewhat more manageable; a surprisingly small number of 'blocks' (a particularly significant day or evening, say) are used, even if within them the Narrator will refer to earlier or later periods. The work as a whole is a rich and varied structure covering the endless changes of characters and society from the 1880s to the Great War, and concluding triumphantly at the end of Le Temps retrouvé. Here, triggered by physical sensations, as when he stumbles on an uneven cobblestone in the Guermantes courtyard, the Narrator's past returns to him in a series of involuntary memories; here, at last, he grasps the coherence of his own personality, and is inspired to immortalize his experiences in his book.

Du côté de chez Swann, if not complete in itself, is an illuminating microcosm of the 3000 pages which make up the novel. It falls into three parts: 'Combray', concerning the Narrator's childhood; 'Un Amour de Swann', a third-person account of the affair, a generation earlier, of an aristocratic family friend and the alluring Odette; and 'Noms de pays: le nom', where the Narrator is in love with Gilberte, the daughter of Swann and Odette. All three parts contribute to the pattern of failure which will be overcome only with the final triumph: the sweet childhood memories slip away; Charles Swann falls for a woman 'qui n'était pas mon genre'; the mature Narrator, revisiting scenes once graced by Mme Swann, admits that 'la réalité que j'avais connue n'existait plus'. At the same time, the other major themes are apparent. Social success, at later stages so important to the Narrator, is in this volume the concern of Swann; the Narrator's love for Albertine, jealous, unrequited and self-deceiving, is prefigured in the Swann–Odette relationship. Clues to the ultimate means of redemption are also apparent. Voluntary memory is of only limited help to the Narrator striving to recreate in his mind his grandparents' house in Combray, but physical sensation – the evocative taste of a 'petite madeleine' dipped in tea – is already hinting at how the past can be recovered. Even this early experience leads him to note: 'J'avais cessé de me sentir médiocre, contingent, mortel.' The values of art are suggested throughout Du côté de chez Swann, as in the Narrator's delight in the theatre ('la première forme . . . sous laquelle se laissait pressentir pour moi, l'Art') and the frequent use of paintings as a term of comparison (the pregnant servant-girl being likened to Giotto's Charity, for example). And even if the young Narrator can only respond inarticulately to the beauties of the sun's reflection on water ('Zut, zut, zut, zut'), he is nevertheless aware of a creative obligation 'de ne pas m'en tenir à ces mots opaques et de tâcher de voir plus clair dans mon ravissement'. In other ways, too, this first volume sets the tone for those that follow: in its rich humour (which brings out to the full tante Léonie's foibles or the snobbery of Legrandin), and in its masterly use of language, whose elaborate syntax mimics the intricate workings of the Narrator's mind, and whose fine-spun imagery confers on all his observations layer upon layer of meaning.

Various criticisms are levelled against Proust: that his style is too precious; that his abstract digressions are sometimes excessive; that his pessimism about human relations is exaggerated. But a common verdict would be that, just as reading him is so much more demanding than reading many other authors (some critics offer detailed advice as to how to go about it), so the rewards are correspondingly greater. Towards the end of le Temps retrouvé, and at last certain of his potential, the Narrator writes: 'Je savais très bien que mon cerveau était un riche bassin minier, où il y avait une étendue immense et fort diverse de gisements précieux.' Proust's unique achievement is to have brought so many of these treasures within the grasp of the reader.

Further reading

G. Painter, Marcel Proust (1959, 1965); G. Brée, The World of Marcel Proust (1967); A. King, Proust (1968); R. Shattuck, Proust (1974); D. May, Proust (1983); V. Minogue, Proust: 'Du côté de chez Swann' (1973).

Workpoints

1 'Il y a, à travers toute l'œuvre, des correspondances constantes' (M. Raimond). How does this apply to the three parts of Du côté de chez Swann?

2 'What gives Proust's novel its unique character is above all its combination of a tough-minded analytical realism with a synthesizing poetic vision' (V. Minogue). Discuss and illustrate.

3 Consider this comment on Proust's characters: 'En tant que personnages de roman, ils ne sont pas victimes de leur complexité. Ils se situent au-delà de la raideur et en deçà de l'incohérence' (M. Raimond).

Alain ROBBE-GRILLET (b. 1922)

Whatever posterity makes of him, Robbe-Grillet is for the moment firmly identified as a prime mover in the changes that overtook the French novel in the 1950s and generated what is usually known as the nouveau roman. He trained and worked in agriculture, and practised in various former French colonies until, in 1955, he took a post with the publishing house Les Editions de Minuit and devoted himself full time to literature.

In his first novel, *Les Gommes* (1953), he was already challenging the assumptions and practices of the conventional novel. *Les Gommes* is a detective story with an attempted murder, a detective and a victim, but the norms are shattered when Wallas, the detective in question, himself turns out to be the real killer; and the reworking of the Oedipus myth adds another disconcerting element. Already, too, Robbe-Grillet is here using the circular plot-structure and the distortions of conventional time which will feature in much of his later work. With *Le Voyeur* (1955) he acquired both the Prix des Critiques and the hostility of the traditionalists, and each of these contributed to establishing his reputation. *Le Voyeur* can be read as a refinement and a development of the earlier novel: Mathias, a watch-salesman visiting a small island, dominates the narrative point of view – whereas in *Les Gommes* this was more varied – and the previously-used interior monologue has now been scrapped. At the same time certain characteristic devices carry over from the preceding work, notably the stress on physical objects to crystallize and convey states of mind, so that a packet of cigarettes or a figure-of-eight pattern will recur obsessively in the course of the text.

By the mid 1950s Robbe-Grillet was complementing his experiments in fiction with the polemical essays subsequently collected in *Pour un nouveau roman* (1963). The very titles are highly indicative: 'Une voie pour le roman futur', 'Sur quelques notions périmées', 'Nouveau roman, homme nouveau'. He argues crisply for a new kind of novel, which would reflect contemporary experience instead of the outlook of Mme de Lafayette or Balzac, who may have been innovators in their own time but should not be allowed to dictate terms to their successors. Accepted notions – characters, plot and the political *engagement* so much discussed in the 1950s – are all held up to question. The crucial issue is the nature of writing itself: 'Au lieu d'être de nature politique, l'engagement c'est, pour l'écrivain, la pleine conscience des problèmes actuels de son propre langage.' Hence Robbe-Grillet's frequent references to other art-forms, such as music and abstract painting, which turn inwards to emphasize their own intrinsic nature, rather than outwards to the world which surrounds them.

La Jalousie (1957) is probably Robbe-Grillet's best-known novel, and perhaps his most typical one. It deals with a triangular relationship between an unnamed plantation-owner, his wife A., and Franck, who may be her lover. The whole text follows the perceptions of the husband, observing the patterns of the banana-trees, studying his wife's movements, scrutinizing her behaviour with Franck over drinks. Time is plastic rather than chronological, shaped according to the husband's thoughts, which dart between the past, the present and a possible future. The psychology of the traditional novel is avoided, but the husband's nagging anxiety that he is being deceived emerges vividly via the recurrent – and growing – image of the squashed centipede. In his introduction Robbe-Grillet explains the pun of his title, incorporating the idea of a blind which, when closed, prevents any view of what lies outside, thus sustaining any and every obsession: 'La jalousie est une passion pour qui rien jamais ne s'efface: chaque vision, même la plus innocente, y demeure inscrite une fois pour toutes.' Since *La Jalousie*, his stress on objective visual images, rather than subjective ideas, has led him increasingly in the direction of another art-form, cinema, as in the 'ciné-roman' *L'Année dernière à Marienbad* (1961). Other novels, such as the symbolically-titled *Dans le labyrinthe* (1959), show him emphasizing ever more strongly the reality of the written text at the expense of the external world.

Further reading

La Jalousie, ed. B. Garnham (1969); *Dans le labyrinthe*, ed. D. Meakin (1983); B. Stoltzfuss, *Alain Robbe-Grillet and the New French Novel* (1964); B. Garnham, *Robbe-Grillet: 'Les Gommes' and 'Le Voyeur'* (1982).

Workpoints

1   On *Les Gommes*: 'Robbe-Grillet has weakened the authority of the omniscient narrator, and placed a much greater responsibility upon the shoulders of his reader, who becomes a creator rather than a spectator' (*B.Garnham*).

2   On *Le Voyeur*: '*Le Voyeur* must be approached without reference to the traditional constraints of meaning, sequence and chronology' (*B. Garnham*).

3   On *La Jalousie*: 'Créer, au lieu d'analyser, la psychologie des personnages, voilà l'essentiel de l'art robbe-grilletien' (*B. Morrissette*).

Antoine de SAINT-EXUPERY (1900–44)

Saint-Exupéry's experiences as a pilot form the basis of nearly all his writing, which he characterized as a 'témoignage'. He lived through the dangerous pioneering days of commercial aviation in the 1920s and early 1930s, first on the mail runs to West Africa, then opening up routes in South America. Despite age and injury he flew with a reconnaissance group in the Second World War, and was eventually lost in action, but not before he had acquired an immense reputation – especially through *Pilote de guerre* (1942) – as a distinctive voice of the free world. Since his death, his books have outsold those of most, if not all, other modern French writers.

His literary career shows a steady progression, defining ever more clearly his main areas of concern, and gradually turning away from secondary issues. *Courrier sud* (1929) presents Jacques Bernis's quest for a real meaning in life as against the claims of material comfort or emotional involvement. In *Vol de nuit* (1931), which draws on the very beginnings of night-flying in Argentina, the virtues of practical action are stressed more forcefully and incarnated in the heroic figure of Rivière, the director of the aviation company, who demands the total commitment of his pilots, even at the expense of their individual happiness. With *Terre des hommes* (1939), Saint-Exupéry leaves behind the novel-form (though, curiously, the book won him the Grand Prix du Roman) in order to reminisce, meditate and philosophize in a series of sketches and essays evoking the Sahara, the Andes and the Spanish Civil War. Conventional contemporary life, if not analysed in any detail, is seen as dull, negative and demeaning; the archetypal bureaucrat is vigorously denounced: 'Tu t'es roulé en boule dans ta sécurité bourgeoise. . . . Maintenant, la glaise dont tu es formé a séché, et s'est durcie.' Everywhere human promise is being stifled; observing the sleeping immigrant workers on the train back to Poland, Saint-Exupéry reflects: 'Ce qui me tourmente . . . c'est un peu, dans chacun de ces hommes, Mozart assassiné.' In contrast, flying offers a fresh view and a broader perspective implicit in the work's ambitious title. The life of Saint-Exupéry and his colleagues is presented as a vocation, and is frequently discussed in religious terms (young pilots are 'novices', night flying is compared with a liturgical rite performed in a temple). Further, and perhaps more important still, aviation brings comradeship and mutual responsibility in 'la grande famille professionnelle' – which completely outweighs all other human relationships. Through Saint-Exupéry's poetic prose, with its rich descriptions of desert, mountain and starry night skies, run the recurrent images of sterility – sand, rock, stones – over which the miracle of human life has the potential to triumph: 'Chaque existence craque à son tour comme une cosse et livre ses graines.' In *Pilote de guerre* the destruction of war and the collapse of civilization which has led to it are both condemned, in a text based on a reconnaissance flight over Arras in northern France. But the central concern remains the affirmation of positive values, now stated as a specifically humanistic creed: 'Je combattrai pour la primauté de l'Homme sur l'individu – comme de l'universel sur le particulier.'

Outside the mainstream of Saint-Exupéry's work, *Le Petit Prince* (1943) uses the manner of a fairy-tale to show how much adults would benefit from the imaginative, intuitive understanding which never seems to outlast childhood. *Citadelle*, published posthumously and incomplete in 1948, is a massively wide-ranging attempt to point up the moral of the previous works through the parables and lessons of a desert chieftain.

Further reading

C. Cate, *Antoine de Saint-Exupéry* (1971); B. Masters, *A Student's Guide to Saint-Exupéry* (1972).

Workpoints

1 *Flying*: 'There have been other writer–pilots, but only Saint-Exupéry has been able to express the poetry of flying' (*B. Masters*). How does he achieve his poetic effects? (Sense-impressions? imagery? appeals to the imagination?) And how important a place does aviation hold in his works?

2 *The modern world*: 'Je n'aime pas qu'on abîme les hommes' (*Terre des hommes*). How effectively does Saint-Exupéry present contemporary threats to human potential? And how convincing are his antidotes?

3 *The moral dimension*: To what extent are Saint-Exupéry's ideas integrated into his literary texts? How far, on the other hand, do the latter simply serve as a platform for him to deliver explicit lessons?

Jean-Paul SARTRE (1905–80)

For thirty years following the Second World War, Sartre was the most influential and internationally celebrated of French writers. His literary work had begun to appear in the 1930s, soon after he had ended his student career at the Ecole Normale Supérieure by obtaining a brilliant first place in the *agrégation*, and for some ten years he was to establish his early reputation as an author of fiction and philosophical essays. During the war, there occurred a perceptible change of direction and emphasis: his immense energy and devastating intelligence were turned increasingly towards theatre and politics. From 1945 onwards, works in which he championed the cause of liberty, attacks on all forms of social and political repression, and frequent interventions in French and international politics earned him considerable popularity and renown, especially among young people and in academic circles. Conversely, he was a particularly uncomfortable thorn for political authorities of a conservative or right-wing flavour; and Sartre's many critics resented his forthright support for communism in China, Russia and Cuba, and his encouragement of insurrection in various African countries. The award of the Nobel Prize for Literature in 1964 is an indication of his importance as writer and philosopher; Sartre's refusal to accept it is a measure of his courage and independence – and also of a disdain for every form of established authority and every sort of conformity.

At the start of his professional career, apart from interruptions for his national service and a further period of study in Berlin, Sartre worked as a teacher of philosophy for several years and began simultaneously to publish his first essays and fictional writings, including *L'Imagination* (1936) and *La Nausée* (1938). Both works reveal a remarkable ability to describe mental abnormality, which is apparent in subsequent works such as a collection of short stories entitled *Le Mur* (1939) and in his major fictional achievement, the series of novels called *Les Chemins de la liberté* (1945–9). The pre-war works already contain the fundamentals of Sartre's philosophy, which came to be known as Existentialism. This term (which Sartre adopted only with reluctance) is often used loosely: it is sometimes forgotten that there exists a form of Christian Existentialism in addition to the resolutely atheistic variety propounded by Sartre (and Simone de Beauvoir) in essays such as his *L'Etre et le néant* (1943) and, more frequently, in fiction and drama. Based on theories which originated in Scandinavia and Germany, the basic tenet of Sartrean Existentialism is that 'existence precedes essence'. Traditional philosophies are, in Sartre's estimation, fundamentally essentialist, and they postulate the notion of some model, some established form of perfection, to which individual humans attempt to conform. For Sartre, this conformity results in a loss of liberty: man is or could be what he makes of himself and his life. Whereas the acorn contains within itself the essential characteristics which will oblige it, by processes of natural change, to develop into an oak (with no chance of becoming a beech or a birch), man creates his own essence, because by living and choosing – or even not choosing – he asserts his own values. Existentialism is therefore a philosophy based on human choice: man, in Sartre's view, is totally free. However, this liberty is also an embarrassment, for where there exists no fatality, and no predetermined standard of moral behaviour, man is responsible for himself and his fellow human beings. Side by side with liberty, there is anguish (*angoisse* is a word which recurs constantly), because where there are no norms and no immutable criteria, man cannot know whether he has chosen well or badly. Sartre refutes all conventional standards of right and wrong, and in their place he offers authenticity and inauthenticity, depending upon whether any chosen action increases or reduces human liberty.

One of the clearest demonstrations of Sartre's philosophy is provided in his first play to be performed publicly, *Les Mouches* (1943). He had been attracted to drama by an experience during his months as a prisoner of war in 1940–1: to entertain his fellow prisoners in Stalag XII at Christmas, Sartre (the atheist!) wrote a nativity play called *Bariona* which, while dealing ostensibly with the birth of Christ, was in fact a comment on the invasion of France presented in the form of the occupation of Palestine by the Romans. On his release from imprisonment, Sartre decided to use the same method to encourage French resistance. For *Les Mouches*, he chose the story of Orestes returning from exile to his native Argos where, in collaboration with his sister, he overthrows the ruler and liberates the inhabitants. The play can be interpreted as a political allegory in which Orestes represents the Free French forces returning to work with the Resistance in the person of his sister, Electre, with the aim of overthrowing the tyrant Aegisthus who murdered their father and usurped the throne. Aegisthus, in this interpretation, represents the German invader, and the widowed Clytemnestra is the personification of those in France who collaborated. There is also a clear philosophical interpretation: *Les Mouches* (like *La Nausée*) can be seen as the Existentialist education of the central character. Other aspects of Sartre's philosophy are treated in his next play, a short and particularly effective work called *Huis clos* (1944). Its original title, *Les Autres*, focused attention upon the central theme: it is a starkly presented, one-hour display of psychological warfare as the three inmates of a sort of self-service Hades reach the conclusion that: 'L'enfer, c'est les autres.'

Thereafter, without abandoning his philosophical stance or his interest in literature, Sartre's work became markedly more political. This new orientation is visible in a critical work, *Qu'est-ce que la littérature?* (1947) and it continued in his studies of individual authors such as Baudelaire, Genet and Flaubert. It is particularly obvious in subsequent plays. *Morts sans sépulture* (1946), about the Resistance, presents the brutal interrogation and torture of *maquisards* by the collaborators. *Les Mains sales* (1948) is a play about political assassination and socialism in an imaginary East European country at the close of the Second World War. After *La Putain respectueuse* (1946), in which Sartre uses the theatre as a platform for flagrant anti-American propaganda, acts of authentic liberty appear to be possible only if they further the most extreme forms of socialism. Although Sartre did not belong to the Communist Party, his sympathies clearly lay with the east, to the extent that he was prepared to condone in Russia what he was quick to denounce in America. His denunciation of capitalism and middle-class morality is severely weakened by his reluctance to condemn Stalinist atrocities. Given Sartre's political preferences and his advocacy of violence as a means of obtaining political change, it is hardly surprising that, during the closing years of his tense and tormented life, he should have been in close association with young Maoist revolutionaries and members of European terrorist organizations.

Further reading

I. Murdoch, *Sartre: Romantic Rationalist* (1953); P. Thody, *Jean-Paul Sartre* (1960); K. Gore, *Sartre: 'La Nausée' and 'Les Mouches'* (1970); F. Jameson, *Sartre: the Origins of a Style* (1984); R. Hayman, *Writing against: a Biography of Sartre* (1986); *Les Mouches*, ed. R. North (1963); *Les Mots*, ed. D. Nott (1981); *Huis clos*, ed. J. Hordré and G. Daniel (1987).

Workpoints

1   *Philosophy and politics*: 'There is a curious tension between Sartre's belief in absolute freedom, which is form of faith, and the tragic negativity he repeatedly arrives at on the level of personal and political relationships' (*J. Weightman*).

2   *Fiction*: 'Great intelligence can sometimes magnify a small creative gift. . . . M. Sartre's natural talent as a novelist is not remarkable, but he is one of the most intelligent men in Europe. With immense determination he has used his powerful intelligence to compensate for other deficiencies. It has done more than compensate, it has given his novels a dignity of their own. You may not like them, for their taste is rank: but you cannot reasonably neglect them' (*C. P. Snow*). Is *La Nausée* a novel, an essay or a metaphysical meditation?

3   *Theatre*: 'With Sartre, character is subordinate to the philo-sophical argument, which is presented skilfully and excitingly' (*G. Brereton*).
    'His best plays are fully committed to left-wing ideology. They have sought to vindicate the inevitability of violence in the struggle for freedom and to decry the "bourgeois morality" which shrinks from such crimes' (L. M. Barker).

6

Continuity and change

Whereas the beginnings of the French literary landscape are difficult to chart in detail because of their remoteness in time, the circumstances in the late twentieth century present the would-be surveyor with very different problems. Precisely because the situation is so immediate and so hazy, there is little chance of a long-term perspective, a detached view. In addition, it is not yet possible to be sure how the terrain will eventually settle, which tracks will turn into main thoroughfares, and which hills or valleys will stay untouched. But perhaps the only reasonable approach, since the present is so obviously the result of an endless process of evolution, is to recognize that the process will continue, and to look forward to an open future rather than try to seal off the past at, say, 1960 or 1980.

Any attempt to look ahead would seem bound to embrace the two contrary principles of continuity and change. On the one hand, French literature will not, any more than the society from which it springs or the language in which it is embodied, become unrecognizable overnight. But on the other, like its cultural setting, it will adapt and alter. Some of the continuities seem clear enough. A striking number of writers whose importance was established decades earlier were still prominent in the early 1980s: Beckett and Sarraute remained active, while Butor and Robbe-Grillet were not out of middle age. An opinion poll in the review *Lire* in 1981 to identify France's most influential intellectuals revealed the enduring prestige of Simone de Beauvoir and Michaux, as well as of a younger writer such as Michel Tournier. Trends detected earlier also persist. Most strikingly, perhaps, the lines which might once have divided literature from non-literature, and one genre from another, seem increasingly blurred. Roland Barthes is by no means the only writer of non-fiction to work creatively in the domain of, to use the fashionable term, 'écriture': the psychoanalyst Jacques Lacan and the philosopher Jacques Derrida, whose deconstructionist readings challenge all fixed textual interpretations, are among many whose writings straddle the old divisions. At the same time, significantly new developments are taking place. The original novels and stories of Jean-Marie Le Clézio, with their powerful evocations of modern cities and exotic deserts, have attracted much interest; René de Obaldia has deeply impressed audiences with an innovative line in comic theatre; Jacques Roubaud's experiments in poetic form are a further sign of vitality. Any number of other names could be mentioned; but none seems immediately to dominate the scene. Perhaps, indeed, the most recent developments might be understood better in relation to movements rather than isolated individuals. In a climate where, as is often pointed out, the writer cannot speak for a whole community or civilization – let alone for humanity as a whole – sectional interests appear to be making themselves heard increasingly. While Marguerite Duras had achieved the undisputed status of a major figure by the 1970s, a rising generation of feminist writers (Monique Wittig, Hélène Cixous and Victoria Thérame among them) had also come to the fore. (One might add that in 1981 the Académie Française elected its first woman member, Marguerite Yourcenar – though doubtless not in response to feminist pressure.) Outside France, the Francophone literatures of Quebec (as in the work of Gabrielle Roy), the Maghreb (Kateb Yacine, Mohammed Dib), Black Africa (Léopold Sedar Senghor) and the West Indies (Aimé Césaire) all assume a growing importance.

The longer one considers the future, however, the more one is forced to resign oneself to its uncertainties. As the mass media claim an ever-increasing share of the public's attention, the status of literature is subject to change, and its very nature comes into question. As early as the 1950s Michel Butor was writing a telling essay about 'le livre comme objet' – a temporary cultural phenomenon which might be about to disappear. According to Butor: 'Le fait que le livre, tel que nous le connaissons aujourd'hui, ait rendu les plus grands services à l'esprit pendant quelques siècles, n'implique nullement qu'il soit indispensable ou irremplaçable.' A noted study of Old French literature is called *From Script to Print* (by H. J. Chaytor, published in 1945) – a clear reminder of the role of technological advance in the literary process; and it would be more than tempting to examine the modern period under the title *From Print to Print-Out*. But there could equally well be a different kind of echo of the past, if, as has been suggested by critics such as Robert Escarpit and Marshall McLuhan, the influence of the audio-visual media comes to reimpose the oral components of culture at the expense of the textual. More apocalyptically, a writer as devoted to the written heritage as Raymond Queneau has envisaged literature itself as 'une chose qui peut disparaître'.

But speculation is of little value when this part of the landscape is yet to be opened up: until the haze disperses, while the environment has still to establish itself and the roads and towns remain to be built, there is no purpose in rushing to put up the signposts here.

Glossary

This glossary is intended essentially to explain some important terms used in the main body of this book. For a comprehensive coverage of literary terms, the following works are recommended: M. Abrams, *A Glossary of Literary Terms* (1981); J. Cuddon, *A Dictionary of Literary Terms* (1980); J. Redfern, *A Glossary of French Literary Expression* (1970); J. Shipley, *Dictionary of World Literary Terms* (1970); H. Bénac, *Nouveau vocabulaire de la dissertation* (1986). Much useful information is also to be found in J. Reid, *The Concise Oxford Dictionary of French Literature* (1976).

Académie Française Started as an unofficial gathering of a few men in a private house: given royal recognition and granted formal status by Louis XIII in 1635 at the instigation of Richelieu. Its original tasks were to compile a dictionary, a grammar, a poetics and a rhetoric, but Richelieu almost immediately interrupted that work to involve the academy in the quarrel surrounding Corneille's controversial play, *Le Cid*. The membership is always forty (referred to as 'les Quarante'); it was originally composed of men of letters nominated by the king, but subsequently replacements have been elected by the academicians and, in the course of three centuries, writers and literary critics have been joined by men of distinction in other spheres: diplomats, scientists, soldiers. Apart from a break in its existence at the time of the Revolution, its work has continued to the present day – even if few of its original tasks have been satisfactorily completed. It now forms part of the Institut de France and is housed in the Palais Mazarin.

Alexandrine The standard line of French poetry since the seventeenth century; the name of this twelve-syllable line is derived from a late twelfth-century epic entitled the *Roman d'Alexandre*; the rhythmic unit is the half-line of six syllables (*l'hémistiche*) and strict rules concerning scansion, metre and

rhyme were imposed in the seventeenth century, notably by
Boileau's *Art poétique*; the classical or binary alexandrine,
consisting of two equal hémistiches with a pause (or caesura)
between them, came under attack from the Romantic poets in
the nineteenth century who revived a ternary alexandrine with
two pauses.

bienséances Conventions based on a respect for what is seemly
and fitting, the *bienséances*, in the context of drama, formed part
of the so-called 'rules' governing classical tragedy; for example,
the duels, murders and physical violence that are enacted on
stage in Shakespearean or French Romantic drama should take
place out of sight and be conveyed to the audience by *récits*.
Like the unities, they contribute to an emphasis upon the
psychological rather than the physical action.

commedia dell'arte A traditional form of comedy imported into
France by Italian companies, where stock characters such as
Harlequin and Columbine, Scaramouche and Pantalone rely
upon improvised dialogue rather than a set text. It was an
important element of the Italian theatrical influence in France
during the sixteenth, seventeenth and eighteenth centuries,
interrupted only briefly when their penchant for excessively
licentious and satirical humour led them to make fun of
Madame de Maintenon in a play called *La Fausse prude*.

confidant(e) (French: **confident(e)**) A trusted companion of
the hero or heroine in classical tragedy whose function was to
receive information of a personal and intimate nature; it is for
example Œnone in Racine's *Phèdre* who learns of the heroine's
incestuous passion; the confidant can have a more active role as
is illustrated by the influence of Narcisse upon Néron in
Racine's *Britannicus*.

dénouement The unravelling of the plot, the final outcome of a
play or novel.

epic (French **épopée**) Originally a long poem celebrating the
exploits of a legendary hero, raised to a symbolic level by
simplification and exaggeration and expressing the ideal of a
whole generation – for example, *La Chanson de Roland* in the
Middle Ages, where the participant in a minor skirmish is
turned into a heroic figure symbolizing the fight of Christendom
against Islam. In the nineteenth century many writers tried to
revive and modernize the epic – Hugo, notably, by varying the
form with a series of short poems arranged chronologically to
narrate the history of mankind. The term is now often applied
to novels as well as poems.

epistolary novel A popular form of fiction in eighteenth-
century England and France in which the action is conveyed by

a series of letters and written messages between the characters. An outstanding example is *Lès Liaisons dangereuses*.

genre The term is often applied to different kinds of literature to distinguish between different modes or forms; comedy and tragedy are separate dramatic *genres*; together they are two components of the dramatic genre. *La séparation des genres* refers to the seventeenth-century practice of avoiding any blend of tragedy and comedy, as recommended in a couplet from Boileau's *Art poétique*:

> La Comique, ennemi des soupirs et des pleurs,
> N'admet point en ses vers de tragiques douleurs.

Jansenism A stern religious doctrine derived from the teachings of St Augustine (fifth century) as propounded by Bishop Jansen of Ypres in the early seventeenth century. Based on the need for Divine Grace, the essential doctrine was one of predestination, according to which the human soul is damned unless touched by the finger of God's mercy. Jansenist beliefs were adopted by the religious community of Port-Royal, on the outskirts of Paris, where Racine received his education. Pascal's *Lettres provinciales* were written to support the Jansenists in their struggle against the Jesuits.

Jesuit A member of the powerful religious order founded by St Ignatius Loyola in the sixteenth century. Originally intended as a religious force to combat the spread of Protestantism throughout Europe, the Society of Jesus became involved in political intrigue and commercial ventures. The term is sometimes used pejoratively to imply a lax and worldly attitude to religion or a use of casuistry to avoid moral prohibitions.

jeu de paume The name of a popular seventeenth-century ball game, and by extension, of the court in which it was played. The enclosed, walled court was an ideal place, like the circular inn-yards of England, for a travelling theatre company to use for performances. It was in such a makeshift theatre that Corneille's first play was produced. One legacy of this practice of building an improvised stage in an enclosed space rather like the court still used for Real Tennis is still visible in modern texts where the *côté cour* and *côté jardin* are used to indicate stage left and stage right.

libertinage Although a libertine can be a loose-living or licentious person, the more usual meaning in the seventeenth century was a free-thinker, a person who disregarded accepted religious beliefs and standards. To distinguish between the two, Bayle coined the term 'libertin d'esprit'. Molière portrayed this spirit of independence in his character Don Juan; Pascal attacked it in his *Pensées*; it can be traced into the work of the *philosophes* in the eighteenth century.

melodrama   Although at the outset melodrama involved the use of music, the term came to mean 'blood-and-thunder' drama, or plays of an unusually (some say excessively) sensational variety, which depend upon an artificial heightening of tension by tricks of plot and use of stage effects. Pixérécourt (1773–1844) was a leading exponent of the genre, and melodrama became particularly popular in nineteenth-century France.

picaresque   A style of action, derived from late sixteenth- and early seventeenth-century Spain, in which a carefree and unscrupulous vagabond wanders from one social milieu to another, his encounters and adventures usually providing a satirical view of society. The eighteenth-century novel *Gil Blas* by Lesape is the most widely-known example. Modern usage often extends to any fiction consisting of loosely connected episodes in the adventurous life of the hero – for example, Stendhal's *La Chartreuse de Parme*.

Port-Royal   The home of Jansenism (q.v.) until destroyed by papal decree in the early eighteenth century.

préciosité   One feature of seventeenth-century efforts to achieve a more cultivated standard of behaviour and diction, for which women were largely responsible. Often considered ridiculous because of the exaggerations and affectations to which it led (see Molière's play *Les Précieuses ridicules*), it began as a genuine attempt to encourage clarity of thought and delicacy of expression, and, as such, is visible in the precise language of Racine's tragedies.

roman-fleuve   A cycle or series of novels, consisting of a sequence of self-contained but interconnected texts relating to a particular individual, family or other social group seen over a period of time. The *roman-fleuve* belongs most of all to the first half of the twentieth century, and includes such works as Georges Duhamel's *Chronique des Pasquier* (1933–45), Roger Martin du Gard's *Les Thibault* (1922–40), and Jules Romains's *Les Hommes de bonne volonté* (1932–47). The term itself comes from Romain Rolland, who likened his *Jean-Christophe* cycle (1906–12) to a river which had not only its dramatic passages but also those quieter zones which 'n'en continuent pas moins de couler et de changer'.

Saint-Cyr   A religious and educational establishment for aristocratic young ladies in the seventeenth century. Racine's last two plays (*Esther* and *Athalie*) were first performed there by the pupils. After the Revolution it was converted to its present use as a military academy, the equivalent of Sandhurst.

scholastic philosophy A philosophical method taught in the schools and universities of the Middle Ages, based on theology and relying on formal arguments and appeals to authority, especially Aristotle. In a pejorative sense it comes to mean an exaggerated formalism without any reference to experience and as such was attacked by Descartes in the seventeenth century.

sensibilité As a reaction to the coldly analytical and excessively cerebral approach to life apparent in the work of many early eighteenth-century writers, there develops a 'courant sensible' which places emphasis upon passion and feeling, upon emotion and instinct. In the pre-Romantic fiction of Rousseau and Bernardin de Saint-Pierre, the focus is moved from head to heart. *La sensibilité* is an important feature of the transition from the Classical concern for *l'homme*, man in general, to the Romantic concentration upon *le moi*, man in particular.

sonnet A form of poem introduced into France from Italy in the sixteenth century. The regular sonnet consists of two verses of four lines (quatrains) and two of three lines (tercets), with a rhyme-scheme abba, abba, ccd, ede, but many irregular forms exist. Major writers of the sonnet include Ronsard and du Bellay in the sixteenth century and, among its later exponents, Baudelaire and Mallarmé.

style indirect libre A way of expressing a character's words, thoughts, and viewpoint generally, without inserting 'she felt that', 'he thought that'. The tenses of indirect speech are used (usually imperfect or pluperfect), but combined with the emotional exclamations and adverbs of direct speech, for example the regrets of Emma in *Madame Bovary*, expressing *her* view of the situation, not Flaubert's: 'Mais, pour elle, rien n'arrivait, Dieu l'avait voulu! L'avenir était un corridor tout noir, et qui avait au fond sa porte bien fermée.' This technique is extensively used by Flaubert and Zola.

unities The unities of time, place and action form an important element of what came to be known as the 'rules' of seventeenth-century French tragedy. The neatest definition is given in Boileau's *Art poétique*:

> Qu'en un lieu, qu'en un jour, un seul fait accompli
> Tienne jusqu'à la fin le théâtre rempli.

What Aristotle had shown in his *Poetics* (fifth century BC) to be the practice of dramatists in Greek antiquity was re-interpreted and misinterpreted by theoreticians in sixteenth- and seventeenth-century France. Whether the unities were adopted out of respect for the drama of antiquity, imposed by critical authority on reluctant dramatists, or willingly embraced by playwrights was a matter of personal judgement or taste. Some dramatists, like Corneille, resented the unities; others, like Racine, derived positive benefits from the effects of compression and concentration.

vers libre   Term applied to modern poetry which has left the traditional rules of versification (rhyme, set number of syllables, strophic patterns etc.), replacing them by assonance, alliteration, rhythm etc. To be distinguished from *vers libres*, a verse-form used by La Fontaine, consisting of rhyming lines with a regular number of syllables, usually eight or twelve, but the rhyme and the length of the line vary throughout the poem.

vraisemblance   Verisimilitude, having the appearance of what is true, genuine. Truth being at times stranger than fiction, the dramatist needs to base his plot not on *le vrai*, the accurate historical fact, but on *le vraisemblable*, so that the action of the tragedy develops in accordance with its own inner logic; where history leaves room for chance, *le vraisemblable* can eliminate the vagaries of external fate and impose its own tragic inevitability. Put simply, *le vraisemblable* is what is true for an audience, if not for a historian.

Bibliography

Historical and cultural background

R. Anderson, *France 1870–1914. Politics and Society* (1977); D. Brogan, *The Development of Modern France (1870–1939)* (1967); J. Bury, *France 1814–1940* (1969); E. Cahm, *Politics and Society in Contemporary France 1789–1971* (1972); *Cambridge History of Modern France*, 6 vols. (1983–5); D. Charlton, *France. A Companion to French Studies* (1979); A. Cobban, *A History of Modern France*, 3 vols. (1957–65); G. Duby and R. Mandrou, *A History of French Civilization* (1964); G. Dupeux, *French Society 1789–1970* (1976); A. Guérard, *France: A Short History* (1946); H. Jackson (ed.), *A Short History of France from Earliest Times to 1972* (1974); R. Magraw, *France 1815–1914, The Bourgeois Century* (1983); D. Potts and D. Charlton, *French Thought since 1600* (1974); F. Roe, *Modern France* (1956); D. Sutherland, *France 1789–1815. Revolution and Counterrevolution* (1985); J. Wallace-Hadrill and J. McManners (eds), *France, Government and Society* (1970); T. Zeldin, *France 1848–1945*, 2 vols. hardback, 5 vols. paperback (1973–7).

Bibliographies

D. Cabeen, W. Brookes *et al.*, *A Critical Bibliography of French Literature*, 6 vols. (1947–80); P. Langlois and A. Mareil, *Guide bibliographique des études littéraires* (1965); D. Mahaffey, *A Concise Bibliography of French Literature* (1975); C. Osburn, *Research and Reference Guide to French Studies* (1981).

O. Klapp, *Bibliographie der französischen Literaturwissenschaft* (1966– , annual); R. Rancœur, *Bibliographie de la littérature française du moyen âge à nos jours* (1966– , annual); *The Year's Work in Modern Languages* (1931– , annual).

Dictionaries

J. Beaumarchais *et al.*, *Dictionnaire des littératures de langue française* (1984); P. Harvey and J. Heseltine, *The Oxford Companion to French Literature* (1959); J. Reid, *The Concise Oxford Dictionary of French Literature* (1976).

General guides and surveys

G. Brereton, *A Short History of French Literature* (1976); P.-G. Castex and P. Surer, *Manuel des études littéraires françaises*, 6 vols. (1967); L. Cazamian, *A History of French Literature* (1955); P. Charvet (ed.), *A Literary History of France*, 5 vols. (1967–74); A. Gill (ed.), *Life and Letters in France*, 3 vols. (1965–70); J. Cruickshank, *French Literature and its Background*, 6 vols. (1968–70); A. Lagarde and L. Michard, 'Textes et littérature', 6 vols. (1970–9); H. Mitterand (ed.), *Littérature: Textes et documents*, 5 vols. (1987–8); Pelican Guides to European Literature, 4 vols. (1971–9); C. Pichois (ed.), Collection littéraire française, 16 vols. hardback, 9 vols. paperback (1968–79).

General literary studies

E. Auberbach, *Mimesis. The Representation of Reality in Western Literature* (1953); G. Brée, *Women Writers in France* (1973); W. Fowlie, *Climate of Violence. The French Literary Tradition from Baudelaire to the Present* (1967); P. France, *Rhetoric and Truth in France: Descartes to Diderot* (1972); W. Howarth and C. Walton, *Explications: The Technique of French Literary Appreciation* (1971); G. Michaud, *L'Œuvre et ses techniques* (1957); P. Nurse (ed.), *The Art of Criticism. Essays in French Literary Analysis* (1969); G. Poulet, *Etudes sur le temps humain*, 4 vols. (1951–68); J. Rousset, *Forme et signification* (1962); R. Sayce, *Style in French Prose* (1953); R. Wellek and A. Warren, *Theory of Literature* (1966).

Poetry

E. Beaumont, J. Cocking and J. Cruickshank (eds.), *Order and Adventure in Post-Romantic French Poetry* (1973); H. Berthon, *Nine French Poets* (1943); A. Boase, *The Poetry of France. An Anthology with Introduction and Notes*, 4 vols. (1964–73); G. Brereton, *An Introduction to the French Poets* (1956); P. Broome and G. Chesters, *An Anthology of Modern French Poetry, 1850–1950*, and *The Appreciation of Modern French Poetry, 1850–1950* (1976); R. Gibson, *Modern French Poets on Poetry* (1961);

M. Grammont, *Petit traité de versification française* (1969); H. Lemaître, *La Poésie depuis Baudelaire* (1965); R. Lewis, *On Reading French Verse* (1982); C. Hackett, *An Anthology of Modern French Poetry* (3rd edn 1967); P. Mansell-Jones, *The Background of Modern French Poetry* (1951); D. Parmée, *Twelve French Poets* (1957); J. Payen and J. Chauveau, *La Poésie des origines à 1715* (1968); M. Raymond, *From Baudelaire to Surrealism* (1950); R. Sabatier, *Histoire de la poésie française*, 8 vols. (1975–82).

Drama

J.-L. Barrault, *Nouvelles réflexions sur le théâtre* (1959); E. Bentley, *The Life of the Drama* (1965); E. Bentley (ed.), *The Theory of the Modern Stage* (1968); G. Brereton, *French Tragic Drama in the Sixteenth and Seventeenth Centuries* (1973); G. Brereton, *French Comic Drama from the Sixteenth to the Eighteenth Century* (1977); K. Elam, *The Semiotics of Theatre and Drama* (1980); W. Howarth, *Comic Drama* (1978); H. Kitto, *Form and Meaning in Drama* (1968); J. Lorcey, *La Comédie française* (1980); A. Nicoll, *The Theatre and Dramatic Theory* (1962); G. Steiner, *The Death of Tragedy* (1961); P. Voltz, *La Comédie* (1964); J. Russell Taylor (ed.), *The Penguin Dictionary of the Theatre* (1970).

The novel

M. Allott (ed.), *Novelists on the Novel* (1959); R. Barthes, *Writing Degree Zero* (1967); L. Bersani, *From Balzac to Beckett* (1970); W. Booth, *The Rhetoric of Fiction* (1983); R. Bourneuf and R. Ouellet, *L'Univers du roman* (1972); V. Brombert, *The Intellectual Hero: Studies in the French Novel, 1880–1955* (1961); H. Coulet, *Le Roman jusqu'à la Révolution* (1967); G. Jean, *Le Roman* (1971); M.Raimond, *Le Roman depuis la Révolution* (1967); E. Showalter, *The Evolution of the French Novel, 1641–1782* (1972); M. Turnell, *The Novel in France* (1950); *The Art of French Fiction* (1959) and *The Rise of the French Novel* (1979); S. Ullmann, *Style in the French Novel* (1957), and *The Image in the Modern French Novel* (1960).

Series

It would be impossible to list here all the series of studies – complete and continuing – devoted to various aspects of French literature, but the following all offer valuable guidance:

On individual texts: Studies in French Literature (published by Edward Arnold), Critical Guides to French Texts (Grant and Cutler), Landmarks of World Literature (Cambridge University Press), Profil d'une œuvre (Hatier), Thèmes et textes (Larousse), Lire aujourd'hui (Hachette), Poche critique (Hachette).

On individual authors: Past Masters (Oxford University Press), Fontana Modern Masters, Twentieth-Century Views (Prentice-Hall), Columbia Essays on Modern Writers, Writers and Critics (Oliver and Boyd), Twayne World Authors, Ecrivains de toujours (Seuil), Classiques du XXe siècle (Editions Universitaires), Poètes d'aujourd'hui (Seghers), Connaissance des Lettres (Hatier).

On literary movements and periods, and on critical concepts: Critical Idiom (Methuen), New Accents (Methuen), Collection U (Armand Colin), Que sais-je? (Presses Universitaires de France), Collection Points.

Index

The index covers literary and cultural movements and figures. It does not include historical or political details. Figures in italics denote the main text for an author.